Senior Management Teams in Primary Schools

This book focuses on senior management teams (SMTs) in primary schools. It shows how team approaches can be effective where members combine energies in working towards shared goals, so achieving synergy. But management has become high risk for headteachers, rendering the quest for synergy problematic. Tasks imposed by national reforms have virtually forced heads to share leadership through a team approach. Yet their accountability for the team tempts them to play safe by retaining tight control.

The book reports research into SMTs in large primary schools which examined how team members work together and relate to other staff and governors. A major barrier to synergy was the tension between belief in the management hierarchy where what the head says goes, and belief that all team members are entitled to make an equal contribution to the SMT. Different ways of coping with this tension determined the level of synergy achieved.

The study provides an evidence-based starting point for improving teamwork. It is essential reading for all concerned with team approaches to school management – staff, governors, trainers, policy makers, academics and students on advanced courses. The research has wider implications for team approaches to management elsewhere in the public and private sectors.

Mike Wallace is Professor of Education Management and Policy at Cardiff University. **Lynda Huckman** is at the University of Bath, where her areas of research include education management.

Senior Management Teams in Primary Schools

The quest for synergy

Mike Wallace and
Lynda Huckman

London and New York

First published 1999
by Routledge
11 New Fetter Lane, London EC4P 4EE

Simultaneously published in the USA and Canada
by Routledge
29 West 35th Street, New York, NY 10001

Routledge is an imprint of the Taylor & Francis Group

Transferred to Digital Printing 2004

© 1999 Mike Wallace and Lynda Huckman

Typeset in Goudy by
J&L Composition Ltd, Filey, North Yorkshire

British Library Cataloguing in Publication Data
A catalogue record for this book is available
from the British Library

Library of Congress Cataloging in Publication Data
Wallace, Mike.
    Senior management teams in primary schools /
Mike Wallace and Lynda Huckman.
        p.   cm. — (Educational management series)
    Includes bibliographical references (p.) and index.
    1. School management teams—Great Britain—Case studies.
    2. Education, Elementary—Great Britain—Case studies.
    3. Educational leadership—Great Britain—Case studies.
    I. Huckman, Lynda, 1943-   . II. Title. III. Series.
    LB2806.3.W37   1997
    372.12—dc21   98–54124

ISBN 0–415–17036–2

Contents

Illustrations

Figures

Tables

Acknowledgements

The research reported in this book was funded by a grant from the Economic and Social Research Council (reference number R000235671).

A special debt is owed to the headteachers, their SMT colleagues, other staff and chairs of governors in the case study schools who squeezed in time for interviews and enabled meetings to be observed. Many staff covered colleagues' classes to release them for interviews during the school day. The readiness of staff and chairs of governors to be involved, despite their already heavy workloads, enabled a detailed picture of a diversity of approaches to teamwork to be built up. A debt is also owed to the headteachers who completed and returned the postal survey, giving a clear indication of just how widespread senior management teams have become in the primary schools sector.

Several people contributed to the research and writing process at different times. Mark Hadfield and Sue Content of the University of Nottingham assisted with designing the postal survey and were responsible for carrying it out. Jan Gray, the project manager at Cardiff, transcribed the interview and observation summary tapes and wordprocessed the first draft of some tables and figures. Lynda Huckman undertook case studies in three schools, analysed the survey returns and case study data and wrote a first draft of chapters reporting the findings. Mike Wallace directed the project (first at the University of Nottingham and later at Cardiff University), designed the survey, undertook one case study, reanalysed the data, and wrote the book.

Mike Wallace would like to thank Pam and Rog Shaw for their hospitality, and to acknowledge the constant companionship, intellectual support and ready humour of Alison Wray which were so instrumental to making this book happen.

Chapter 1

A risky business

These days primary school management is a high-risk enterprise. Once a career in teaching meant a job for life, but not any more. Reforms introduced by the past and present central government have dramatically raised the stakes for headteachers and their colleagues on the professional staff in the UK, as in many other western countries. Not only have ministers expected staff faithfully to implement their imposed agenda of innovations but also, with the advent of new external accountability measures, the consequences of resistance or failure to attain externally determined standards of pupil learning can ultimately be job threatening. The performance of schools is now much more likely to be found wanting and publicly exposed. Where the marketisation thrust of past central government reforms has taken hold, parents may vote with their feet by withdrawing their children, resulting in a reduction in the school budget based on pupil numbers from which staff salaries are paid, and the possibility of redeployment or redundancy.

While all teachers are increasingly being held to acccount for the quality and outcomes of their work, the going is particularly tough for headteachers. They, alone among the professional staff, are charged with responsibility for managing the school within the oversight of the governing body. The sheer weight of tasks, initially to implement multiple innovations and subsequently to work in the new context as reforms become embedded, has forced most headteachers to delegate. In the past primary school heads, in contrast to their secondary counterparts, could reasonably claim to have expertise in most or all areas of schoolwork. Yet longer serving heads in all but the smallest institutions (where they retain class teaching responsibility) have been left behind by other staff who have direct experience of implementing externally imposed changes in the curriculum and its assessment. External pressure continues to intensify under the present central government which has, to date, been characterised by an even stronger centralising tendency than its predecessor. Policies designed to strengthen central government control over primary education include setting national targets for raising attainment of primary school pupils coupled with the threat of external intervention if targets are not met, and the imposition of daily periods dedicated to literacy and to numeracy.

Primary heads have therefore become – comparatively recently – more dependent on their staff, and many are following the example of secondary heads by sharing the management burden through some form of team approach. In small schools, the entire professional staff may be conceived as a single team while, in larger institutions, the creation by heads of school or senior management teams (SMTs) is becoming commonplace. Distinguishing features of SMTs are as follows: first, that their members represent a subgroup of the professional staff as a whole which includes the head, deputy or deputies and one or more teachers with a promoted post carrying substantial management responsibility; and second, that SMT members are involved in making policy and administrative decisions on behalf of other staff, whose views are represented to a varying degree. Sharing by means of an SMT offers potential to bring heads much needed support. *Synergy* may be achieved where all members combine their energies in working towards shared goals. Here the team amounts to more than the sum of its parts, making more of a difference to management than individual members could on their own. Not only are heads empowered through the assistance of colleagues, but so too are other SMT members who are able to contribute to management decisions which reach beyond the bounds of their individual responsibility.

A team approach may also have its downside. In a climate of increased external accountability, heads are placed at considerable risk if the team effort fails to perform effectively. From heads' perspective, if all members of the team commit themselves to pulling together in a unified direction with which the heads are comfortable, all well and good. But what if they don't? Heads are uniquely vulnerable compared with other SMT members as they are the school level manager where the buck stops. If either heads or other SMT members do not commit themselves fully to teamwork or fail to carry out their responsibility competently, or if SMT colleagues pull together in a direction that, in the heads' judgement, courts disaster, who will get the blame? Since heads are responsible for SMTs' performance as team leader – and often team creator – the finger is likely to be pointed at them. Moreover, whichever approach to management is adopted, should standards of teaching and pupil learning be judged as below par, the quality of management – and therefore heads' leadership – will be called into question.

The 1997 annual report of the central government's Office for Standards in Education (OFSTED) stated that standards of pupils' achievement had been judged as 'poor' in one in twelve primary schools at key stage one and one in six at key stage two. The report also noted that:

> Most schools are led well but in about one in seven the leadership is weak and fails to give a clear educational direction. Schools which are otherwise well led often do not evaluate their own performance with any rigour. Too few headteachers monitor and influence classroom teaching.
> (OFSTED 1997: 17)

It is hard to see inspectors taking the view: 'Great SMT; pity about teaching and learning.' Central government ministers have signalled their intention to make it easier for school governors to dismiss heads and other staff whom inspectors judge incompetent.

The major risk for heads presented by a team approach to management is the possibility that synergy will not be achieved and the SMT will add up to rather less than the sum of its parts. Heads may find themselves disempowered, in a position where they could achieve more by relying on their authority to direct colleagues. They may then be inhibited from taking a strong lead, or attempt to do so and precipitate debilitating conflict with their SMT colleagues. The more heads share through teamwork, the more empowerment they and other SMT members stand to gain but, on the other hand, the more they stand to lose through mutual disempowerment if teamwork should flounder. A central theme of this book is that heads are uniquely placed to make incremental decisions about how far to venture along the potentially high risk but also potentially most effective and ethically justifiable road of a team approach which features extensive power sharing. They can also decide when to play safe by confining power sharing within strict limits through a more restricted form of teamwork, a strategy offering less potential for effectiveness than the high risk alternative, but providing the safeguard of a lower risk of teamwork failure leading to ineffectiveness.

So the reforms have sharpened a longstanding dilemma for heads: their greater dependence on professional colleagues draws them towards sharing management tasks through some kind of team approach; in a climate of increased external accountability, however, they may be wary of sharing in ways that might backfire if colleagues turn out to be empowered to act in ways that produce low standards of pupil achievement, alienate parents and governors, bring negative media attention, or incur negative judgements by inspectors. In short, how much sharing dare they risk?

This dilemma is reflected in the complexities of SMT practice, for the process of working together is characterised by a chronic contradiction between two sets of incompatible beliefs and values held by senior primary school staff, affecting their use of resources to achieve goals within a team approach. The notion of sharing management through teamwork overlays a long tradition in primary schools where heads have been viewed as the sole members of the professional staff with formal management responsibility. The increase in external accountability brought by reforms accords with this tradition, where headteachers were set apart from other primary school staff through their differential salary, status and authority as managers. Over the last few decades, an expanding range of intermediate posts has been created with different levels of enhanced salary linked, in the main, to differential management responsibilities. There is a strongly held belief among professional staff in a *management hierarchy*, often with five or more levels, where senior staff are entitled to oversee and direct the work of the junior colleagues for whom they are responsible. Headteachers top the hierarchy since they are ultimately accountable for the work of the school. They have unique ability to affect colleagues' careers through their contribution to staff selection, appraisal and development, and the allocation of responsibilities and salaries.

Sharing through a team approach resonates with the growth of egalitarian beliefs and values about primary school management which have become widespread, fostered during the 1980s by publications of central government groups, especially Her Majesty's Inspectorate (HMI), and national and local committees of enquiry (Wallace 1989). The implicit model of good management practice embedded in such documents embraces the notions both of hierarchy and of entitlement to participate in curriculum decision making. It is asserted that curriculum management tasks should be shared among professional colleagues who work collaboratively through a variety of consultation procedures. There is considerable overlap between management responsibilities, especially those relating to curriculum and assessment, since most teachers are responsible for a class of pupils and teach most or all subjects. The model leaves unclear who has ultimate responsibility if consensus cannot be attained: whether the class teacher, a colleague with the relevant area of management responsibility, or the head.

A collaborative approach to management has also been widely advocated by academics and trainers. One argument rests on democratic values: all staff are entitled to have their say in matters that affect their work (Bottery 1992; Blase and Anderson 1995; Southworth 1995). Another is based on views of managerial effectiveness: in making complex decisions, a group is likely to challenge a head's initial idea that may otherwise fail to take important considerations into account (Evers 1990). More generally, managers are interdependent: whatever their position in the management hierarchy, every member of staff has a contribution to make since managerial tasks can only be fulfilled with and through other people. Gaining staff commitment to policy decisions is therefore necessary (Bell and Rhodes 1996). Like headteachers, other managers also depend for their success on the performance of those they manage. All teaching staff are deemed managers under the official model of good practice, so everyone depends on everyone else. Alongside belief in a management hierarchy lies a paramount belief that in contributing to teamwork, whether of an SMT or the whole staff team, all members have an *equal contribution* to make to decisions irrespective of their position in the management hierarchy pecking order. While heads are creators, developers and leaders of their teams, they are also team members whose opinion is worth no more and no less than that of colleagues.

This study of primary school SMTs reveals how they were affected by a team culture which included a variable balance between beliefs and values associated with a management hierarchy and those connected with making an equal contribution as SMT members to the work of the team. SMT members worked together harmoniously while there was congruence in the beliefs and values guiding their actions. Working towards a team decision could reflect a belief in the entitlement of each member to contribute as an equal to discussion preceding a consensual decision, complemented by an equal obligation to accept commitment to its subsequent implementation. The decision-making process might alternatively reflect unified belief in a management hierarchy among team members, where the head could legitimately choose whether and how far to consult, make the decision, and then expect team colleagues to put their energies into its implementation. Conditions for open conflict or passive resistance arose where team members differed over whether they were operating within the framework of a management hierarchy or as SMT members with equal entitlement to contribute to the team's tasks. A head might make a unilateral decision where other members believed that it should have been a consensual team effort. Conversely, a head might seek the equal contribution of colleagues where they believed that the head should make the running.

Putting SMTs in perspective

This theme highlights the complexity of teamwork in hierarchical organisations whose professional culture may also support a measure of egalitarianism and points to the centrality of interaction both inside teams and between team members and outsiders. To tease out patterns in this complexity we need a perspective on interaction which is sophisticated enough to address contradictory beliefs and values underpinning individual and group actions (and withholding from action), the different capabilities of SMT members to use power according to their beliefs and values, and the expression of power in both synergistic and conflictual situations. Most importantly, such a perspective must enable us to grasp how each SMT member has differential power to develop, reinforce or change beliefs and values constituting the team culture, which both shape and are shaped by interaction. A cultural perspective provides a lens for investigating how far beliefs and values of team members are shared; a political perspective provides a lens for analysing how individuals and groups have access to different resources in achieving their ends within the team. Blending cultural and political perspectives into a dual perspective offers a more comprehensive set of concepts than either single perspective alone which link beliefs and values with synergistic or conflictual use of resources. Accordingly, the combined cultural and political perspective on interaction has been employed which was developed in an earlier study of secondary school SMTs (Wallace and Hall 1994). The mix of concepts and their articulation trialled in that research formed the conceptual starting point for the present investigation.

The book has three purposes. First, an account is given of the outcomes of this study, designed to explore the prevalence and working practices of SMTs in large primary schools through a survey of headteachers and case studies of four teams. Some kind of team approach has become the most common way of managing schools in both sectors that are too large for all staff feasibly to make major policy decisions face to face. If we assume that the quality of primary school management can make a positive impact on the quality of pupils' education, it becomes important to know what SMTs do and how well they do it in a fast changing world. The investigation sought answers to such questions as: what part do heads play in creating and leading SMTs? What practices do SMTs embrace within the conception of teamwork that their members adopt? What are the trials and tribulations of working as a team? How can SMT members and other staff get the best from a team approach? Second, the cultural and political perspective is outlined and employed to illuminate the complexities of SMT operation in reporting the research findings. Third, tentative consideration is given to what makes for effective teamwork in primary school SMTs within the frenetic and insecure environment of unrelenting reform. This chapter sets the scene. Key concepts connected with teams and management are defined; changes are tracked in the national policy context fostering belief both in a management hierarchy and in collaboration among primary school staff while forcing them to coordinate their work; how primary sector SMTs originated within this rapidly evolving context is discussed; what is known about teamwork inside and outside the education sphere is assessed; and the remainder of the book is introduced.

When is a team not a team?

The research task was to investigate how SMT members conceived their team approach and how they attempted to work together, rather than assess SMTs against some prespecified notion of what teams should be and what they should or should not do. Nevertheless, there have to be limits to what may count as a team if it is to be distinguishable from a group or other loose association of individuals. There is some sense in which a team must be conceived of as an entity over and above the aggregate of individuals who constitute it. A useful starting point is the broad definition of a *team* offered by Larson and LaFasto (1989: 19): 'A team has two or more people; it has a specific performance objective or recognisable goal to be attained; and coordination of activity among the members of the team is required for the attainment of the team goal or objective.' The complementary definition by Katzenbach and Smith (1993: 45) is more exacting: 'A team is a small number of people with complementary skills who are committed to a common purpose, performance goals, and approach for which they hold themselves accountable.' Implicitly, part of what makes an effective team a distinctive entity is the synergy arising from complementarity of its members' contributions, entailing shared commitment extending beyond goals and their achievement to acceptance of mutual responsibility for the team's performance.

The SMTs in this study were certainly teams in name, but were they teams in practice? On the face of it, they all matched up to the first definition: the SMTs consisted of several members with complementary responsibilities typically covering the whole school; they had been established by heads to help them manage the institution; this purpose could not be achieved unless members pulled together. The match did not necessarily bear closer scrutiny, however: who was a full member could be ambiguous; while heads formally prescribed the purpose of the team, other members might not view their corporate goals in compatible terms; the espoused team purpose might be diffuse; and outsiders including other staff and governors might not share any sense of purpose team members possessed. It was not a foregone conclusion that teams would demonstrate the unified internal commitment, performance goals and sense of shared responsibility for the team's performance that the second definition demands.

SMTs represented a particular kind of team: they were conceived as permanent entities whose membership related more to senior levels of managerial responsibility than to the characteristics of individuals who might hold such responsibility at any time; and as having an ongoing purpose – SMTs' managerial work is never done. Their constitution and working practices differed, therefore, from project teams commonly referred to in team manuals drawing on private sector experience (Kharbanda and Stallworthy 1990). The latter are more like the working parties which are increasingly a feature of larger schools (including some in this research): a temporary arrangement set up to achieve a one-off goal within a specified period, after which the team is disbanded (West 1992).

Team members may *collaborate* where they combine their individual resources to achieve agreed goals that cannot be fulfilled as effectively by individuals working alone (as in the case of a major policy decision where no member has a monopoly on ideas about the best way forward). Collaboration implies a process of 'joint work for joint purposes' (Hall and Wallace 1993) which, when it is successful, produces synergy. *Teamwork* refers to collaboration within the SMT to realise a jointly held purpose. It should be noted that collaboration does not necessarily mean the experience is all sweetness and light. SMT members may share a commitment to reaching a policy decision but disagree strongly about its content. Nevertheless, collaboration entails a unified commitment to working towards a compromise which all members feel ready to support. Nor is collaboration the prerogative solely of equals: the differential status of SMT members does not stop them from maximising use of the resources available to them to contribute to achieving a jointly held goal. Examples of close collaboration were identified in the secondary school SMT study, and Nias *et al.* (1989, 1992) found instances where the whole staff in medium-sized primary schools subscribed to a 'culture of collaboration' encompassing the curriculum.

Individual SMT members' motivation to work together may be voluntary, especially in the case of heads who can choose whether to adopt a team approach even where, on appointment, they inherit an existing team. It may also be a response to compulsion by others, as where heads create an SMT and one or more other members (particularly deputy heads) are included because of their existing position in the management hierarchy, whether or not they feel committed to a team approach. They may be expected to act according to certain ground rules as a condition of membership, yet may respond by seeking ways of resisting compliance. Ultimately, North American research suggests that people can be forced to work together while the heat is on, but not to give more fully of themselves as close collaboration requires (Joyce *et al.* 1989; Fullan 1991; Hargreaves 1994).

The formal *leaders* of SMTs are headteachers, who use their resources to develop teams' working practices by sharing this leadership role in some way with other members. A simple definition of *leadership*, following the usage of Louis and Miles (1990), is actions which set the course for the organisation, whether to maintain the *status quo* or to initiate change across the organisation or a team within it. Such leadership actions include making strategic plans, stimulating and inspiring others to act, creating conditions favourable to their action, and monitoring progress. In the eyes of OFSTED inspectors, as the earlier quotation illustrates, poor leadership among primary headteachers is judged partly in terms of failure to monitor other staff.

Leadership may usefully be subdivided along lines suggested by Burns (1978) and applied to primary schools by Southworth (1998). *Transactional* leadership implies negotiation between leaders and followers, who often have different priorities, where each party makes compromises where necessary to ensure the smooth running of the organisation. Heads and other staff may settle on a unified procedure for curriculum planning or for supervising pupils in the playground. *Transformational* leadership refers to the attempt to set a new course for the organisation by gaining support for a vision of a desirable future and facilitating others' efforts to realise it. Reaching beyond transactions necessary to keep the school on the road, transformational leadership implies winning the hearts and minds of colleagues to work synergistically towards a goal to which all are persuaded to subscribe. Whose vision comes to be shared is not specified. Restricted sharing through an SMT allows for the possibility of one-way transformational leadership through which heads try to implement their ready-made vision through harnessing the efforts of other SMT members towards engendering staff support. More extensive, multi-directional transformational leadership is also possible, where heads enable SMT colleagues and staff outside the team to contribute to the articulation of a shared vision which is an outcome of their joint efforts. In the UK, whether transformational leadership is restricted or extensive, the content of any shared vision will be bounded by the necessity – to survive inspection – of conforming with central government reform policies. By design, central government reforms have narrowed the parameters within which a school-level vision must lie.

Hierarchy, participation and classroom autonomy

Most staff in primary school SMTs will have pursued a teaching career for a decade or more, and many will remember what teaching was like before the central government reforms. Experiences of various management structures, individual levels of managerial responsibility, salary differentials, any gap between management decisions and classroom practice, the amount of participation by teachers in management, and any team-building component of management training will, together, have left a legacy of assumptions informing their perceptions connected with their present post. As Alexander (1984) demonstrated in respect of primary teachers' educational beliefs, individuals may subscribe to ambiguous or contradictory assumptions. The sequence of individual professional experiences within an evolving national context will have sedimented current beliefs and values about a management hierarchy, how far team members should be treated as equals in contributing to teamwork, whether they should monitor other staff, how far team members and outsiders should participate in policy decision making and, possibly, the degree to which teachers (including SMT members) should be left to their own devices in the classroom. Primary heads have generally been – and in small schools remain – class teachers. A characteristic distinguishing most primary SMT members other than heads from those in secondary SMTs is that they continue to sit firmly on both sides of the teacher/manager fence: they may be senior managers but, except in the largest institutions, they retain responsibility for a class.

Aspects of this historical legacy help explain why SMT members and other staff may hold contradictory beliefs and values that affect team operation and the relationship between the SMT and other staff. Today's climate resonates with the bad old days of 'payment by results' in the last century, when external accountability really did mean jobs on the line: elementary school pupils were examined annually by HMI, and school finances depended on getting required grades. A significant difference was the strong consensus over curriculum and pedagogy which lasted until the 'progressive' movement of the 1960s. Staff in elementary schools were allowed increasing classroom autonomy during this long consensus period (Maclure 1970), when perhaps ministers and inspectors did not consider that teachers might experiment beyond the bounds of acceptability. A pre-war central government 'handbook of suggestions for teachers' stated that the final decision on curriculum and pedagogy rested with heads, adding:

> The only uniformity of practice that the Board of Education desire to see in the teaching of Public Elementary Schools is that each teacher shall think for himself [sic], and work out for himself, such methods of teaching as may use his powers to the best advantage and be best suited to the particular needs of the conditions of the school. Uniformity in details

(except in the mere routine of school management) is not desirable even if it were obtainable. But freedom implies a corresponding responsibility in its use.

(Board of Education 1937: 3)

Teaching staff were thereby empowered to experiment, facilitating disintegration of the pre-war consensus about the primary school curriculum and teaching methods. The diversification of practice which blossomed during the 1960s eventually brought a right-wing backlash with publication of the first Black Paper (Cox and Dyson 1969), continuing on and off until the present day (Alexander 1997). Belief in teachers' right to a high degree of individual classroom autonomy, despite heads' efforts to shape their practice behind the classroom door in line with the values they developed during their class-teaching days, has proved enduring but has been significantly eroded as a consequence of reform.

Headteachers have been set apart hierarchically from other teachers since elementary schooling began. For many years a rudimentary management structure existed, consisting of just two levels: head and class teachers. A training manual first published in 1882 included in the role of the head 'superintendence and conduct of the work of his assistants'; the head was also required to 'examine into the work of his [sic] subordinates' (Langdon 1905). There is abundant evidence that, while heads were exclusive formal leaders, their impact on colleagues' classroom practice was often limited. For many years, elementary schooling in the UK and North America could be interpreted as characterised by what Lortie (1969) called a 'balance between autonomy and control', where heads established a broad direction for teachers' work through 'low constraint decisions' at the level of school-wide policy. It was tacitly accepted that teachers had leeway to decide how far to implement policies affecting what and how they taught. Decisions about curriculum and teaching in principle were confined to the policy-making zone, and those about curriculum and teaching in practice were made in the largely separate zone of the individual classroom. To the extent that these zones remained distinct, as where heads did not monitor to see whether policy decisions were reflected inside the classroom, harmony could prevail. Conflict could arise where monitoring revealed an implementation gap and teachers' right to determine classroom practice was questioned (Wallace 1986a).

By the 1980s when, in the aftermath of right-wing criticisms of 'progressivism', central government ministers wished to rein in the diversity of practice, direct legal powers had been removed and indirect means were therefore initially employed. A key lever was the range of promoted posts for teachers which could be deemed to carry responsibility beyond the classroom. The gradual emergence of salary and responsibility differentials among teachers during the middle years of this century was commonly linked in primary schools with posts carrying responsibility for advising on particular curriculum areas (Campbell 1985). Creating posts carrying curriculum responsibility across the school was regarded by HMI (DES 1978) as a means of gaining consensus on classroom practice through consultation, enabling staff other than the head to participate in policy decisions which would then be reflected in their classwork. Advocating such a strategy represents an attempt to increase the overlap between the zone of decisions about practice and the zone of decisions about policy. This differentiation of posts actually reflected contradictory purposes from the outset, however, connected as much with sectional union concerns and the vagaries of teacher supply as with management responsibility, and resulting in secondary school staff receiving the bulk of promoted posts (Wallace 1986b).

The first 'posts of special responsibility' for teachers were introduced in 1945, though very few went to the primary sector. Of these, many were used to attract, retain, or reward valued teachers rather than for responsibility beyond the classroom (Hilsum and Start 1974). The position of deputy headteacher for schools over a minimum size was established as late as 1956. At the same time, three levels of graded post were created and, as innovation took hold in the 1960s, deployment of staff with graded posts as curriculum advisers began to be encouraged by, among others, the Plowden Committee (CACE 1967). Graded posts were succeeded in 1971 by five overlapping incremental scales, merged into four in 1974. They were replaced in turn, after various adjustments, by a main professional grade and up to five levels of 'incentive allowance' after central government imposed a pay and conditions structure for teaching staff (DES 1987). This move was part of the central government strategy to curb the power of teachers' unions and pave the way for large-scale reform. The incremental pay spine for teaching staff in operation at the time of the research was introduced in 1993, criteria for award of extra points remaining virtually unchanged.

The picture emerges of repeated tinkering at policy level with a system of salary differentials, official reasons for allocation of promoted posts remaining diverse. A recent document setting out the pay and conditions of teaching staff (DFE 1994: 18) allows for the award of 'up to five points to a classroom teacher who undertakes specified responsibilities beyond those common to the majority of teachers', 'up to three points for excellent performance, having regard to all aspects of the classroom teacher's professional duties but in particular to classroom teaching', 'up to two points . . . to a classroom teacher who is employed to teach subjects in which there is a shortage of teachers, or in a post which is difficult to fill', or one point for a classroom teacher with substantial responsibility for children with special educational needs.

Evidence is patchy on the actual reasons for allocating posts in primary schools. Major surveys (DES 1978, 1982, 1985; ILEA 1985), coupled with research examining the role of curriculum and other post holders and deputy heads (e.g. Robinson 1983; Campbell 1985; Wallace 1986a; Nias et al. 1989, 1992; Wallace and McMahon 1994; Webb and Vulliamy 1996a; Alexander

1997) suggest the majority of posts have, at least since the 1980s, carried head-teachers' expectation that incumbents have a duty to make an impact on col-leagues' work. The system of posts may therefore be regarded as favouring belief in a more extended management hierarchy in all but the smallest pri-mary schools. Under 'the reasonable direction of the headteacher', conditions of service for any teacher now include the possibility of 'coordinating or man-aging the work of other teachers; and taking such part as may be required of him [sic] in the review, development and management of activities relating to the curriculum, organisation and pastoral functions of the school' (DFE 1994). This same body of evidence suggests, conversely, that many such teachers remain unwilling to monitor colleagues' classwork in their area of manage-ment responsibility (Webb and Vulliamy 1996a). As later chapters will show, belief in individual teachers' classroom autonomy continues to inhibit some SMT members other than heads from monitoring colleagues for whose work they are responsible within the management hierarchy. Reticence appears to relate to their conception of their responsibility as being merely advisory and the wish to avoid transgressing colleagues' autonomy behind the classroom door; the old professional culture dies hard.

The status of heads as top managers is reflected in research into their work-ing practices. Investigations of medium-sized primary schools at the onset of central government reforms by Nias and her colleagues showed how heads were powerful leaders, often with considerable impact on practice. They were variably supported by delegated leadership activity of the deputy and other teachers (Nias et al. 1989, 1992). A range of evidence testified to heads' ability to set parameters for colleagues' involvement in management, some who iden-tified closely with 'their' school adopting a go-it-alone 'paternalistic' approach (Alexander 1984; Coulson 1990; Southworth 1995) facilitated by acquiescence of other staff but denying deputies the management role many desired (Coulson and Cox 1975). Others encouraged a mutually supportive but hier-archical head–deputy partnership (Wallace 1986a; Nias 1987; Southworth 1998). Conditions for more directive management were fostered, according to Coulson (1980), by the advent of innovations like team teaching and open-plan classrooms, enabling heads and staff with management responsibility to increase informal surveillance of their colleagues. It is not clear, however, to what extent any information gathered in this way was followed up in attempt-ing to reduce diversity of classroom practice.

The terms within which conditions of service of heads and deputies have been set out since 1987 are strictly hierarchical, reflecting intentions of past central government ministers through this reform and others to reinstate legally backed power to restrict individual classroom autonomy. Subject to legislation and articles of government for the school, 'a headteacher shall be responsible for the internal organisation, management and control of the school' with the proviso that 'a headteacher shall consult, where this is appro-priate, with the [local education] authority, the governing body, the staff of the school and the parents of its pupils'. Deputies are accorded an intermediate role between head and other staff, being required to participate in management 'under the overall direction of the headteacher' (DFE 1994).

The tone of this central government document is that headteachers should direct other staff (albeit being receptive to their ideas) in exercising their management responsibility. The same assumption is echoed in criteria used by OFSTED inspectors to judge effectiveness of management, though senior staff (as in the case of SMTs) are accorded a supporting role in the management hierarchy. Guidance for inspectors, while claiming that 'there are many acceptable styles of leadership', summarises good leadership practice against which schools are to be judged as follows:

> the governors, headteacher and senior staff provide positive leadership which gives a clear direction to the school's work. Staff understand the role they are encouraged to play in the development and running of the school and also know that their contribution to the school is appreciated. Pupils learn effectively and efficiently.
>
> (OFSTED 1994: 63)

More 'junior' teachers should know their place: to contribute little ideas within the big idea or vision for the school originating with senior managers within curriculum and financial parameters set by central government. Further, 'the implementation of [development] plans is monitored', implying that steps should be taken to ensure the zone of decision making about policy pervades the zone of decisions about classroom practice. Not surprisingly, a consistent view of headship is adopted by the Teacher Training Agency (TTA), the central government quango responsible for training of new headteachers and the National Professional Qualification for Headteachers (NPQH) scheme for assessing and training aspiring heads. The TTA (1997: 4) national standards for headteachers state that amongst heads' leadership skills should be the ability to 'direct and coordinate the work of others; build and support a high performing team; work as part of a team; devolve responsibilities; delegate tasks and monitor practice to see that they are being carried out'. Heads' responsibility for promoting and participating in teamwork is here framed by their overarching directing and monitoring role.

Pressure reducing individual classroom autonomy has come not only from the spread of a hierarchical view of management but also from the opposite direction – class teachers themselves. Hoyle (1986) claims that emergence of this egalitarian form of pressure was related to the wider political climate highlighting individuals' right to have a say in the running of social affairs; the need for coordination resulting from curriculum changes; increasing complexity of schools; and provision of in-service training which promoted the idea of participation. Ironically perhaps, certainly since the 1960s, many staff have pushed for substantial involvement in policy decision making, including decisions connected with curriculum, teaching methods, and promoting coherence and progression for pupils throughout the school. Reaching out from the zone of decisions on classroom practice into the zone of decisions on school-wide policy is seen to impose an obligation on those involved in making a policy decision to collaborate over implementation in the classroom. As with engagement in team teaching, commitment to implement school-wide policy decisions constrains individual teachers' autonomy to make their own decisions about classroom practice. Yet extensive participation in decision making is consistent with the belief that individuals contribute as equals.

The case for participative management has received scant official acknowledgement beyond conditions of service provision noted above that other staff should be consulted by heads 'where this is appropriate'. On the other hand, participative approaches to management have been promoted by academics and trainers, many practical handbooks targeted at primary headteachers extolling the virtues of gaining staff commitment through encouraging their participation, while variably noting possible difficulties, such as the time participative decision making can require (e.g. Day *et al.* 1985; Hill 1989; Harrison and Gill 1992; Davies and Ellison 1994; Bell and Rhodes 1996). There is similar emphasis in much management training for primary heads and other staff with management responsibility, especially since the advent of major central government initiatives in the early 1980s (Wallace and Hall 1989; Wallace 1991a; West 1992).

A major study of inner London primary sector schools (the largest with over 500 pupils) in the mid 1980s suggested that effective primary school leadership lay in the middle ground between the extremes of strictly hierarchical and perennially participative approaches. Effective heads enabled deputies and other staff to contribute to management, but their appropriate level of involvement was contingent on the decision at hand. The prescription for heads' pre-decision about how much involvement to allow in a particular decision was to

> divide the decisions they are required to make into two groups: those which it is quite properly their responsibility to take and for which any attempt at delegation to a staff decision would be seen as a dereliction of duty, and those which, quite properly, belong to the staff as a whole. In some cases it will be perfectly clear to which group a certain decision belongs; in others, it will be extremely difficult to decide. Mistakes will be made and the consequences – as when the staff discover that a decision affecting their way of working has been taken with no opportunity for them to voice an opinion on the matter, or where there is a conflict of interests between individual teachers on the staff – will have to be suffered. However, if the head is perceptive and sensitive she or he will soon learn to distinguish which decisions are which.
>
> (Mortimore *et al.* 1988: 281)

Scant detail was offered as to what 'purposeful leadership' might look like, and subsequent observational investigations (e.g. Hayes 1996) have revealed just how complex, unpredictable, and highly context-dependent the process of managing decision making can be.

Teamwork in response to education reform

The dramatic increase in external accountability and in primary heads' dependence on other staff brought about by central government reforms has added strength to the pincer movement whereby the establishment of a management hierarchy and the increase in staff participation in management had already reduced teachers' individual classroom autonomy. The link between zones of decision making about policy and about classroom practice has been further tightened. Part of this process is the adoption by heads in larger primary sector schools of team approaches to management as they look for support to increase their impact on what happens in classrooms. Embedded in the reform package, as exemplified by conditions of service for teaching staff and inspection criteria, is a strongly hierarchical view of management. Research documenting the early impact of reforms in primary schools (Pollard *et al.* 1994; Webb and Vulliamy 1996a; Menter *et al.* 1997) suggested that the response of most heads was twofold: opting for more directive approaches in line with belief in a management hierarchy while at the same time encouraging staff to collaborate in implementing reforms, consistent with the more egalitarian belief in participative management promoted during the 1980s. Reforms introduced by the mid 1990s, bringing many new management tasks, included:

- the national curriculum, divided into separate subjects in contrast with the integrated approach that used to be widespread in primary schools, and phased in over several years;
- tighter regulation of religious education and a daily collective act of worship;
- nationwide assessment of the national curriculum and publication of results for pupils completing key stage one at age 7 and key stage two at age 11;
- a national rolling programme of external inspection entailing publication of results, whereby schools may be publicly judged as 'failing';
- publication of national curriculum assessment results and truancy rates in the form of 'league tables', through which schools may be ranked;
- a code of practice governing provision for pupils with special educational needs;
- new arrangements for supporting pupils from minority ethnic groups;
- an increased proportion of parents and local community representatives on governing bodies;
- responsibility for financial management and the appointment and

dismissal of staff falling to governors and headteachers under the local management of schools (LMS) initiative;

- nationally imposed salaries, conditions of service and promotion structure (see above);
- more open enrolment of pupils to promote greater parental choice, providing conditions for competition between neighbouring primary schools resulting in a new emphasis on marketing;
- the possibility of schools opting out of local education authority (LEA) control and being funded directly by central government;
- the expectation that each school will have an annually updated development plan which is used to inform inspections;
- a budget for staff development with an annual entitlement of five 'training days' for in-service training;
- biennial appraisal of all teaching staff;
- a national system for assessment and training of aspiring and new headteachers;
- the requirement that LEAs develop local schemes within central government reforms such as LMS and appraisal and support schools with implementation of all reforms;
- pressure on LEAs to remove surplus pupil places where substantial spare capacity exists, stimulating LEA reorganisation schemes which may involve school closures and mergers.

As the 'policy hysteria' (Stronach and Morris 1994) of education reform gathered pace, primary heads were faced with a multiplicity of innovations – designed elsewhere, imposed on schools, and subject to an externally determined timetable for implementation – alongside other work (Wallace 1992; Wallace and McMahon 1994). The sequence for introducing particular reforms affected the rate at which primary heads' dependence on colleagues rose relative to their external accountability. At first, dependence came to the fore as staff worked together on the core subjects of the national curriculum and trialled the national assessment arrangements, many seeking to adapt the reforms to reflect their existing professional beliefs and values. Later, accountability loomed larger as reporting of assessment results became incorporated in national league tables, new style inspections with published results were imposed and targets for pupil attainment were set.

One consequence of the reforms has been to alter the balance between two subroles that make up headteachers' role. Hughes (1985) distinguished between the two subroles of *leading professional*, focusing on leadership connected with the core activity of teaching and learning, and *chief executive*, stressing management to provide suitable conditions for teaching and learning to take place. This conception is inevitably a product of its time, developed when major curriculum content decisions were made in schools but most financial decisions were made at LEA level, and the substance and balance of the two dimensions has shifted since. The leading professional subrole is divided into two dimensions. The 'traditional' embraces internal school activities including teaching and pastoral support for pupils, and nurturing productive relationships with other staff. The 'innovating' component is about connecting with the external environment, whether through being open to outside influences, taking part in educational activities outside the school, and encouraging colleagues to experiment with new ideas originating inside and outside the institution. The chief executive subrole is similarly split. The 'internal' dimension refers to allocating responsibilities and coordinating and controlling work through such means as setting up management structures and monitoring other staff. The 'external' relates to the level of status and individual autonomy that heads are accorded by outside agencies.

There is evidence (Garrett 1997) that the balance has been altered by central government intervention in the direction of the chief executive, though a somewhat diminished leading professional subrole does remain – many heads hold onto a professional culture where they expect to express their educational values through headship (Southworth 1998). The chief executive subrole is enhanced through additional responsibility for internal activities like finance and staff selection, monitoring and appraisal and greater freedom from external control at LEA level. Heads' autonomy is also constrained by an increase in external power over schooling through greater authority and accountability of governing bodies coupled with the 'steering at a distance' approach of the past central government (Kickert 1991) and the even more directive approach of the present one, mandating reforms and introducing accountability measures for policing their implementation. Both traditional and innovating dimensions of the leading professional subrole are left some space by the reforms, but central government now largely calls the shots by imposing parameters for most curriculum content and the priorities for staff development.

As changes heralded by reform policies have been implemented, it has become apparent how they augment each other in increasing primary heads' external accountability and internal dependence on other staff: here the overall thrust of the reform package amounts to demonstrably more than the sum of component parts. Table 1.1 illustrates some ways whereby changes in practice connected with reform policies launched by the middle of the decade raise the accountability and dependency stakes for heads. Interaction between reforms is evident. For example, the national curriculum is subject to national testing; results are published in league tables which will be compared with central government targets; they may be taken into account by parents in choosing a school for their child; they provide a basis for national comparison when the school is inspected; and the size of the LMS budget, and therefore the employment of staff and their ability to purchase curriculum resources, depends on the number of pupils attracted to the school. Where heads do not have responsibility for a class, they must rely on other staff for resourcing and teaching the national curriculum, achieving as high a standard as possible,

Table 1.1 Cumulative impact of reforms on primary headteachers' accountability and dependence

Change connected with reform	Impact on headteachers	
	External accountability	Dependence on other staff
National curriculum	basis for assessment and external inspection	implementation by class teachers, led by curriculum post holders responsible for writing policies and for support
Religious education and collective worship	basis for judgement by parents and inspectors of provision and its quality	implementation by class teachers, led by post holder responsible for RE
Assessment of national curriculum	basis for judgement by parents, governors and inspectors of standards achieved	implementation by class teachers, especially in Year 2 and Year 6
External inspection, results published	basis for judgement by parents and governors of standards achieved and quality of teaching and management	quality of all teachers' work inspected, including policies developed by post holders
League tables of national curriculum assessment results and truancy rates	basis for comparative judgement by parents, governors and inspectors of standards of pupil learning and discipline	all teachers' work contributes directly or indirectly to assessment results and truancy rates
Code of practice for pupils with special educational needs (SEN)	basis for judgement by parents, governors and inspectors of quality of provision and its management	class teachers with pupils who have SEN and SEN coordinator must ensure compliance with code of practice
New arrangements for supporting pupils from minority ethnic groups	basis for judgement by parents, governors and inspectors of quality of provision and its management	specialist teachers and support staff must provide support for pupils within new arrangements
Higher proportion of parents and local community representatives on governing bodies	accountability to greater number of lay people on governing bodies	teacher governors represent professional view to greater number of lay people on governing body, all teachers' work contributes to judgements by governors of quality of heads' management
Heads and governors responsible for financial management and staff appointment and dismissal under LMS	governors and inspectors scrutinise LMS budget and its management, governors approve budget	where budgetary management delegated by head, staff concerned are responsible for day-to-day management, all teachers' work contributes to parents wishing to send their child to the school. Size of LMS budget depends on number of pupils

Table 1.1 Continued

Change connected with reform	Impact on headteachers	
	External accountability	Dependence on other staff
More open enrolment of pupils	parents are more able to choose whether to send their child to the school within a quasi-market	all teachers' work contributes to parents wishing to send their child to the school
Ability of schools to become grant maintained, funded by central government	where school becomes grant maintained, head is accountable to governors, without LEA support	all teachers' work contributes to judgements by governors of quality of the head's management
Expectation that schools have a development plan	basis for judgement by governors and inspectors of quality of planning and implementation	all teachers' work contributes to quality of planning and implementation
Staff development budget and training days	basis for judgement by governors and inspectors of quality of staff development and its management	where budgetary management delegated by head, staff concerned are responsible for day-to-day management, teachers organise staff development activities
Appraisal of teaching staff	basis for judgement by governors and inspectors of quality of scheme and its management	where senior staff are appraisers, their work contributes to quality of the scheme

managing assessment, giving parents a good impression that will encourage them to send their child to the school, and pulling out all the stops for the inspection.

Taken together, the number and scope of reforms, the speed of their introduction, and the strategy for implementation adopted by central government ministers created conditions where it was to be expected that heads in larger primary schools might perceive the need for a new management structure. They had to share the burden of new management tasks and at the same time ensure that colleagues' contribution to the work of the school maximised the chances of its survival and, ideally, success in a context where interested parties other than staff were increasingly able to make the running.

SMTs hit the primary scene

Exactly when primary heads began to opt for team approaches involving an SMT is uncertain. Some indication is offered by research conducted from around 1988 when the reforms began in earnest. One local stimulus was the creation of the promoted post of 'primary needs project (PNP) coordinator' in Leeds primary schools during a major LEA initiative between 1985–89. Alexander (1997), who led the project evaluation, identified several types of management structure. They included a form of SMT, where some heads incorporated the PNP coordinator into a team of three along with themselves and the deputy head, and a more complex 'management matrix' in larger institutions consisting of head, deputy, PNP coordinator, curriculum and year leaders. He noted how changing management structures reflected the way many heads were involving colleagues in decision making and delegating tasks to cope with the introduction of LMS.

From 1990, reports from various sources suggest the sporadic emergence of SMTs in larger institutions across the country, generally representing three or more of the upper levels of the management hierarchy: the head, deputy and one or more other senior staff. In an account of her headship, Smith (1991) described how she overhauled the management structure, creating an SMT consisting of herself, the deputy and the lower school coordinator. Team members were released from teaching for a weekly meeting covering policy and more detailed matters, and were also enabled to visit classrooms to observe or work alongside colleagues. Fieldwork during 1991 for a study of perceptions of effective management reported that six out of seven primary schools investigated in depth had an SMT. There was evidence of synergy in three, where other staff reported that 'team members appeared to work well together and without undue conflict, that the work of the team led to sound management and decision making and helped keep the school on course, and that the overall style of management was consultative' (Bolam et al. 1993: 93). The potentially risky nature of team approaches highlighted earlier was indicated by problems reported in the remaining SMTs, interpreted by teachers outside them as a result of poor interpersonal relationships and poor communication. Teachers with promoted posts in one case were unclear as to whether they were members of the team. The SMT was viewed as creating an unhealthy division between the team and other staff. In a second team the deputy was uncommitted to a management role. In the third, team members other than the head perceived that conflicts of personality inhibited members from engaging in productive teamwork. The researchers stated that, alongside SMTs, there could also be a close head and deputy partnership, and that these teams were a forum for discussion of policy issues.

Passing reference to SMTs is made in other studies from this time. There was an SMT in all six case study schools (with between 240 and 450 pupils) in a study of planning for change (Wallace and McMahon 1994) whose fieldwork was carried out in 1991–92. The managerial contribution of SMTs to planning varied, half making up the major policy decision-making group, while the role of the rest was confined to being consulted prior to decisions taken by the head, either alone or with the deputy. Five SMTs met weekly or fortnightly, but four of these had to meet at lunchtime or after school because of a lack of non-contact time. Investigations where fieldwork was conducted up to 1994 also mention SMTs. The study of nine schools by MacGilchrist *et al.* (1995) implied that, in a small majority, an SMT was involved in development planning; one of the three female primary heads investigated by Hall (1996) had opted during her first headship for an SMT as a strategy for working round a deputy she perceived to be ineffective, whereas the other heads relied more on a head–deputy partnership; and the case study by Hayes (1996) of one head's attempt to introduce collaborative decision making indicated how she created an SMT as part of the management structure. An account in the education press of the management structure in a primary school with over 750 pupils (similar to the matrix structure identified by Alexander) included a senior team – the head, deputy and two teachers with the highest level of management responsibility – to which curriculum coordinators and year leaders brought proposals (*Times Educational Supplement* 1993). The head preferred to call this team a 'reference group' as the term had less hierarchical connotations than 'SMT', suggesting an egalitarian belief which belied the seven-level hierarchy of promoted posts carrying differential management responsibility in the school.

Webb and Vulliamy (1996a) conducted relevant research on fifty primary schools. They noted a trend towards heads' creation of SMTs. While the deputy was still the main assistant for heads in medium-sized institutions, one or two teachers with promoted posts were also incorporated into a team whose members worked with individual curriculum coordinators to formulate policies. In large schools, the greater number and range of hierarchical levels of promoted posts available enabled heads to create SMTs which included senior staff with responsibility for coordinating the work of pupils within a particular age range, resulting in a very few cases in a matrix structure involving curriculum coordinators similar to that noted in Alexander's evaluation. The management structure in the largest schools approached the multiplicity of levels found in the secondary sector. Here heads had allocated substantial promoted posts to curriculum coordinators, that 'formed a managerial layer in a three-tier management structure which, while it made policy formulation speedier and more streamlined, reduced the influence of class teachers over decisions on whole school issues' (Webb and Vulliamy 1996a: 150). Two examples were found of large schools with an SMT where a second deputy had been appointed to support heads with their wider range of management tasks.

More recent research (Menter *et al.* 1997), conducted in 1993–96, reported that two out of twelve schools had an SMT. The heads' rationale for adopting a team approach included ensuring that the new managerial workload was covered: in one, the head replaced a deputy who was leaving the school by requiring two senior teaching staff to take on the deputy's responsibilities; in the other, the head was attempting to compensate for a deputy who was underperforming by creating an SMT which included both this deputy and two other senior staff. The two SMTs faced an onerous workload with little non-contact time for carrying out their management tasks, and interviews with team members suggested a common perception that heads retained the balance of control over the SMTs' work.

Managerialism: are heads guilty till proven innocent?

These researchers and Webb and Vulliamy interpreted headteachers' response to the pressures of reform, including the adoption of such team approaches, as embodying the new 'managerialism'. This concept is often used pejoratively and is variably defined, though there is a general emphasis on empowerment of managers in public sector institutions (Clarke and Newman 1997) to co-ordinate the work of professional colleagues at the expense of their individual and collective autonomy so as to realise externally derived policy goals, and to provide efficient services subject to the discipline of strong external accountability. A managerialist thrust was avowedly intrinsic to education reforms, where private sector management structures and procedures were applied to the public sector as state-funded education was reconceived as a market-place commodity (Grace 1995). Managerialism is held responsible for unjustifiable erosion of teachers' collective autonomy. For Webb and Vulliamy, it means top-down hierarchical behaviour: a response 'characterised by the creation of systems, an emphasis on document production, accountability based on criteria external to the school and more directive controlling leadership by headteachers' (Webb and Vulliamy 1996b: 442). They argue that 'increasingly a tension between collegiality and managerialism is resulting in concepts like "whole school" being hijacked by a managerialist ethic'.

SMTs are apparently viewed as headteachers' strategy for tightening their grip on class teachers' practice, despite increased emphasis on cooperative working to implement reforms. Webb and Vulliamy suggest that such cooperative approaches, the initial response to reform, are being overtaken by 'managerialism and the directive management styles of headteachers associated with it, which undermine the feasibility and credibility of teachers working together collegially to formulate policies and promote continuity of practice' (Webb and Vulliamy 1996b: 455). Greater autonomy for heads under LMS, league tables of national curriculum test results, inspection reports, appraisal, internal monitoring of teaching as reflected in conditions of service and inspection criteria: such reform-linked changes combine with strategies like the creating of SMTs as elements of managerialism favouring increasingly directive management by heads.

Menter and his colleagues define managerialism more globally as a means of marketising education through 'manufacturing consent' of staff to implement this change:

> We see management, or more properly managerialism, as charged with bringing about the cultural transformation that shifts professional identities in order to make them responsive to client demand and external judge-

ment. Managerialism promotes the flexible and post-Fordist provision of education by operationalising it within the educational workplace. Managerialism acts discursively to internalise and justify very fundamental changes in professional practice, and to harness energy and discourage dissent.

(Menter *et al.* 1997: 9)

This version of managerialism implies mutually reinforcing practices which surreptitiously engender a shift in beliefs and values held by heads and other staff. They come to accept and voluntarily – but unwittingly – collude in implementing changes that undermine their ability as education 'producers' to decide on the curriculum and how it should be taught. Creating an education market requires teachers to respond to wishes of parents as the new 'consumers', rather than expect to be entitled as professionals to teach according to their educational beliefs and values. Heads have become more directive, whether by overt or more subtle means. Even if strategies like reducing the number of hierarchical levels in management structures and opting for team approaches (including creating SMTs) reflect heads' egalitarian beliefs, they empower other staff only in so far as they work together synergistically to achieve the goals of marketisation. Teachers, in other words, are being manœuvred into contributing voluntarily to the downfall of their collective autonomy to determine classroom practice.

Are SMTs in larger primary schools merely the tools of managerialist headteachers, themselves dupes of politicians? More evidence is needed: neither study focused on SMTs or involved observing SMTs at work. There is counter-evidence from Hall's observational study of women primary and secondary headteachers which suggests heads' behaviour may not be simply determined by managerialist forces. She concluded that, while heads she observed were entrepreneurial in striving for the school to succeed in the reform context, their leadership style was not managerialist. Far from being strongly directive and intolerant of opposition, they

> sought to act with others rather than exert power over them. They encouraged a culture based on caring and reciprocal relations and resisted the push towards corporate managerialism that government reforms have instigated ... the integrity of their leadership styles would appear to have given them the strength to transform (through working with rather than against) New Right educational reforms.

(Hall 1996: 192–3)

Hall's research implies that some heads at least have sufficient room to manœuvre to mediate the 'managerialist' thrust of the reforms, a conclusion supported by self-reports of the majority of primary headteacher respondents surveyed by Bell *et al.* (1996). The charge of managerialism must be taken seriously but so, equally, must the possibility that heads and other staff may have variable power to mediate managerialist policies according to beliefs and values that run counter to the spirit of reforms. It is clear, though, that investigation at the institutional level must take the wider social and political context into account.

Teamwork: the knowledge base

This account of the emergence of primary sector SMTs foregrounds the lack of detailed knowledge about their prevalence or practice. There is no shortage of practical handbooks promoting teamwork inside schools, whether in the UK (e.g. West 1992) or North America (e.g. Maeroff 1993; Harvey and Drolet 1994; McEwan 1997), and in the private sector (e.g. Blanchard et al. 1992; Spencer and Pruss 1992). The basis of the authors' prescriptions is primarily their experience or that of their sources as headteachers, trainers or consultants. Valuable as this experience undoubtedly is, the knowledge produced remains largely untested by research. A genre with what passes as a form of research backing is particularly popular in North America (e.g. Peters and Waterman 1982; Larson and LaFasto 1989; Katzenbach and Smith 1993), but the methods used are questionable. Teams of some kind are located which are judged according to some outcome criteria to be effective, and team members are then interviewed about factors making for success. Informants' accounts are limited to factors of which they are aware, and suffer from the 'well, they would say that' syndrome – possibly overplaying their personal contribution – which authors rarely cross-check by other methods, such as observing the teams in action.

Methodological weaknesses abound elsewhere. One British handbook (Belbin 1993) is based on an influential piece of research on individuals' preferred team roles (Belbin 1981), and written in the light of feedback from users of the approach and Belbin's own extensive consultancy experience in the years since his original experiments. The prescriptive edifice is built on analysis of roles emerging when individuals attending a management training course played a simulation game. No follow-up research seems to have been done to ascertain whether such behaviour holds good in real management teams tackling their normal tasks in real time, where – unlike the simulation – repercussions of managers' mistakes do not disappear once the game is over.

It seems likely that generalisations from this literature to primary SMTs can legitimately be made at only a high level of abstraction. For if transferability of knowledge across education sectors in the UK cannot be assumed, the contextual differences between countries in respect of the same sector, or between primary SMTs and the array of management and other kinds of team investigated outside the education sphere render the likelihood of transferability even more problematic. Consistent messages from this body of work, which may have wider applicability, include:

- teams can achieve more than their members could do individually if team tasks are such that one person could not carry them out so well without support, but close teamwork is not straightforward to develop or sustain. Many factors may inhibit synergy which cannot always be predicted or avoided;
- the quality of team leadership is critical – formal leadership of the team establishes conditions for teamwork. Informal leadership during the team-work process can be more fluid, circulating according to expertise and task;
- shared beliefs and values about how team members should work together, including their approach to coping with disagreement, underpin synergistic teamwork;
- beliefs and values about what is good for the team and what is good for the individual member may not coincide, but teamwork implies some subjugation of individual interests for the sake of the team interest;
- where there is a management hierarchy, it can inhibit equal contribution of team members but integrate work across structural boundaries;
- teamwork requires competence of all members in their substantive expertise and ability to work with other people including the psychological strength to receive feedback, but their contributions may be complementary rather than identical;
- collaboration and unified commitment require trust and mutual respect which can be fostered but not made to happen;
- team approaches are necessarily goal oriented, and shared clarity and commitment promotes synergistic teamwork;
- the experience of working in teams is likely to be evaluated by members according to its intrinsic worth for their job satisfaction and personal development, and its instrumental value in facilitating achievement of the team's purposes;
- reaching team decisions through consensus is widely preferred to other approaches, but it can be time consuming and may require unified commitment to compromise and resolving disagreements.

These generalisations relate to the culture of teams and the use of power by their members. Unified commitment signals a culture shared throughout the team, leading to synergistic use of resources by team members; leadership suggests empowerment of those acting as leaders, depending on beliefs and values of other members about the appropriateness and quality of their leadership.

Structure of the remaining chapters

So much for generalisations from elsewhere; what about primary school SMTs? The rest of the book gets on with the story, beginning in Chapter 2 with a summary of the research design and an outline of the cultural and political perspective which informed data collection and analysis. Outcomes of the initial survey of headteachers are summarised in Chapter 3. Remaining chapters are devoted to themes connected with case studies of four SMTs. The account begins in Chapter 4 with an introduction to the SMTs and exploration of the relationship between their location within the management structure and their perceived role in managing the school. Attention shifts in Chapter 5 to analysis of why the headteachers opted for a team approach involving an SMT, and how they and other members attempted to establish shared working practices and develop the team. Chapter 6 focuses down on the process of teamwork, examining how far team members adopted complementary individual team roles, how they conducted SMT meetings, and their experiences of decision making. SMT members achieve their purposes with and through other staff and governors, and their relationship with these groups is discussed in Chapter 7. The issue of team effectiveness is taken up in Chapter 8, where insiders' and outsiders' perceptions are reviewed, complemented by reference to judgements made by inspectors. In the light of the research findings, issues raised in this introductory chapter are revisited and practical and policy implications of the study are considered.

Chapter 2

A cultural and political toolkit

As a researcher, the answers you find depend on the questions you ask. The social world is infinitely complex, and researchers are, intrinsically, part of it. The stimulus for researchers interested in investigating social phenomena relates to their initial interpretation of the experience of people they elect to study; and the ideas and generalisations they develop may – by design or by default – impact on the practice of those same people where the researchers' ideas and generalisations filter down to them (Giddens 1976) through, for example, publications like this book. Whether implicitly or not, researchers begin a study with some conceptual baggage or orientation. The theoretical orientation of this study was explicit, the purpose of the present chapter being to unpack the baggage which framed the investigation to explain why certain questions were asked which led to particular kinds of answer.

The chapter begins with an account of the research design and data collection effort, and a brief consideration of the limitations of the study. Then a case is made for combining cultural and political perspectives that have been widely employed separately elsewhere as the conceptual framework for exploring and interpreting the operation of SMTs. Perspectives are conceived as loose metaphors, providing a lens for viewing the social world and making sense of what we see, and examples are critically discussed of research on school management from either of the perspectives to be combined. The concepts incorporated in the proposed dual perspective are defined and brief examples of their application are given to induct readers into the tricky business of doing two things at once. Finally, the importance is asserted of linking the little picture of SMTs' practice – the main focus – with the big policy picture that these SMTs are bound to reflect, and to which, in their small way, they contribute.

Design and methods

Central concerns were to determine how widespread SMTs had become in larger primary sector schools and to build on the earlier secondary school SMT research in three ways: methodologically, by employing methods of data collection and analysis developed there; substantively, by considering how far key features of secondary SMTs were replicated in their primary sector equivalents; and conceptually, by applying the cultural and political perspective to a new setting. It was decided to restrict attention to schools of medium to large size because SMTs in them would probably constitute a subgroup of the teaching staff, as is the case in secondary schools. The original study and other research (e.g. Wallace 1996) had suggested that an unintended consequence of creating an in-group of SMT members could be to foster a perception among other staff that they were an out-group, some distance from the hub of managerial action. The present investigation could examine whether teaching staff lower in the management hierarchy and their senior colleagues had become more remote from each other since the advent of the reforms, a trend other researchers claim to have found in secondary (e.g. Bowe *et al.* 1992) and primary schools (Webb and Vulliamy 1996a). Since there would not be a precise size of school below which SMTs might include the whole teaching staff, the cut-off point for the smallest schools eligible for inclusion in the research was taken as catering for 300 pupils. There are likely to be more than ten teaching staff in schools of this size or over, and four or more levels of promoted post including head and deputy. In Wales, just 12 per cent of primary sector schools had over 300 pupils in 1994/95 (Welsh Office 1996), while in England this proportion was 22 per cent, the two largest institutions having over 800 pupils (DFEE 1997).

The project began in May 1995 and was funded by the Economic and Social Research Council for eighteen months. It was designed to address the question:

> How, within a context of educational reform, do SMTs in large primary sector schools operate where all members perceive themselves to be committed to teamwork as their core strategy for managing the school, and to what effect?

It was possible to study only a few teams in depth, so the decision was made to go where the going was likely to be good for exploring teamwork by seeking SMTs whose members expressed a positive attitude at the onset of fieldwork towards the idea of working as a team. The literature discussed in the first chapter made it clear that teams in name may or may not act as teams in deed, and it was judged that most would be learned about practices, problems and successes of primary school SMTs by working where a sustained effort was being made to operate according to some conception of teamwork. To allow for the possibility that the headteacher's gender might be a significant factor affecting how primary SMTs worked, investigation was planned of an equal number of SMTs with female and male heads. There are over 20,000 primary sector schools in England and Wales and, as 51 per cent of heads were female in 1994 (DFEE 1996), the gender balance superficially appears even. This statistic belies the fact, however, that women are under-represented among primary sector heads given that, at the time, 82 per cent of all primary teaching staff were female. Just 7.3 per cent of women teaching staff were heads, compared with 31.3 per cent of men. It is likely that women are also under-represented in the other senior posts from which SMT membership tends to be drawn.

The fieldwork consisted of two phases. First, in the summer term 1995 a postal questionnaire survey was conducted of 150 headteachers in randomly selected schools of 300 or more pupils in south Wales and south-west England. It established the prevalence of primary sector SMTs and also enabled data to be gathered on headteachers' perceptions of teamwork and its effectiveness which informed subsequent data collection. After two reminder letters, a total of sixty-five returns (representing a 43 per cent response) was received. This response rate is consistent with that for other postal surveys conducted since central government reforms. Three respondents reported that their pupil numbers were now below 300 and it was decided to include them nevertheless. Follow-up telephone calls to 79 non-respondents indicated that the proportion of those who did respond and who also stated that they had an SMT approximated the proportion in the wider sample. A few returns were incomplete, but such information as was given was included in the analysis. Second, four focused and interpretive case studies (Merriam 1988) of contrasting SMTs were conducted, informed by the secondary SMT study and initial survey of heads. The four schools, all with more than 300 pupils, were selected from the area covered by the survey. Data were collected over the four terms between autumn 1995 and autumn 1996. Criteria for selection of schools to approach included existence of an SMT, professed commitment to teamwork among its members, variation in size of school, and ensuring an equal number of women and men headteachers.

Data collection and analysis were informed by qualitative techniques developed by Miles and Huberman (1994), including tabulation to summarise findings. Methods for gathering data were semi-structured interviews with each SMT member, a sample of other teaching staff with and without promoted posts, and the chair of governors; non-participant observation of SMT meetings and other meetings where team members were present; and creation of a document archive. The extent of interview and observation data collected for the case studies is summarised in Table 2.1. Case study fieldwork was supported in all four schools, and no restriction was placed on access to SMT and other meetings. It was agreed that no individual, school or LEA would be identified in any published work arising from the study. Feedback was offered to the four schools after fieldwork was completed but the offer was taken up in only one instance. Staff most centrally involved in the case studies were invited to comment on the draft of this book.

The integrated approach to data collection and analysis facilitated progressive focusing as the study unfolded. An initial literature review and the

Table 2.1 Case study database

Data collected autumn 1995– autumn 1996	Case study school				Totals
	Winton	Pinehill	Kingsrise	Waverley	
Interview with headteacher	2	2	2	2	8
Interview with other SMT members	3	5	8	4	20
Interview with chair of governors	1	1	1	1	4
Interview with other staff	6	6	7	7	26
Observation of SMT meetings	6	1	3	2	12
Observation of meetings between SMT members and other staff	2	4	2	2	10

conceptual framework and findings of the secondary SMT study were the main sources of research questions, to which the detailed survey and interview questions related. Survey data were tabulated, responses to open-ended questions being categorised inductively. Notes were taken during observations and interviews, and the latter were tape recorded. Summary tapes were prepared with reference to fieldnotes, the interview schedule and interview tapes which included the researchers' interpretations and direct quotations to back them up. Summaries were transcribed and collated. Interview summaries were made, feeding into site summaries which formed the basis for cross-site analysis. Matrices were developed to display qualitative data, and the data set was scanned to tease out broad themes and explore the contextual complexity of particular situations.

Limitations of the research

There is no such thing as the critique proof research design, and several limitations of this study are worth bearing in mind. First, the project was of moderate scope and conducted over a relatively short period, meaning that the findings amount to a snapshot of practices and perspectives rather than a profile of team evolution. Second, the orientation was sociological, and psychological variables, including those connected with personality, were not addressed. What individuals who were interviewed might view as a 'personality clash' was interpreted according to the cultural and political dimensions of the conflictual interaction between the protagonists concerned. Third, though an attempt was made to ensure that the survey sample of headteachers was likely to be reasonably representative through random selection of schools in two regions, the response rate was low. Further, the research design did not allow for cross-checking the accounts of headteachers who did respond against accounts that other staff in their schools might give. Fourth, reliance on qualitative methods and a small number of case studies provided depth of understanding at the expense of generalisability in terms of representing primary SMT practice in larger schools across the country. An element of generalisation is, nevertheless, possible in the sense that the impact of central government reforms on these SMTs could be tracked, constituting a major factor stimulating the move towards team approaches. The variety of structures and processes featured in just four cases also suggests that, on one hand, there is room for different approaches to teamwork within certain parameters while, on the other, primary SMTs share some features with those identified in the literature on teams elsewhere. In so far as heads and other SMT members have an element of agency and their interaction is not totally predetermined by wider structural forces such as reform policies, they have room to manœuvre over the form, role and purpose adopted by the SMT. Fifth, presence of a researcher in the case study schools may have contributed to a 'halo effect'. The stance adopted was to be non-aligned in terms of immediate staff concerns, but the investigator would be uniquely privileged in the sense of observing what went on inside SMT meetings and gathering, in confidence, views of individuals about each other's performance. A response was made to occasional requests to give generalised feedback while respecting confidences, which could have had some effect on the subjects of the research. However, SMT members reported that any such input had made little impact on teamwork during the fieldwork period.

Finally, when considering SMT effectiveness, it must be noted that the causal linkage from SMT practice to pupil learning was followed only as far as the direct outcomes of teamwork, so relevant conclusions must be regarded as tentative and based on impression (see Chapter 8). Data were gathered on perceptions of effectiveness from inside and outside the SMTs; behaviour was observed indicating team members' varying commitment and other factors facilitating or inhibiting teamwork, how far ideas from different sources were taken into account in making SMT decisions, and the extent to which an overview of the school was sustained; and views expressed in school inspection reports were noted. This database is, arguably, sufficient to highlight significant practical, policy and theoretical issues.

Metaphorically thinking

Any quest for one best super-theory to explain the entire social world is probably futile. Social phenomena are too complex for such reductionist explanation and theories in the social sciences are both normative and culturally relative, reflecting beliefs and values of their creators who cannot escape their location inside the social and political climate of their time. Theories orientate us towards phenomena in particular ways; it seems more realistic to regard them as perspectives (House 1981) amounting to lenses for scrutinising the social world, or as metaphors (Morgan 1986) which foreground some features of social phenomena while neglecting aspects that other metaphors would pick up. If no metaphor can be taken as gospel, it follows that analysis may be deepened by using more than one metaphor to look at the same phenomenon. Mixing metaphors born of different traditions is increasingly advocated as a strategy for overcoming the myopic tendency of a single metaphor: Cuthbert (1984) identifies five; Bolman and Deal (1991) opt for four; and Bush, drawing on Cuthbert's work, goes for six in the second edition of his book. Bush claims that these perspectives or metaphors

> represent conceptually distinct approaches to the management of educational institutions. However, it is rare for a single theory to capture the reality of management in any particular school or college. Rather, aspects of several perspectives are present in different proportions within each institution. The applicability of each approach may vary with the event, the situation and the participants.
>
> (Bush 1995: 146–8)

He argues, further, that the validity of applying any metaphor depends on organisational characteristics like size of the institution. The political perspective, for instance, is deemed less relevant to the informal decision-making process in a small primary school than in large secondary schools and colleges where groups of staff tend to compete for resources. This stance implies that examining uses of power in the case study primary schools would be doomed to find next to nothing! Bush assumes, first, that each perspective addresses an exclusive proportion of the total 'reality' of particular organisational phenomena; and second, that certain phenomena may be present or absent in different situations under investigation. This view of metaphors seems overly restrictive. If metaphors are no more than alternative lenses for examining the social world, they can surely be used either one after the other, as in a *mixed metaphor* approach, or at the same time, as in a *multiple metaphor* strategy.

Any perspective may also be brought legitimately to bear on any empirical situation in the social world. One limitation of much research on primary and secondary schools from a single perspective stems from the possibility of interpreting, from alternative perspectives, the same phenomenon (such as decision making) in both kinds of institution. Secondary school staff no more have a monopoly on political conflict over decisions connected with scarce resources than their primary school colleagues have a monopoly on cultural cohesion leading to consensus decisions. The contrasting mixed-metaphor approach of Bolman and Deal is directed towards helping managers improve their practice by trying different ways of reflecting on their experience. It rests on the assumption, unlike Bush, that the same organisational phenomena may fruitfully be interpreted from more than one perspective or 'frame' where they are employed sequentially. Bolman and Deal argue that most managers become stuck in the habit of using their pet frame, where they could free themselves up by looking at their experience from alternative points of view:

> The ability to reframe experience enriches and broadens a leader's repertoire and serves as a powerful antidote to self-entrapment. Expanded choice enables managers to generate creative responses to the broad range of problems that they encounter . . . it can be enormously liberating for managers to realise that there is *always* more than one way to respond to any organisational problem or dilemma. Managers are imprisoned only to the degree that their palette of ideas is impoverished.
>
> (Bolman and Deal 1991: 4, original emphasis)

Each frame contains a bundle of concepts enabling managers to build up their interpretation and a normative image of how organisations should be managed, giving them something to emulate or reject according to their professional values. By switching between alternative frames, managers enlarge the potential basis of understanding that informs their practice. Bolman and Deal suggest managers should use one perspective at a time for simplicity's sake, but note that some research and theory employs concepts from two or more perspectives together in working towards a sophisticated analysis (e.g. Cohen and March 1974; Perrow 1986), transcending limits of a single perspective interpretation through a 'multiple frame' strategy. The approach adopted in the present study represents a step along this road, according to the assumption that two or more perspectives can be rolled into one as a multiple metaphor where concepts from the constituent perspectives are employed together.

There is not a one-to-one relationship between concept and perspective: typologies of perspectives differ in the number of metaphors they create, and there is some divergence over which concept belongs to which perspective. Here, concepts commonly located in cultural and political perspectives are combined in a dual metaphor for interpreting interaction in an organisational setting. The key to fitting two perspectives together so closely is to adopt stipulative definitions of concepts drawn from each constituent perspective which are mutually compatible. This strategy is likely to be rejected by many who opt for a single metaphor or mixed metaphor approach, because incompatible versions of concepts connected with cultural or political perspectives have been widely employed, leading to opposing interpretations of similar phenomena. Table 2.2 compares approaches towards theorising and analysing interaction adopted by several researchers who have used one or other perspective, or both, to examine school management.

It should be borne in mind that this depiction is offered solely to point up certain contrasts and does not reflect the conceptual sophistication of each approach. Nevertheless, it throws into relief how the orientation towards

Table 2.2 Comparison between approaches to cultural and/or political perspectives

Criterion	Nias et al. 1989	Ball 1987	Southworth 1995	Blase and Anderson 1995	Bolman and Deal 1991	Wallace and Hall 1994
Purpose of theorising	understanding leading to advice about action	critical evaluation	critical evaluation leading to alternative approach to leadership and advice about action	critical evaluation leading to leadership theory	advice about action	understanding leading to advice about action
Type of metaphor	single	single	single	single	mixed, including separate cultural and political	multiple: combined cultural and political
Assumptions about key concept in main perspective(s)	culture becomes widely shared among staff	power is conflictual	power is largely conflictual	power may be conflictual or synergistic	culture: leaders promote widely shared staff culture through vision building, ceremonies etc., power: conflictual	culture: beliefs and values variably shared between subcultures. power: may be conflictual or synergistic. Interaction entails differential use of power according to beliefs and values, affecting how and by whom staff culture is shaped
Use of concepts from alternative perspective (single and mixed metaphors)	use of power, especially by headteachers	norms and rules govern routine interaction	normative control by head and other staff	principals attempt to manage staff culture through manipulation	sequential use of alternative frames including cultural and political	simultaneous use of concepts from both cultural and political perspectives
Interpretation of synergistic interaction between head and other staff	cohesion due to shared beliefs and values	headteachers dominate other staff through controlling activity, so avoiding potential conflict	headteacher dominates other staff through controlling activity, so avoiding potential conflict	empirically most principals dominate other staff (cf. Ball 1987), a few principals share power democratically with other staff	cohesion due to shared beliefs and values promoted by leaders	cohesion due to shared beliefs and values resulting from use of power by heads and other staff.
Interpretation of conflictual interaction between head and other staff	shared beliefs and values about compromise enable conflicts to be avoided or resolved	each protagonist uses power in struggle to realise incompatible interests	head resolves conflicts, through normative control or personal interventions	each protagonist uses power in struggle to achieve incompatible interests	each actor uses power in struggle to realise incompatible interests	each actor uses power according to beliefs and values to realise incompatible interests

perspectives facilitates and constrains interpretation of findings, and also how concepts employed in different single perspectives must be rendered compatible before they can be combined in a multiple metaphor. The first three groups of writers investigated schools in Britain: Nias and her colleagues conducted an observational study of staff relationships in primary schools; Ball investigated secondary school management, focusing largely on teachers' views of headteachers' behaviour; and Southworth, who had worked with Nias, subsequently observed a primary head's approach to management. The studies of Blase and Anderson are based on US teachers' perceptions, including those about principals, and case studies of two principals. The work of Bolman and Deal, introduced above, and the study of secondary SMTs conducted by Wallace and Hall are also included.

There are six criteria for comparison. First, these writers have differing purposes for engaging in theory development which affects their use of whichever perspective. In the context of theories about organisations, Hoyle (1986) distinguishes between 'theory for understanding', whose purpose is primarily to provide explanation (which may be antithetical to practical action) and 'theory for action', aimed at guiding workplace practice. The category of theory for understanding could helpfully be subdivided further, according to the writers' value orientation towards the phenomena they examine empirically. Some investigators have adopted an explicit critical stance either from the beginning, framing their theory building and empirical efforts, or in the light of their findings. Others have retained a more distanced orientation towards what they variably acknowledge as value-laden fields of enquiry, seeking explanations which constitute a platform for themselves and others to make judgements according to a range of possible value positions. It therefore seems useful to separate 'theory for understanding', where a distanced orientation is adopted, from what may be labelled 'theory for critical evaluation' where commitment to an overtly critical stance is made. Second, the different perspectives are associated with varying approaches towards metaphors – whether single, mixed or multiple. Third, assumptions differ about the compass of central concepts underlying each perspective employed, with consequences for the interpretation constructed. Fourth, where single or mixed metaphor approaches are adopted, examples of concepts brought into the analysis are listed which could be construed as belonging to the alternative metaphor. The final two criteria address contrasting interpretations of interaction between headteachers and other staff which is either synergistic (where people apparently work together harmoniously), or conflictual (where individuals and groups struggle against each other).

Captured by the perspective?

The analysis of Nias and her co-workers employs a cultural perspective to explain interaction observed among primary school staff, portraying how the entire staff group developed and sustained a shared set of beliefs and values about how staff members related to each other. The analysis majors on the myriad subtle ways in which all staff contribute to developing and maintaining the shared staff culture. These researchers may have been captured by their perspective in the sense that their attention is drawn away from the possibility of differential use of power by heads and other staff in moulding this shared culture, of the emergence of subcultures, or of conflict as the bottom line explanation for some interactions. Others investigating primary schools have questioned the lack of purchase on power within this cultural perspective (e.g. Newman and Pollard 1994). Power may be underplayed, but it does creep into the account, suggesting the notion of organisational culture is inadequate to grasp all that was found significant from this perspective. For example, they state:

> normative *control* was so pervasive that it is easy to lose sight of the fact that it too was the product of a *power differential*. Each school had a head with a strong 'mission' and well developed *political skills* who had been in post for at least ten years and to whom had accrued during that time a con-siderable amount of personal *authority*.
>
> (Nias *et al*. 1989: 15, emphasis added)

The power related concepts in italics have surfaced in the analysis because they are needed to explain how heads were uniquely placed to persuade other staff to accept their managerial values and so achieve value consensus, even in situations of cultural accord. Synergistic interaction is explained as expressing shared beliefs and values, whereas conflicts are interpreted as being confronted or avoided in line with underlying shared values about, say, working towards compromise solutions.

A stark contrast is provided by Ball, whose purposes include providing an alternative to prevailing analyses of schools employing systems theory, and informing consideration of how to improve education consistent with explicit values:

> An understanding of the way that schools change (or stay the same) and therefore of the practical limits and possibilities of educational develop-ment, must take account of intra-organisational processes. This is partic-ularly crucial in examining developments which are related to the achievement of more equal, more just, as well as more effective education.
>
> (Ball 1987: 3)

His single metaphor approach is based on a type of political orientation he terms a 'conflict perspective': 'I take schools . . . to be *arenas of struggle*; to be riven with actual or potential conflict between members; to be poorly co-ordinated; to be ideologically diverse' (Ball 1987: 19, original emphasis). By definition, power means struggle, whether overt or suppressed. This analysis also appears captured by the perspective. The narrowly conflictual view of power favours an interpretation of all interaction as embodying conflict, even if it is not readily apparent. Ball acknowledges this danger: 'having set an agenda for the study of micropolitics and institutional conflict in schools, I do not want to fall into the same trap as the social system theorists, of seeing conflict everywhere, where they saw consensus.' Conflict, however, is given the dominant role in the analysis. What passes for harmonious interaction is interpreted as masking implicit conflict, and concepts related to culture find a place in the explanation:

> interaction is centred upon the *routine*, mundane and, for the most part, uncontroversial running of the institution . . . .routine organisational life is set within the *'negotiated order'* . . . a patterned construct of contrasts, *understandings, agreements* and *'rules'* which provides the basis of concerted action . . . In this way conflicts may remain normally implicit and subterranean, only occasionally bursting into full view.
>
> (Ball 1987: 20, emphasis added)

Secondary heads are viewed as using overt and covert strategies resting on their unique access to power to realise their interest in retaining control over other staff while, to achieve this goal, they must secure staff commitment. SMTs are viewed as a means of supporting this interest, members other than heads being orientated towards them. Other staff perceive the SMT as 'the hierarchy' who exclude teachers from important aspects of decision making. The SMT's ability to control other staff is reinforced by the 'norm of cabinet responsibility' where team members withhold from publicly criticising SMT decisions. Yet the analysis stops short of exploring how teachers may also use power to 'manage the boss', whether through acquiescence, support or resistance. The cultural concepts in the quotation placed in italics are subordinated in his analysis but have close affinity with those featuring centrally in the interpretation of Nias and her co-workers. In both single metaphor analyses, concepts relating to the perspective that was *not* employed are therefore present in the account. The 'norm' of cabinet responsibility articulated by Ball is a cultural notion; the 'personal authority' of the head in the analysis by Nias and her colleagues is a political idea. Both analyses have used concepts from an alternative perspective in a subsidiary position to grasp the range of phenomena found.

Southworth's single metaphor approach grew out of his case study, and was developed to interpret and evaluate key findings. It draws on that of Ball and appears similarly constrained by the perspective adopted, but his purposes reach further towards construction of an alternative normative theory. Ball (1987: 280) concludes with the statement: 'the alternative lies in the direction of *school democracy*. But that, as they say, is another story' (original emphasis).

Southworth begins to tell such a story by working towards articulation of his preferred critical approach to school leadership and offers advice on how to support heads in learning to develop this orientation to their practice. A conception of power as essentially conflictual takes his analysis of a primary headteacher's management practice along parallel lines with that of Ball, developing the idea of 'normative control' to explain how the head used subtle means to get his way with other staff, such as promoting teachers who shared his values to management positions. The 'normative' element of the concept has cultural overtones, linked here with the political notion of control. Harmonious interaction is interpreted as resulting from the head's successful 'domination', acting to deflect or pre-empt most potential conflict and, on the rare occasions when disputes between other staff did arise, using normative control strategies such as intervening or deploying other senior staff on his behalf.

The opposing interpretations of interaction following from these separate cultural and political perspectives are indicative of their incompatibility. One researcher's cultural cohesion is another's political domination. The claim made earlier that cultural and political perspectives can be combined into a dual metaphor rests on the assumption that concepts drawn from the constituent perspectives can be rendered compatible. This job clearly cannot be done with a cultural perspective restricted to cohesion and a political perspective restricted to conflict. How is a marriage of a theorist's convenience to be achieved? One response is to broaden the constituent perspectives: the cultural orientation may allow for conflict between subcultures, while the political orientation may allow for synergistic use of resources to achieve shared interests. The political perspective adopted by Blase and Anderson goes part way. Their purposes are aligned with those of Southworth, and they construct a compatible normative theory of 'democratic, empowering leadership', but their theory embraces a more comprehensive definition of power. It is conceived as expressed in all interaction which may vary from the conflictual ('power over'), through the facilitative ('power through') to the synergistic, where individuals participate as equals ('power with'). This conception has potential to get round some limitations of the narrower conflict perspective where power disappears unless some actors are interpreted as wielding power over others, whether up front through conflict or behind the scenes through domination. It underpins the approach developed by Lindle (1994) towards supporting practice-related learning of school managers.

The critically evaluative purpose of Blase and Anderson leads them, however, to interpret much empirical interaction between principals and other staff as amounting to domination by principals whether through overt, authoritarian means or the covert, manipulative means of more facilitative approaches. In the latter case, principals secure commitment of other staff to their own – rather than a shared – agenda. Their single metaphor approach also results in cultural concepts appearing in a subordinate role in the analysis. They argue that collaborative or 'diplomatic' interactions among teachers reflect a mutually supportive culture: 'the politics of diplomacy were consistent with the norms of equitable exchange and mutual benefit. Diplomatic actions, such as support among teachers, promoted networks of indebtedness and mutual assistance' (Blase and Anderson 1995: 69). Principals' approach to power has a significant impact in 'setting the political "tone" of the school', either promoting collaborative and reciprocal or conflictual and self-oriented interactions by other staff. Yet, consistent with the critique above of other adherents of a single perspective, they postulate that both forms of interaction are likely to coexist in any school – the bottom line interpretation of interaction here is not predetermined by the perspective as being necessarily either synergistic or conflictual.

A more comprehensive view of power therefore avoids the problem that conflict perspectives face over allowing for occurrence of synergistic interaction. Expanding the single metaphor can take us only so far, as even a political perspective allowing for synergistic as well as conflictual interaction gives limited purchase on why individuals and groups employ power. Blase and Anderson appear to resort to cultural concepts because they help to explain the uses of power by making inferences about the beliefs, norms and values guiding principals and other staff, about the degree to which they are shared, and the contribution that the uses of power by different individuals and groups may make to changing or sustaining their own beliefs and values and those of other parties to interaction. Culture and power are intimately connected.

The mixed metaphor approach of Bolman and Deal seems attractive because they allow for sequential interpretation from different conceptual orientations. Yet they are forced into the position of employing one perspective at a time precisely because their version of each perspective makes it incompatible with others. The cultural perspective, for Bolman and Deal, is about the shared implicit beliefs, norms and values that promote cultural cohesion as a largely irrational and unconscious process. The political perspective is restricted to conflict, so never the twain shall meet. By contrast, the multiple metaphor approach to integrating the cultural and political perspectives relies on the assumptions that interaction may be synergistic or conflictual; relevant beliefs and values may or may not be shared with other parties to interaction; and particular versions of concepts can be taken from each constituent perspective which are mutually compatible. In seeking to explain synergistic interaction inside SMTs, the interpretation focuses on how far beliefs and values about teamwork are shared, how past use of power by team members has brought about this shared culture and how the culture guides use of power to achieve shared interests in the present. Conversely, conflictual interaction is explained by examining differing beliefs and values guiding the use of power by team members in attempting to achieve incompatible interests. The unique position of authority accorded to heads, discussed in the opening chapter, gives them greater power than their SMT colleagues to shape the SMT culture relating to teamwork, but the latter also have informal sources of power to buy into or reject the model of teamwork and its cultural assumptions on offer from heads.

Drawbacks of combining perspectives in this way are that the analysis is complicated, with potentially double the number of concepts of either single perspective, and that these concepts must articulate with each other. It follows that any theoretical orientation is bound to be reductionist because of the effort to find patterns to render complex social phenomena comprehensible. The corollary of attempting a more sophisticated and so less reductionist orientation to capture more of the phenomena at hand is a more complex interpretation which runs the risk of burdening the analyst – and reader – with conceptual overload. This point is well illustrated by juxtaposing the cultural concepts employed by Nias and her colleagues with the political concepts adopted by Ball (Table 2.3). To keep the conceptual load within bounds, selection of concepts is restricted to those which proved in the secondary SMT study to provide deepest insights when enquiring into teamwork. Another drawback of the approach then becomes apparent: some fine grain of the analysis possible from within each single perspective is lost, since the full range of concepts they offer is not employed. The multiple metaphor approach follows Giddens' (1976) view that culture and power are integral components of interaction, where individuals communicate meaning within a context of normative sanctions and relationships of power. Since all three elements are

Table 2.3 Key concepts employed within different perspectives

Cultural (Nias et al. 1989)	Political (Ball 1987)	Cultural and political
culture of collaboration	power	culture of teamwork
beliefs	control	subculture
values	goal diversity	beliefs
understanding	ideology	values
attitudes	conflict	norms
meanings	interests	role
norms		status
symbols		rituals
rituals		consensus
ceremonies		power
negotiation		resources
consensus		hierarchy
		interests
		dialectic of control
		authority
		influence
		conflict
		contradiction
		coalitions

intrinsic to interaction they are empirically inseparable, though analytical distinctions can be made.

Concepts drawn primarily from a cultural perspective

Meanings and norms lie within the compass of a *culture*, shared symbols, beliefs and values expressed in interaction – in short, 'the way we do things around here' (Bower 1966). The SMTs in this study variably developed a '*culture of teamwork*' consisting of shared beliefs and values about working together. Beliefs and values include those about *norms*, or rules of behaviour, a common norm being that SMT decisions must be reached by coming to a working consensus, having acknowledged dissenting opinions. Where the meanings and norms held by individuals are shared, they belong to a common culture. In an organisation there may be distinct and overlapping groups who share different sets of beliefs and values, each forming a *subculture*. SMT members may share a subculture exclusive to the SMT, while those members responsible for the infant or junior department may also share the professional subculture of staff in their department.

Some shared meanings take the form of *myths*: stories and rumours passed between individuals and whose authenticity may be based on hearsay or hard evidence. Certain myths relate to the institutional history. SMT members who had worked in the school for some years had a store of anecdotes about people and events from the past which could be a basis for interpreting the present. Meanings which may or may not be shared include those relating to the *role* of an individual or group. When individuals occupy a social position their actions are determined both by their perception of what others expect of any person in that position according to their formal responsibilities and by individuals' idiosyncratic preferences. This study considers the group *role of the SMT* in managing the school: the aggregate of beliefs and values about a team's purpose among SMT members and others. It also looks into the preferred individual *team roles* occupied by different SMT members. People may occupy several roles, leading to the possibility of *role conflict* where beliefs and values do not coincide. Many SMT members other than heads had class-teaching responsibility. They could experience some conflict between their beliefs and values as SMT members, where they were expected to serve the interests of the whole school, and those as class teachers where they legitimately wished to promote their sectional class-teaching interests. A third realm of shared meaning of significance for SMTs is *status*. This term refers to the relative position of a person on a socially defined hierarchy of social worth. It was unanimously perceived in the case study schools that differential salary awards among teachers, allocated for increasing levels of management responsibility, represented an indicator of their relative status. Membership of SMTs did not remove status differentials connected with salaries, management responsibilities and conditions of service. The larger salary and very different conditions of service of headteachers secured their higher status within the management hierarchy than their SMT colleagues, whatever the strength of any egalitarian values guiding the team approach.

Symbolic elements of culture are those where actions represent something else, typically a shared value. Such actions include *rituals* – routinised and habitual (such as the seating arrangements for SMT meetings which might demonstrate a value placed on everyone's contribution) – and, within this category, *ceremonies* implying some kind of celebration. Members of one SMT occasionally socialised together. Hoyle (1986) suggests that much interaction between staff is symbolic since actions may have both an explicit managerial purpose and signify a shared value.

Concepts drawn primarily from a political perspective

The notion of *power* refers to individuals' capability to intervene in events so as to alter their course, and is defined by Giddens (1984) as 'transformative capacity': use of resources to secure desired outcomes. These *resources* vary, including incentives and rewards, sanctions, reference to norms of behaviour, knowledge, and skills and attitudes linked to individual personalities. Within SMTs, aspects of individuals' personality were expressed through their preferred use of power according to their beliefs and values, in a pattern which may be encapsulated as their personal style as managers and teamworkers. The status and the opportunity for career advancement offered by SMT membership were incentives for some staff, motivating them to seek membership. Heads were empowered to reward such individuals by enabling them to join the SMT. Sanctions included heads' potential to take disciplinary action while other SMT members could withdraw their commitment to the team and undermine its work, perhaps by leaking confidential information.

Diverse forms of knowledge are a resource which may be used to alter the course of events. Individuals may use contextual knowledge in considering when to offer or withhold information. All team members drew on their knowledge of the school to contribute to SMT debates, and each member had expertise associated with his or her individual management responsibility. Some members of SMTs actively sought opinions of other staff and relayed them to the team. Power may be manifested in interaction yet may also remain latent, since resources like the ability to apply sanctions may still exist when they are not in use. Moreover, power is relational since one person's action to secure particular outcomes involves others' responses or their potential to act. The goals of each team member could be met only through actions of colleagues inside (and often outside) the SMT.

For Giddens, power may or may not relate to conflict. His conception contrasts with the 'zero-sum' definition offered by Dahl (1957) who viewed power as 'the ability to get someone to do something that he or she would not otherwise do'. The conception of power employed by Giddens allows for each actor in a conflict situation to use transformative capacity in trying to achieve interests which contradict those of others. It also suggests that, where consensus exists, individuals have great capacity for collaborating to promote change or to maintain the *status quo* inside and outside the SMT. Unanimous agreement among SMT members on decisions tended to result in a concerted effort to implement them. This view of power is consistent with the version adopted by Blase and Anderson and implies that individuals use power synergistically where they pull together to achieve a shared goal and there is no resistance. Zero-sum conceptions of power, widely associated with conflict theorists, do not accept its existence where one person persuades others to do what they would also like to do, but perhaps had not previously considered.

Following Bacharach and Lawler (1980), two types of power may be distinguished. *Authority* means the use of resources to achieve goals in a way perceived by an individual to be legitimated by beliefs and values linked to formal status. It includes the right to apply sanctions to secure compliance. The conditions of service of headteachers give them extensive managerial authority. According to Bacharach and Lawler, individuals have either overall or delegated authority. In the area of education, however, the balance of authority is not so clear cut. The authority of headteachers, even though the reforms have much reduced the authority of LEAs, is still delegated by the governing body of each school. Heads are entitled to delegate to other staff aspects of their own delegated authority, as where they adopt a team approach, and to distribute only as much delegated authority to SMT colleagues as they wish.

The SMT tended to be regarded as a group with high status in the school management hierarchy. Members other than the head held delegated authority accompanying their individual management responsibilities and the variable expectation that they should contribute as equals in the team. The head retained authority to overrule other team members, make decisions unilaterally, or withdraw whatever had been delegated. There was no recourse to formal sanctions if the head temporarily took back delegated authority by belatedly removing a decision from the SMT brief. Beliefs and values about differential status in the management hierarchy were associated with levels of delegated authority: in one team the head was responsible for the SMT; the deputies were responsible for the infant and junior departments; and an experienced teacher with a substantial extra allowance was responsible for pupils with special educational needs throughout the school. The possibility of contradictory perceptions of relative delegated authority could arise from SMT members' overlapping responsibilities. In the example above, responsibility for pupils with special educational needs could be construed as belonging to the allowance holder, to the deputy in whose department particular pupils were placed and, ultimately, to the head. Beliefs and values may therefore differ on how much authority is delegated in the school, to whom, and when and how it should be used.

Influence means the informal use of resources to achieve goals where individuals perceive there are no sanctions available linked to delegated authority accompanying their status in the management hierarchy. There may be other sanctions, such as holding back from contributing to SMT deliberations. The less delegated authority actors hold, the more they will be reliant on influence. Heads may also use influence in situations not covered by their authority, as when asking a favour of an SMT colleague. Actions involving influence may be overt, as in this example, or more covert, as where an individual's intentions are not made fully explicit. It should be noted that the data collection methods employed offered limited access to any actions where intentions may have been covert.

The concept of 'micropolitics' has sometimes been restricted to covert use of influence, following Hoyle (1986). While his definition of micropolitics encompasses the continuum from conventional management procedures to 'almost a separate organisational world of illegitimate, self-interested manipulation', his description of micropolitical strategies is largely confined to those which are covert and contentious. Hoyle suggests that bargaining is 'more micropolitical to the degree to which it is implicit rather than explicit, outside rather than inside formal structures and procedures, and draws upon informal resources of influence'. Other writers who refer to micropolitics, like Blase and Anderson, adopt a broader conception which underlines the intrinsic nature of power in all interaction, whether open or underhand, synergistic or conflictual. To avoid confusion arising from such contrasting uses of the term, the micropolitics label has been avoided in the present study. A related term is manipulation, often employed pejoratively to imply covert and illegitimate behaviour. Action (or withholding from action) may be defined as *manipulative* either where an actor intends, covertly, to influence events through means or towards ends that are not made explicit; or where the action is regarded as illegitimate, whether overt or not. Bullying, on this account, is as manipulative as back stabbing. The analysis of interaction is complicated because implicit or explicit means or ends may be perceived by different actors as legitimate or illegitimate. Reitzug and Reeves analysed how leadership actions of an elementary school principal were manipulative but legitimated by his intention to empower teachers by stimulating them to try new approaches:

> Perhaps the closest example to manipulative behaviour is provided by the incident where Mr. Sage placed an 'out of order' sign on the copy machine that was still operating so as to force teachers to consider alternative means of instructional delivery. Although this action could be interpreted to lack straightforwardness and certainly promoted Mr. Sage's personal instructional beliefs, it provided an opportunity for teachers to improve their educational situations by examining and critiquing their methods of instructional delivery.
>
> (Reitzug and Reeves 1992: 208)

The principal's action could be construed as manipulative, since his intentions about means and ends were covert. Yet it was legitimated for the principal because he wished to stimulate teachers to explore avenues beyond copying worksheets. The teachers might not have agreed, if they ever found out. Depending on the view of different parties to interaction, an action may conceivably be overt and legitimate; manipulative because it is covert, but still legitimate; or manipulative since it is illegitimate, whether overt or covert. Legitimacy of action inside a team rests on the norms that constitute the culture of teamwork. Case study school heads fostered a climate in SMT meetings conducive to collaboration. They did not make their aim explicit to colleagues yet, for the heads, their actions were a legitimate part of their role as team leader. Individuals attempt to realise their *interests*, outcomes that facilitate the fulfilment of their wants. The connection between realisation of interests and culture lies in individuals' use of resources in action to realise interests reflecting the beliefs and values to which they subscribe.

Power relationships

When individuals interact, each is partly autonomous and partly dependent on the other, however asymmetrical the power relationship between them. In other words, all parties to interaction normally have access to at least a modicum of resources amounting to influence; and some, especially heads, also have authority. As argued in the last chapter, despite the increase in authority accruing to them, heads are ever more dependent on their colleagues in school and do not have anything like complete control over them. Although distribution of power is unequal, it is distributed throughout the institution. When interacting, each person may be viewed as engaged in a multidirectional *dialectic of control* (Giddens 1984) – a network of power relationships between the interdependent individuals and groups involved. Rather than assume that individuals may enjoy total control – the power completely to determine the actions of others – they may alternatively be regarded as having variable power to *delimit* these actions. Where heads create conditions which expand the opportunities for SMT colleagues to take initiatives, they also monitor and are ready to step in where they deem it necessary to avoid colleagues overreaching the boundaries of their 'comfort zone'. The idea that control is dialectical implies a sequence of action and response between individuals and groups where each enables the other to choose what to do, but within limits. The dialectic of control inside SMTs works all ways: members other than heads may empower the head to operate as team leader where her or his mode of operation is acceptable to them. Where a head does step beyond the bounds of acceptability to other members, they have recourse to influence in delimiting what the head can do, such as when they might make it clear they will not support the head in implementing his or her favoured course of action for the

SMT. Similarly, there is a dialectic of control between the SMT and outsiders, whether they are other teaching and support staff or governors.

Power as transformative capacity links with conflict where individuals endeavour to realise irreconcilable interests. *Conflict* implies a zero-sum-style power struggle between people expressed through interaction. Yet conflict does not automatically follow from the existence of incompatible interests. Actions may be taken to realise *contradictory interests* without conflict if action to realise one interest is separated from action to realise the contradictory interest (Wallace 1991b). Equally, no clash may ensue where people are either not aware of their interests or the consequences of their actions, or are unwilling or unable to act on their interests. As heralded in the introduction to this book, a key factor underpinning SMT operation was the contradiction between the norm that team members contributed as equals and the norm that they held differential status within the management hierarchy. Mostly, action according to these contradictory norms was kept separate and interaction proceeded smoothly. Team members subscribed to both norms but usually only one was expressed at any time. An image of how these norms related is offered in Figure 2.1.

The degree to which each norm prevailed in particular SMTs differed

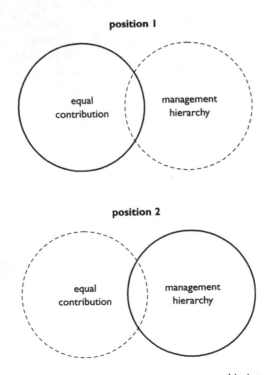

Figure 2.1 Contradictory norms expressed in interaction within SMTs

markedly. Where all members acted according to the norm of contributing as equals (Position 1), the opposing norm relating to a management hierarchy remained in the background. Where heads were more directive and their authority to act in this way was accepted by other members, the norm that there was a legitimate management hierarchy linked to status was expressed, and the norm of equal contribution as team members (Position 2) was latent. On occasion, a head might shift between norms. One way was to move from adherence to the norm of contributing as an equal in the team to the norm linked with the head being at the top of the management hierarchy. As long as other members could switch happily between norms and, temporarily, revert to adherence to the norm of a management hierarchy, harmony was retained. In a similar vein, if a newly appointed head in a school whose previous head had worked hierarchically promoted teamwork by inviting SMT colleagues to engage in discussion on an equal basis, they might take up the offer and switch to allegiance to the norm of equal contribution.

Conflict could arise if different SMT members adhered to different norms in the same interaction. Other SMT members might refuse to accept a head's authority to act unilaterally (according to the norm of a management hierarchy) in an area they regarded as within the SMT remit (according to the norm of equal contribution). A head might attempt to open up team debate (according to the norm of equal contribution) while other members refused to contribute on the grounds that the head was solely responsible for the decision concerned (according to the norm of a management hierarchy). While the norm of a management hierarchy was potentially supported by sanctions associated with heads' authority, the norm of equal contribution was not: other members were, ultimately, empowered to engage in teamwork at the behest of the head. They did, however, have recourse to considerable influence by withdrawing their commitment to teamwork.

The tension between the contradictory norms of a management hierarchy and equal contribution as team members within SMTs is endemic. Figure 2.2 portays how the uneasy balance between these norms may not only differ between SMTs but also change over time within a team. The extent to which one norm is expressed in comparison with the other corresponds to different positions along the continuum representing the differing balance between the two norms. Interaction is framed by factors relating to these norms, like:

- the number of levels of formal status among members;
- the parameters set by heads, such as who is involved in which part of the team decision-making process;
- how far members with lower status in the management hierarchy perceive they should defer to those with higher status;
- who contributes to setting the SMT's agenda;
- who excludes what from this agenda;
- the extent to which all SMT members are committed to teamwork.

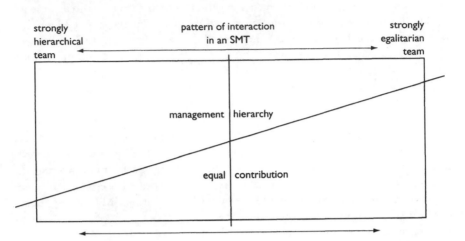

Figure 2.2 Shifting balance of contradictory norms within SMTs

SMTs may vary over how far the enduring *pattern* of interaction in them expresses one norm or the other. The left-hand extreme position represents the most hierarchical team situation, where heads make full use of their authority to direct other SMT members. Such heads conform to the spirit of the official discourse discussed in the previous chapter which has emanated from central government and its agencies. The right-hand extreme position represents the balance of contradictory norms most heavily weighted towards equal contribution within a team, where heads encourage other members to participate as equals to decision making and withhold from directing them or placing constraints on the SMT agenda. It is likely that the pattern of interaction in different SMTs will reflect different positions between these extremes, and that this pattern may shift incrementally. Interaction may become more egalitarian or hierarchical as the *team history* within the wider institutional history evolves. A new head may promote teamwork in accordance with the norm of contributing as equals; where another SMT member does not accept the implied commitment to teamwork, the head may change tack and be more directive with this person, their interaction becoming more hierarchical.

Gender and teamwork

Recent studies of headteachers (Grace 1995; Southworth 1995; Hall 1996) have highlighted gender as a factor with a significant bearing on their beliefs and values and associated use of power. Research outside education also suggests that the experiences of women and men in organisations differ (e.g. Hearn *et al.* 1989; Coleman 1991). While the present study was not centrally concerned with gender factors, the possibility was considered that behaviour in SMTs might be gender related. Ethnic background might also be relevant; small-scale research based on self-reporting (Powney and Weiner 1991) suggests that management styles of black and white women may differ but, as all SMT members in the case study schools were white, this factor could not be explored. The importance was recognised of avoiding 'androcentrism' (Hall 1993), where experiences of both women and men are viewed from an exclusively male perspective. An equal number of case study schools with women and men headteachers was chosen and the level of awareness of SMT members about any gender factors impinging on their own and others' behaviour was investigated. Within a combined cultural and political perspective, it was possible to consider the beliefs and values of women and men connected with teamwork and their associated use of resources with an eye to the wider social forces, such as assumptions about careers and child-care responsibilities, that have resulted in the disproportionate over-representation of men in senior posts in the primary sector.

The study encompassed both women and men who had expressed some form of commitment to teamwork. Most held professional values about team operation which took precedence over whatever their private beliefs about men's and women's behaviour at work might have been. They demonstrated little awareness of gender as having much impact on teamwork and no observations were made of overt sexism, such as stereotypical expectations about the distribution of management responsibilities, patronising behaviour, or sexual harassment. The varied socialisation experiences of women and men may have had a bearing on their approach to teamwork. Yet the dominant factors explaining their interaction were more directly linked to beliefs and values about working in teams than concerned with gender. Some disagreements or conflicts might have had gender-related aspects, but they were not articulated in such terms. Differences in levels of participation in teamwork among SMT members owed more to their differential position in the management hierarchy than to their gender. Multiple allegiances were based on job roles rather than gender affiliation. Politically, both men and women drew idiosyncratically on resources associated with their personalities, skills and status. Although there were differences in delegation by heads, patterns were not gender specific. Nor were women any less likely than men to use power overtly or covertly, or to opt for a more hierarchical or egalitarian team approach.

SMTs in context

The beliefs and values guiding the use of power inside SMTs and between them and other groups neither emerged from nowhere nor exist in a vacuum. The discussion in Chapter 1 illustrated how individual schools are embedded in a wider social and political environment which both affects and is affected by interaction inside every institution. Headteachers, SMT colleagues and other staff draw on the discourses of this wider context, including the discourse of educational reform, and, equally, contribute to their perpetuation or evolution. The discourse of reform with its incentives for compliance and sanctions against resistance entered a primary school arena already populated by beliefs and values. They encompassed, as already noted, perceptions of headteachers' authority, entitlement of other staff to participate in management, equal contribution to teamwork, a management hierarchy, management responsibilities, collaboration, and individual classroom autonomy. The encounter between these beliefs and values and the discourse of reform is likely to have had diverse consequences to the extent that power is distributed between levels of the education system. If central government ministers cannot guarantee fully to determine actions of school staff, it may be expected that some may have mediated the thrust of reform to a certain extent, adapting new practices in line with their old beliefs and values; others may have internalised the new beliefs and values on offer and actively endorse the strongly hierarchical 'managerialist' approach to management envisaged in the discourse of the official documents discussed in the previous chapter. The possibility of variable mediation will be reviewed in the light of the findings.

Chapter 3

Headteachers' story

Headteachers, as creators and leaders of their SMTs, were the first port of call in exploring the emergence and practice of SMTs in primary sector schools. Their account is 'headocentric' yet, of all the players involved, they are perhaps the ones whose perspective counts most as a starting point. They can decide whether to create an SMT and, if they do so, to establish the SMT's membership, its links with other elements of the management structure and its procedures. Where seeking to set a new course for the school and to respond to central government directives, they may choose how restrictive or extensive an approach to transformational leadership to adopt.

The survey findings reveal a combination of diversity within limits, and of commonalities of perspective and reported practice. Since a few respondents did not complete all questionnaire items, there are slightly different totals for responses relating to particular topics summarised in the tables below. The size of institutions, as measured by the number of children registered on school rolls, ranged from 239 to 689. The list of schools to which the questionnaire was sent was generated using a commercial database, so inclusion of three with under 300 pupils was due to a fall in the number on roll since this database was compiled. While it had not been intended to include such institutions, the survey returns from these schools proved informative for the research. They showed that, even in schools with fewer than ten teaching staff, SMTs had been created whose members constituted a subgroup of the total teaching complement, and their reported structures and working practices were similar to those in larger institutions. The large majority of schools catered for between 300 and 500 pupils (Table 3.1). School types were equally varied, including primary, separate infant and junior schools, and middle schools for pupils up to 13 years old.

Emergence of a new orthodoxy

The survey evidence suggests that what heads conceive of as an SMT has become a dominant feature in the management structure of larger primary and middle schools, there being a management team of some kind which included

Table 3.1 School size and prevalence of SMTs

Number of pupils on roll	Schools with an SMT	Schools without an SMT
Not specified	1	1
200–299	3	—
300–399	26	—
400–499	25	4
500–599	2	—
600–699	3	—
Total	60	5

the head and senior staff in over nine out of ten sample schools. This proportion was in line with the ratio that the follow-up telephone calls confirmed also existed in survey schools whose heads did not respond. Three of the five heads in the sample without an SMT reported that they were considering creating one. Further details supplied about the operation of SMTs does, however, imply that their contribution to management in practice varied from central to quite marginal, as will be discussed. The number of members comprising SMTs ranged from three to nine, most teams featuring four to six. The size of SMT bore little relationship to the number of staff in the school. Criteria for membership were based primarily on the structure of individual management responsibilities, salary and status levels among teaching staff, as opposed to any specific ratio between the number of staff and those representing them in the SMT. The number of full-time teaching staff gives a rough indication of the variation in ratios. Table 3.2 shows how the size of the SMT ranged widely in schools with similar numbers of full-time teaching staff. The largest schools, whose size enabled two deputies to be employed, had small SMTs and one of the smallest schools featured a team of seven.

Few SMTs were very long in the tooth. While several teams had been set up during the year leading up to summer 1995 when the survey was carried out, the oldest had been established fifteen years before. Almost five out of six teams had been created since the Education Reform Act of 1988, and over half of these had been set up between 1990 and 1993 when external pressure to implement reforms was at its height (see Table 3.3). One explanatory factor may have been the length of time that present heads had been in post. While a few indicated they had inherited an SMT, most implied that the team was their creation. It is likely that emergence of SMTs during the reform period amounts to more than mere coincidence (an interpretation supported by analysis of team members' responsibilities below).

The rationale behind creation of SMTs was manifold, a substantial minority of heads giving more than one reason, as typified in these two accounts:

Table 3.2 Size of SMT

No. of full-time teaching staff	No. of SMT members including headteacher						
	3	4	5	6	7	8	9
up to 10	1	—	—	—	1	—	—
11–15	4	7	9	8	3	2	—
16–20	1	8	2	2	3	1	1
21–25	—	2	1	—	—	—	—
26–30	1	1	—	—	—	—	—
Total	7	18	12	10	7	3	1

Note: Not specified = 2; total no. of SMTs = 58

Table 3.3 Time since SMTs were established

When SMTs established		No. of SMTs
No. of years (to summer 1995)	Academic year	
<1	94/95	6
1+	93/94	5
2+	92/93	10
3+	91/92	10
4+	90/91	12
5+	89/90	5
6+	88/89	2
7+	87/88	0
8+	86/87	3
9+	85/86	1
10+	before 85/86	3
Total no. of SMTs		57

Note: Not specified = 3

To move responsibility away from the centre; to share decision taking; to improve the communication network; to more accurately reflect school needs in devising the development plan; to spread knowledge of management issues and develop staff for promotion.

A think tank; a sounding board for the head; a channel of communication to and from year teams; and a coordinating and overall planning body.

The one suggests a relatively egalitarian, extensive transformational leadership approach fostering wide participation which embraces making key decisions; the other suggests a more hierarchical, restrictive transformational leadership approach, directed towards the headteacher's interest in extending his or her knowledge of and impact on the work of other staff. The authority vested in their position enabled heads to act on values underlying such rationales, including those connected with belief in a management hierarchy and in equal contribution, by formulating new management structures incorporating an SMT and determining team membership. Responses were grouped into four main categories (Table 3.4). First, the concern to involve staff other than heads in management figured large, reflecting a value placed on sharing the management load. A third of heads alluded to the contribution that skills and expertise of colleagues could make, consistent with the notion of complementary skills in the second definition of teams outlined in Chapter 1. In contrast, around a fifth placed top value on their perceived need for support to fulfil their management agenda, setting up an SMT explicitly to assist them and suggesting that in the reform context they were becoming more dependent on colleagues' contributions. One stated simply: 'I needed it!' The priority of promoting two-way communication across the school led almost a quarter of heads to give responsibility to a team of senior staff for making it happen. One male head, whose deputy was also a man, had instituted an SMT in part to redress the gender imbalance among those with a central management role by creating a larger group which included two senior women teachers. He was able to use his authority, driven by his belief in promoting gender equity, to bring woman colleagues more centrally into the management domain.

Second, the experience of participating in a management team was perceived by a quarter of heads as a staff development opportunity, whether for individual colleague SMT members or for the whole team, one head creating an SMT in part 'to help develop a sense of team spirit'. (It is noteworthy that none of the respondents focused on the possibility that teamwork might offer themselves a professional learning experience.) Another head reported that the SMT was designed to 'provide a good role for staff', implying that it would contribute to cultural leadership through the work of its members – in both their managerial and teaching roles – which would symbolise good practice and offer an example for others to follow.

Third, reference was made to the impact of educational reform. Over a sixth

Table 3.4 Headteachers' reasons for creating an SMT

Reason given	No. of responses
Involving staff in management	
share responsibilities and harness expertise	18
increase participation in decision making and ownership of decisions	14
improve school-wide communication	13
assist the headteacher	11
improve gender balance among senior staff	1
Providing a staff development opportunity	
on the job opportunity for individual development and team building	14
exemplars for other staff	1
Implementing reforms	
direct link – e.g. group for strategic planning including development plan	10
indirect link – response to multiplicity of changes	3
monitor staff performance	2
School-level factors	
coping with large school	7
opportunity created by merger of schools	4
change of headteacher	3
Total no. of reasons given by 58 heads	101

of heads mentioned specific reforms or activities associated with them, including creating a group to conduct staff appraisal, meeting the expectations of OFSTED inspectors, and leading formulation of the school development plan. One indicated that the SMT was created 'because of the increasing number of management tasks as a result of LMS and the national curriculum', consistent with the view of other researchers reported in Chapter 1 that reforms have expanded the chief executive element of headteachers' role. A few made more oblique reference, stating that the SMT was a response either to the range of recent changes, or to the need to monitor staff performance (consistent with the thrust of central government). One head hinted at the impact of managerialism, stating that the team approach was an attempt to 'reflect current industry practice'.

Fourth, school-specific factors also played a part for a minority, one-fifth of heads indicating how the sheer size and complexity of the school had stimulated them to adopt a team approach. The head of an institution with just under 400 pupils commented: 'In a big school there is a need to break down the organisation into manageable units.' School merger was a strong stimulus for heads of the reorganised institution. One wrote: 'The school is an amalgamation of an infant and a junior school. The change in status and style of the school gave the opportunity to create a complete new management structure.' A few had set up an SMT to support them as a new head, one respondent indicating how a team had been created where there was an acting head and acting deputy prior to new permanent appointments being made.

Built-in hierarchy

In headteachers' rationale for creating an SMT, the emphasis on sharing contrasted with the way the composition of their teams reflected a belief in offering membership to staff with the highest salary and status levels and the most substantial individual management responsibilities. All teams included the head and deputy or deputies. With one exception, as summarised in Table 3.5, they also included one or more teachers and, in two cases, a bursar (reflecting the impact of LMS). Evidence of a hierarchy among the teacher members was provided where headteachers indicated how many salary increments teachers in the SMT were awarded above the basic level for all class teachers. Many referred to the superseded system of fixed incentive allowances which, as related in Chapter 1, had recently been replaced by increments along a single pay spine.

In all instances where teacher members' salary levels were mentioned, they were paid one or more increments above the basic teachers' rate. Other respondents who did not give this level of detail did indicate there was a hierarchy of levels of management responsibility shouldered by teacher members of the SMT. The number of hierarchical levels ranged from two to five, about two-thirds of SMTs containing three levels: head, deputy or deputies, and one or more teachers at the same level as each other. A quarter included teachers at two levels. Figure 3.1 illustrates the different numbers of levels in examples of SMTs. There was another form of built-in hierarchy for the one in six teams

Table 3.5 Number of salary, status and responsibility levels in SMTs

No. of levels	Composition of salary and status levels	No. of SMTs		Total
		Salary levels stated	Salary levels not stated	
2	head, deputy	1	—	1
3	head, deputy, 1 level of teacher	25	16	41
4	head, deputy, 2 levels of teacher	8	6	14
5	head, deputy, 3 levels of teacher	2	1	3
	Total No. of SMTs			59

Note: Not specified = 1

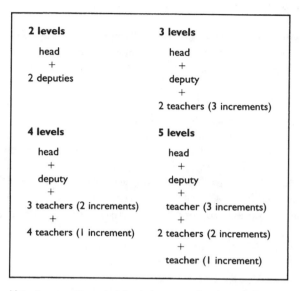

2 levels

head
+
2 deputies

3 levels

head
+
deputy
+
2 teachers (3 increments)

4 levels

head
+
deputy
+
3 teachers (2 increments)
+
4 teachers (1 increment)

5 levels

head
+
deputy
+
teacher (3 increments)
+
2 teachers (2 increments)
+
teacher (1 increment)

Note: increment = salary level above rate for class teachers

Figure 3.1 Examples of SMTs with different numbers of levels

featuring a two-tier arrangement. A subgroup of the most senior staff in these teams held regular meetings alongside those involving the full SMT. What might be termed an 'inner cabinet' consisted of a coalition between the head and deputy or deputies alone, or head plus deputy and the teacher with the highest salary and status level.

Individual management responsibilities of SMT members were generally differentiated in line with salary and status levels and, where respondents spelled out their own brief, they took overall responsibility for the school. While respondents supplied different amounts of detail, it was possible to divide the types of management responsibility into three:

- *cross-school* organisation – for major coordination tasks potentially affecting all teaching staff, often linked with reforms. They included curriculum development, assessment and record-keeping, staff induction, development and in-service training, staff appraisal, the school development plan, pupil discipline, child protection, information technology, finance, provision for pupils with special educational needs, and library administration. In the two SMTs with a bursar, this person was responsible for routine financial administration;

- *departmental* organisation – for coordinating the work of two or more classes of pupils within a particular age range. Arrangements included responsibility for parallel classes in the same year group and responsibility for larger departments, commonly divided in line with national curriculum key stages;

- *curriculum* coordination – school-wide responsibility for one or, in a few cases, two curriculum areas, labelled in accordance with national curriculum subjects (plus religious education).

Cross-school responsibilities featured in three-quarters of SMTs, departmental responsibilities in two-thirds, and curriculum coordination in half. Most teams had a matrix structure, reflecting the increasing organisational complexity of larger primary schools noted by Alexander (1997) at the beginning of the reform period, which consisted of cross-school responsibilities and either one or both of the other types (Table 3.6). Over a quarter featured all three types, a sixth combined cross-school with departmental responsibilities and an equal proportion combined cross-school and curriculum coordination responsibilities.

It is probable that some SMT members and other teaching staff in many schools had some curriculum coordination responsibility, and therefore SMT membership would not necessarily be designed around this type, especially where a senior member of staff had overarching cross-school responsibility for leading curriculum development. Every SMT featuring departmental responsibilities covered all age groups in the school. Taken together, the span of individual responsibilities in each SMT provided the basis for the team to operate within an overview to which each member could contribute, embracing most aspects of school activity. It also provided a spread of responsibilities for promoting school wide implementation of decisions. An example of each combination from three of the largest SMTs is given in Figures 3.2a–c.

The structural hierarchy of SMTs was reflected in the distribution of posts at different levels according to gender, consistent with the national picture for headships outlined in the previous chapter. About three-quarters of respondents specified the gender of each team member. Overall, 72 per cent of these SMT members were women, yet they predominated in the lower salary and status levels and were under-represented amongst deputies and heads (Table

Table 3.6 Areas of individual management responsibility covered in SMTs

Types of individual responsibility	No. of SMTs
Cross-school + department + curriculum coordination	17
Cross-school + department	11
Cross-school + curriculum coordination	11
Cross-school only	5
Department only	11
Curriculum coordination only	2
Total no. of SMTs	57

Note: not specified = 3

SMT member's salary and status level	Individual management responsibilities		
	Cross-school +	Department +	Curriculum coordination
Headteacher	curriculum overview, budget overview, staffing, assemblies		religious education
Deputy headteacher	staff development, pastoral care overview		personal, social and health education
Teacher (3 increments)	assessment, reporting and record keeping, planning		English
Teacher (2 increments)	home–school links	early years	music
Teacher (2 increments)	special education needs	key stage one, cross-phase links	mathematics
Teacher (2 increments)		key stage two	science, physical education
Teacher (2 increments)	community links, safety		design and technology
Teacher (1 increment)	library		art

Figure 3.2a **3-type matrix of SMT members' management responsibilities**

3.7). The inequitable distribution of posts did not appear to reflect gender-related prejudice in the allocation of management responsibilities. Amongst the deputies whose gender was specified, about three-quarters of women and men held cross-school responsibilities and individuals of either gender were responsible for major areas like special needs or staff development. Rather, factors leading to the under-representation of women – they accounted for merely a third of the headteachers – probably lie deeper. This low proportion in larger primary and middle schools is related to the practice widespread among governors of appointing experienced headteachers from smaller schools. Quite a high proportion of women teachers take a career break to have a family (Evetts 1990). As a result, fewer women than men may have had the length of experience at higher levels in the management hierarchy, including headship of a smaller institution, widely deemed by governing bodies to be advantageous for candidates seeking the headship of a large school.

Just one in ten women SMT members were heads, compared with half the team members who were men. At the other end of the hierarchy of posts in these SMTs, two-thirds of women team members were teachers, compared

SMT member's salary and status level	Individual management responsibilities	
	Cross-school +	Department
Headteacher	almost anything!	
Deputy headteacher	assistant headteacher, special educational needs	
Teacher (3 increments)	assessment, adults in training	
Teacher (2 increments)	home–school links, child protection	
Teacher (2 increments)	resource coordinator	junior department coordinator
Teacher (2 increments)		first department (nursery and infant) coordinator
Teacher (2 increments)		in-service training coordinator

Figure 3.2b 2-type matrix involving departments

SMT member's salary and status level	Individual management responsibilities	
	Cross-school +	Curriculum coordiination
Headteacher		
Deputy headteacher	deputising for headteacher	language
Teacher (2 increments)		mathematics, physical education
Teacher (2 increments)	planning	art
Teacher (2 increments)	in-service training	religious education
Teacher (1 increment)	information technology	
Teacher (1 increment)		history
Teacher (1 increment)		science
Teacher (1 increment)		geography

Figure 3.2c 2-type matrix involving curriculum coordination

Table 3.7 Distribution of status levels in SMTs according to gender

Status of SMT member	Women		Men	
	Number	%	Number	%
Headteacher	16	10	30	50
Deputy head	34	21	16	27
Other teachers	107	67	14	23
Bursar	2	2	—	—
Total	159		60	

Note: Percentages rounded to nearest whole number; not specified = 14 SMTs; total no. of SMTs = 46

with a quarter of men members. Over-representation of women at the lower levels was illustrated in the restricted range of SMT gender profiles: while one third of teams consisted of female deputies and teachers led by a male head-teacher, there were no instances of male deputies and teachers led by a female head (Table 3.8). The most common profile for women heads was an all woman team, making up one in five of the SMTs. If primary school teaching is mainly a women's world, among SMTs in larger schools it remains a women's world

Table 3.8 Gender profile of SMTs

Gender profile of SMT members			No. of SMTs
Headteacher	Deputy/deputies	Other teachers and bursar	
Female	female	female	9
Female	female	female and male	5
Female	male	female	1
Female	male	female and male	1
Male	male	male	1
Male	male	female	6
Male	male	female and male	4
Male	female	female	16
Male	female	female and male	1
Male	female and male	male	1
Male	female	—	1
Total no. of SMTs			46

Note: Not specified = 14 SMTs

with a glass ceiling which is not shatterproof, but where the top positions in the hierarchy of salary, status and management responsibility are still disproportionately occupied by men.

A hierarchical SMT role

Individual SMT members' responsibilities were directed towards a corporate team role in contributing to the management of each school. Heads' statements of this role varied over how far they emphasised a 'top-down' hierarchical orientation towards management where the head – alone or with other SMT members – took most initiatives, and a more 'bottom-up' orientation, where the SMT responded to issues raised by staff outside the team. Most implied an approach which was essentially top-down in that the SMT was responsible for shaping the direction of school policy and practice but, within this thrust, room was allowed for seeking the views of staff outside the team and, to a lesser extent, of governors. Their input was apparently restricted to raising issues that SMT members might take up and develop into a school policy, or to giving their views on matters originating with the SMT. A strictly hierarchical view was expressed by one respondent, summarising the team role as being to:

- assist the headteacher in decision making;
- assist the headteacher in dealing with long-term aims;
- provide constant feedback on school performance on day-to-day issues;
- alert the headteacher to possible difficulties likely to arise;
- provide a team approach to problem solving;
- enable a consensus view to be presented to staff;
- thrash out problems in a professional manner.

The SMT acted here as the 'eyes and ears' of the head, enhancing her or his knowledge of what was or was not going on throughout the school and working towards agreed team decisions on policy which were then handed down to other staff for implementation. The traffic in management initiatives was routed along a one-way system from head to class teachers. Another respondent's account made allowance for the flow to come from other staff, but was explicit in acknowledging how most traffic flowed from the head, empowering her to achieve her vision for the school (rather than a vision to which all staff might contribute):

> To decide ways of leading the staff in the direction of the school's aims/mission statement; how to respond to perceived needs; to raise issues they've [SMT members] had brought to them or have observed themselves; to form a support group for the head in implementing her vision.

One statement highlighted the cultural leadership role of the SMT in working to put policies into practice alongside readiness to respond to other staff. The SMT role here was 'to lead; to filter information; to lead by example on policy implementation; to be sensitive to staff views'. The statement giving strongest emphasis to serving the needs of staff other than the head pointed both to team responsiveness and to the part SMT membership played in staff development. The role was to:

- coordinate the smooth running of the school;
- ensure good communication;
- enable issues raised by staff to be discussed in a school-wide context;
- provide middle-management/leadership experience for colleagues.

The SMT was also regarded by this head as a 'good way of communicating urgent information'. Other than being implicitly more or less hierarchical in orientation, respondents' broad conceptions of the SMT role did not differ markedly. While different elements were mentioned in particular statements, there was great overlap. As the above examples suggest, most statements covered more than one element, and they could be classified into relatively few categories (Table 3.9).

Table 3.9 Major elements of the SMT role

Element of SMT role	No. of times mentioned
Making major decisions (with cooperation of governors)	22
Strategic planning (including school development planning and budgeting)	21
Sustaining an overview through internal monitoring, and reviewing practice (including curriculum and pupil discipline)	20
Leading staff within the framework of school aims (including leading teams of other staff and chairing meetings)	14
Maintaining smooth day-to-day running (including pupil discipline)	14
Disseminating outcomes of SMT decision making and ensuring implementation	14
Supporting the head (including acting as a 'sounding board')	11
Contributing ideas to the SMT and taking initiatives	10
Promoting two-way communication across the school	9
Contributing to issues raised by other staff and consulting them	7
Providing a development opportunity for SMT members	5
Total elements mentioned for 57 SMTs	147

Note: Not specified = 3 SMTs

These elements are sufficiently complementary to be brought together in a composite model (Figure 3.3). At the heart of the SMT role lay shared *team tasks*: participating in long-term planning (connected in part with the school development plan) and day-to-day planning within the parameters of declared school aims. This school-wide planning work entailed extensive decision making whose compass ranged from formulation of major policies – implying some form of transformational leadership, to details of routine organisation – the very stuff of transactional leadership. The *teamwork process* enabled members other than the head to offer support, especially by contributing ideas. At the same time the team experience offered individuals a professional learning opportunity which would be likely to improve the promotion prospects of those aspiring towards a more senior management post in future. Since SMTs constituted the core group responsible for taking the lead

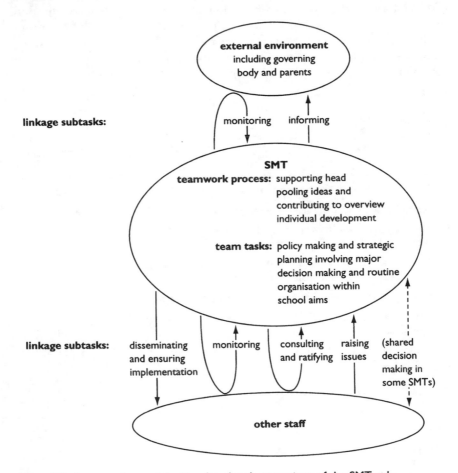

Figure 3.3 A composite model of headteachers' perceptions of the SMT role

in school management, and management implies achieving tasks with and through other adults, team tasks were inevitably achieved with and through colleagues outside the SMT. An integral element of the team role was relating with outsiders – mainly other staff, and to a lesser extent governors and parents – through what may be termed *linkage subtasks*. They constituted a means of bringing together the zones of policy and practice: SMT members could inform themselves proactively by monitoring colleagues, consulting them and asking them to ratify SMT proposals. They could also keep informed responsively by encouraging other staff to raise issues while attempting to impact on them through working to implement team decisions. According to these accounts, SMTs were internally focused in that their work was largely oriented towards the work of staff. They were also affected by factors in the external environment, operating through linkage subtasks within the oversight of governing bodies, which included parent representatives. This model formed the framework for analysing the four case study SMTs in chapters to come.

Diversity and contingency in decision making

The strong element of hierarchy in the spread of individual responsibilities among SMT members and their formal team role could, potentially, be tempered by working practices allowing for more equal contribution to management – and especially decision making – by SMT members other than heads and by staff outside the team. How far participation was shared related to who was enabled to contribute to which parts of the decision-making procedure adopted and for which kinds of decision. Seven out of eight respondents stated that the SMT normally made decisions on behalf of other staff, the remainder reporting that the SMT did not. However, a substantial minority added qualifications to what might otherwise seem a clear-cut division between two practices, dominated by a hierarchical approach. One respondent stressed how SMT decisions were made, 'but not with an air of dictation'. Reserving decision-making power for the SMT turned out to be not entirely a matter of preference for heads. Their limited control over the context was suggested by one respondent who reported that there was not always sufficient time to consult staff across a large school. Another pointed to limited control over the attitude of colleagues, commenting that two team members were unwilling to accept shared responsibility for team decisions. Almost half the headteachers whose SMTs regularly made decisions noted that other staff were involved at some point. The latter were either:

- consulted before any decision was formulated (one head commenting that decisions were made 'in full consultation with other staff and often about issues raised by them – it is not always a top-down agenda');
- invited to approve or modify a proposed SMT decision (another head

adding that 'these decisions are always referred back to whole staff meetings for possible amendment');
- both consulted and invited to approve or ratify a proposal (a third respondent reporting that 'the team consults colleagues and takes decisions – however the opposite can apply where the team proposes strategies or innovations and the whole staff decide').

Most heads whose SMTs did not make decisions stated that the team met first to develop a proposal, then presented it to other staff for a formal decision. As one respondent put it: 'Initial discussion takes place with SMT members and then opinions and thoughts are sought from staff.'

A contingency approach to involvement of other staff was indicated by two-fifths of respondents, depending on the topic under consideration and how far other staff would be affected by it. One head described how SMT decisions 'would be at a day to day management level. They would not make major decisions about policy without consulting staff and looking for common agreement.' The topic, in turn, determined whether other staff would be consulted or asked to approve an SMT proposal, and who would participate in making the decision itself. In the words of another respondent:

> We work collegiately as much as possible so decisions are made in a variety of ways. All staff who are going to be affected by a decision will always be consulted. Decisions may be made by the head, head and deputy, management team or whole staff.

In their more detailed description of the SMT contribution to decision making, a minority of heads indicated that different procedures were employed in different circumstances. According to one head, decisions were generally made

> via consultation on an individual, group or whole staff basis. Usually democratically, occasionally unilaterally by the head and deputy; this is usually in response to a legal requirement where the issue is *how* we tackle something rather than *whether* we tackle it.

Recourse by central government to legally backed mandates to ensure implementation of reforms created a contingent situation where, by ministers' design, decision-making power at school level could be restricted to options connected with strategies for compliance. Studies of primary schools during the early reform period (e.g. Wallace 1992; Pollard *et al.* 1994; Webb and Vulliamy 1996a) also indicated how management decisions were becoming increasingly dominated by the priority of implementing compulsory innovations originating with central government.

While some respondents gave more details than others of their decision-making procedures, there appeared to be a sequence of five possible stages, not all of which featured in every case:

1   initiation – identifying an issue for which a decision was required;
2   consultation – seeking the views of staff, inside or outside the SMT or both, prior to any decision being formulated;
3   proposal – the formulation of a proposed or tentative decision;
4   ratification – inviting staff to endorse or recommend modifications to a proposal;
5   making the final decision – making a commitment to a course of action designed to resolve the issue identified.

Procedures were classified according to which stages were included and who participated in them, showing marked variation in the relative involvement – and therefore the power to affect decision outcomes – of individuals and groups at different levels of the management hierarchy. Table 3.10 summarises the diversity of approaches to decision making. (In this table a dash inside a cell indicates that a possible decision-making stage was not included in a procedure.) The key dimension emerged as a different balance of control over decisions between heads, deputies, other SMT members, and other staff outside the team. This balance of control can be depicted as a varied combination of two opposing orientations adopted by heads, whose unique authority as managers enabled them to introduce decision-making procedures in line with

Table 3.10 Variable involvement in SMT decision-making procedures

Type of procedure	Stage in decision-making procedure					No. of times mentioned
	Initiation	Consultation	Proposal	Ratification	Final decision	
A	(not specified)	all SMT	—	—	head	1
B	head	head and deputy	head and deputy	—	all SMT	1
C	head and deputy	all SMT	—	—	all SMT	4
D	(not specified)	—	—	—	all SMT	20
E	all SMT and other staff	all SMT and other staff	—	—	all SMT	14
F	(not specified)	—	all SMT	all SMT and other staff	all SMT	2
G	SMT	all SMT and other staff	all SMT	all SMT and other staff	all SMT and other staff	4
H	all SMT and other staff	—	all SMT	all SMT and other staff	all SMT and other staff	17
I	other staff	—	all SMT	all SMT and other staff	all SMT and other staff	1
Total no. of procedures mentioned						64

Note: Procedures not specified = 2; total no. of SMTs = 58

their beliefs and values. Under the most 'top-down' orientation, heads restricted others' involvement to colleagues at the highest levels of the management hierarchy; whereas under the most 'bottom-up' orientation, they encouraged all staff to initiate debate and participate in making decisions.

These relatively bottom-up procedures suggest that the model of the SMT role does not tell the full story for teams whose heads fostered more egalitarian practices. Where staff outside the SMT did participate in making final decisions, the model could be amended through the addition of a two-way link (as indicated by the dotted lines) between the SMT and other staff to represent their shared participation at this stage of the decision-making procedure. In all cases, however, it is notable that decision making was both hierarchical and included some involvement of colleagues including, at least, other SMT members. Even the most egalitarian procedure was at the behest of the headteacher, who had authority to introduce and override it. At the most top-down, hierarchical end of the continuum (procedure type A in Table 3.10), one head consulted SMT colleagues but made the actual decision. About one in twelve procedures (types B and C) were slightly less hierarchical where the deputy or deputies were sometimes also able to initiate decisions, but full SMT involvement was confined to responding to these ideas. For a third of procedures (type D) it was not clear who could initiate discussion but the full SMT made final decisions. Other staff began to get a look in where, in a fifth of procedures (type E), they could initiate debate and might be consulted early on, though not about any proposed decision, actual making of the decision remaining exclusively in the SMT domain. Involvement of other staff at a later stage was allowed in the procedure followed by a small minority of heads (type F), where they were invited to ratify a proposed SMT decision but the team retained responsibility for making the decision in the light of this feedback. A few heads enabled other staff to be consulted before any decision, to ratify the SMT proposal following this input, and to participate in making the final decision (procedure type G). Slightly fuller involvement was allowed in a quarter of procedures (type H), where other staff could initiate debate, ratify an SMT proposal and contribute to the staff decision which ensued. Finally, in one case, staff outside the SMT alone could initiate corporate decision making, the team acting solely in a responsive mode, and other staff participated both in ratifying the SMT proposal and in making the final decision (type I).

The procedures may be ranked along the top-down/bottom-up dimension, both orientations being present in every instance. Speculatively, the top-down orientation reflects norms about who may contribute and when, following from headteachers' belief in a management hierarchy, while the bottom-up orientation reflects the opposing belief in the potential of SMT members and of other staff to make an equal contribution to decisions that affect their work. (Decision-making procedures are therefore being interpreted as reflecting the varying balance between norms governing SMT practice associated with these contradictory beliefs outlined in Figure 2.2 in the previous chapter.) Figure 3.4 portrays impressionistically the different balance between these orientations expressed in procedures. Some heads indicated that the level of involvement of colleagues was contingent on the factors outlined above; it may be conjectured that individual heads would set norms for different procedures depending on the circumstances, but within a more or less restricted range determined by the balance between their belief in a management hierarchy and in the equal contribution of colleagues. The two procedures summarised by one headteacher quoted earlier were type E (the team consults colleagues and takes decisions) and type G (the team proposes strategies or innovations and the whole staff decide), suggesting that procedures might vary, but within limits – here according to the norms that other staff should be included, minimally, in the consultation stage before the SMT made a final decision and, maximally, in the ratification and final decision-making stages.

This model of the varying balance between top-down and bottom-up orientations is consistent with the version put forward by Tannenbaum and Schmidt (1958). As adapted by Hoyle (1986), that model portrays how the more headteachers use their authority within the management hierarchy to make decisions alone, the less subordinates are able to contribute. Conversely, the more freedom subordinates (implying the other teaching

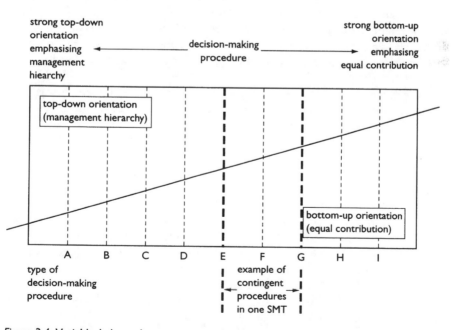

Figure 3.4 Variable balance between contradictory orientations in SMT decision-making procedures

staff) are allowed to participate in decision making, the less headteachers use their authority to control the process and outcomes of decision making. The adapted Tannenbaum and Schmidt model lumps all subordinates together, but the present model elaborates it by distinguishing between hierarchical levels among subordinate staff. In a context where heads create SMTs and delegate some authority to the deputies and teachers occupying different salary, status and responsibility levels who make up the other members of the team, the two opposing dimensions incorporate a sliding scale representing a differing balance amongst a hierarchy of subordinates with whom heads share their authority. At the most hierarchical end of the continuum, heads go it almost alone, with a little help from the deputy or deputies; at the most egalitarian end, heads delegate a substantial amount of authority to staff outside the SMT, but have overarching authority to take back this delegated authority.

A strong value placed on equal contribution was suggested by the norms governing the minimal level of agreement for decisions to be made, as mentioned by forty-three respondents. Finding a working consensus within the group was the most widely preferred approach, followed by three out of four of these respondents, of whom one summarised the process as 'discussion, suggestion, reasoned argument, agreement and/or compromise; finally a common front'. One in ten referred to reaching a majority view, a head in this group indicating that the relevant norm had been established as an accepted ground rule: 'All decisions are arrived at through discussion. A majority view is taken and, though some may not agree totally with the decision taken, we have all agreed the majority view is to be upheld.' Just two respondents indicated how the norm of making majority decisions was formalised by voting on proposals.

Allegiance to norms reflecting belief in a management hierarchy was also implied by one in ten of these respondents, surfacing if the minimum level of agreement could not be reached or if the majority view lay outside heads' comfort zone, especially in a context where their external accountability for consequences of decisions had increased. One respondent noted how 'the head has the final say – he is accountable for all that goes on in the school', while a second spelled out the boundaries of her comfort zone:

> Following consultation with all staff in their departments, and discussion by the SMT, a majority decision is taken unless the headteacher feels that the decision will be against school or LEA or government policy, in which case her decision is final.

She was apparently willing to use her authority, according to her belief in a management hierarchy, to withdraw the decision from the SMT arena if it looked as if these boundaries would be overstepped, and so delimit the contribution of SMT colleagues.

Resolving conflicts of view in making decisions

While a minority of respondents reported that it had always proved possible to reach a working consensus or majority view, over half the forty-nine heads who described how conflicts of opinion were addressed referred to their power of veto if the contingency of unresolvable disagreement arose. One stated, 'The head has the final decision. This is understood but as yet hasn't had to be employed!' A second commented: 'The headteacher has never had to overrule – I would avoid this!' A third highlighted the norm that all SMT members should commit themselves to the head's decision in such circumstances: 'In the final analysis the head would decide and expect the backing of the management team.' This view implies that other SMT members must switch from their belief in equal contribution to the decision towards one where the head was entitled to act unilaterally as the most senior member of the management hierarchy, and their duty was to comply. A fourth described a hierarchical approach, but involving the deputy: 'There is final consultation between head and deputy – the decision is finally made by the head.' A fifth implied that different strategies, moving towards the more hierarchical, could be invoked contingent on the head's perception of the seriousness of potential consequences: 'Matters are generally resolved through a trial period. If the matter is crucial to the benefit of the school, the head would make the ultimate decision, keeping the deputy informed (and the rest of the SMT later).'

A quarter of heads reportedly postponed the decision or continued with debate until a working consensus could be reached, suggesting that they were prepared to stick with norms connected with a belief in equal contribution of SMT members. As one put it: 'We agree to revisit the issue at the next meeting, giving time to reflect.' Another invoked the norm that a first principle should provide the basis for arbitration in 'adopting the philosophy of what is in the best interest of the pupils'. About one in ten headteachers normally went with the majority, some also indicating that there was a norm about instituting a trial period (which minimised the risk of having to live over the long term with a decision they did not support). In the words of one respondent: 'As head I have given a commitment that the majority decision will carry even if I am not particularly happy about it. However, all decisions are subject to rigorous review in the light of implementation.'

The pattern of team meetings

Some form of regular meeting involving SMT members was universal, a substantial minority, including the two-tier teams, having more than one kind. The purposes of meetings were most commonly stated to be a mixture of long-term planning and day-to-day organisation. They embraced management tasks following from reforms including school development planning, curriculum planning and budgeting. Over four out of five meetings were for the entire SMT, though in two-tier teams the inner cabinet consisting of the head and deputy – in two cases joined by the most senior of the teacher SMT members – also met separately. A small minority of respondents reported that individual teacher members also led meetings of other teams of teaching staff for whom they had management responsibility. One primary school with an SMT of seven staff featured a complex matrix structure of meetings: a combination of a two-tier arrangement within the SMT, alongside meetings led by the four most junior SMT members with vertical cross-phase teams of teachers who had classes of pupils of different ages, and with year group teams whose teachers were responsible for parallel classes (Figure 3.5). Here strong formal links were made, on paper at least, between the SMT and other staff; yet the full team did not meet regularly, suggesting weaker internal coordination.

The duration of meetings ranged from less than half an hour to a whole day. Three-quarters of the meetings lasted between half and one and a half hours, the majority of these taking over an hour, suggesting it was comparatively rare for SMTs to meet for an extended period of uninterrupted time. Frequency of meetings varied from every day to twice a year. About half took place weekly, one in six fortnightly and a similar proportion once a month. The severity of the time constraints under which SMTs had to operate was indicated by the timing of meetings. Table 3.11 summarises the time slots which were used. Six out of seven meetings occurred outside the school day and a third of the remainder took place partly inside and partly outside lesson time. Over half the meetings were arranged after school when, according to one head: 'As meetings need to take place after school for financial reasons (no non-contact time), thoughts are not at their sharpest.' More than a quarter of meetings were evenly divided between some time during the hour before the school day began and during the lunch break, so subject to the deadline imposed by the

Duration of meeting	Timing	Frequency	Membership	Purpose
I hour	in school hours	weekly if possible	head, deputy and senior teacher SMT member (2 increments)	matters of current concern, planning school development, timetabling, etc.
I½ hours	after school	monthly	4 teacher SMT members (I increment)	planning curriculum continuity and development
I hour	after school	weekly	each teacher SMT member (I increment) and her teaching team	planning curriculum

Figure 3.5 Matrix structure of meetings in one school

Table 3.11 Timing of team meetings

Timing of meeting	No. of meetings
Before school	12
Lunchtime	11
After school	50
Evening	1
Weekend	1
Training day	1
Inside and outside lesson time	7
Entirely inside lesson time	4
Total no. of meetings for 58 SMTs	87

Note: Not specified = 2 SMTs

start of morning or afternoon lessons. The middle schools enjoyed a slightly higher rate of funding through their LMS budget than primary schools, reflected in greater potential availability of non-contact time during the school day for SMT meetings. Yet the large majority of SMT meetings in the middle or combined first and middle schools, which made up a fifth of the sample, were held outside lesson times. The additional funding did not appear to be significant enough to affect timing of meetings.

Analysis of the time commitment to these meetings revealed great variation. If coordination of activity between members is a hallmark of teams, as one definition discussed in Chapter 1 requires, then the amount of time spent in meeting together will be indicative of the importance or otherwise of the SMT as an approach to school management. At the minimalist extreme, one respondent reported that the SMT met for thirty minutes at lunchtime every half term to 'plan for the next half term', while a second head stated that the SMT came together after school or at lunchtime 'at least once a term' for 'planning and development'. It is questionable how far SMTs whose members so rarely met could constitute more than teams in name. At the other extreme lay teams whose members put several hours into working together every week. The arrangements of two such teams are depicted in Figure 3.6, one a two-tier team involving separate meetings of the head and deputy, the other a single-tier team. Members of both SMTs engaged in daily meetings before school for day-to-day organisation and longer, less frequent meetings for medium- to long-term planning.

A further sense of variation in commitment to meeting was gained by calculating the time spent per week for the fifty-eight responses where heads had given a breakdown of the duration and frequency of meetings. Amongst the

Duration of meeting	Timing	Frequency	Membership	Purpose
Two-tier SMT				
15 minutes	before school	daily	head and deputies	daily organisation
30 minutes	before school	weekly	SMT	urgent issues
1½ hours	after school	weekly	SMT	long-term planning
Single-tier SMT				
30 minutes	before school	daily	SMT	organisation for the day, communicated to staff with SMT present
1½ hours	inside lesson time	weekly	SMT	organisational planning/ issues for coming week
6 hours	weekend	half-termly	SMT	development planning, long-term strategies

Figure 3.6 Arrangements for two SMTs with a strong commitment to meetings

single-tier teams, the time spent per week in SMT meetings ranged from less than five minutes to almost five hours (the single-tier SMT whose meeting structure was summarised in Figure 3.6.). One in six teams spent under thirty minutes and only one in seventeen took up two or more hours, the mean length of time coming to fifty-five minutes per week. In two-tier teams, the head, deputy or deputies, (and most senior teachers in two SMTs) forming the inner cabinet spent between thirty minutes and two hours meeting together, averaging seventy minutes per week. Meetings of the full SMT for them and their SMT colleagues in the lower tier occupied between ten minutes and two hours (and, in one instance, the more junior members met together alone), with a mean time of fifty minutes per week. Therefore, inner cabinet members committed themselves on average to around two hours per week in full SMT and inner cabinet meetings. Having to hold most meetings outside the school day because of constraints on non-contact time imposed by the LMS budget may explain why the amount of meeting time was comparatively short given the extent of the SMT role as conceived by respondents.

Perceived effectiveness of SMTs

Team effectiveness was considered in two ways: first, by examining the reported degree of commitment of all SMT members to a team approach which the earlier secondary school research had shown to be crucial to achievement of synergy within such teams; second, by exploring the criteria employed by respondents. About five-eighths of the fifty-six heads who gave an indication of individual commitment stated that there was unified commitment among team members, one going so far as to claim that 'they share a total commitment to a team approach'. Almost half of these respondents pointed to what lay behind this level of commitment and its perceived benefits to the school. Some hinted at the importance of SMT membership providing representation of other staff, as where a head commented: 'Staff within teams represented like to feel that there is a forum for issues to be raised and for consultation to take place.' Others pointed to sharing beliefs and values, one stating that commitment was 'total – there is clearly a shared common purpose and philosophy', while another pointed to a shared sense of responsibility for management: 'All members feel a responsibility for developing and managing the work of the school – to work as a team, mindful of their own areas of responsibility, was a joint decision stemming from the head's proposal.' Comments from the remainder suggested either that the team had achieved a 'whole' approach, where members were able to act in concert (reflecting their shared culture of teamwork), or that other SMT members were content to operate under the leadership of the head (sharing the head's belief in a management hierarchy) or were willing to compromise their judgements for the good of the institution. One head reported: 'All members of the team are able to discuss sensibly for the benefit of the school and not let personal views affect their decisions.'

Of the three in eight respondents who perceived commitment to the team to be less than complete, about a third commented that commitment was growing. One head indicated that team members were becoming more able to put team interests first instead of 'fighting one's corner' (suggesting that there was a transition towards a more widely shared culture of teamwork). Variable commitment or non-commitment in remaining teams was attributed to individual members pursuing their sectional interests first and foremost; senior teacher members leaving initiative-taking to the head and deputy (perhaps using influence according to belief in a management hierarchy to hold back from actions expressing commitment to teamwork); engaging in an internal power struggle, one head commenting that 'some are power people and want to get one up on others'; or failing to support the rest of the team when a proposed team decision was presented to other staff for feedback. A head stated: 'Occasionally there are problems because a management team decision will be undermined, or certainly not supported fully, by members of the team with year group colleagues or at discussion in a full staff meeting.'

These accounts may be viewed as reflecting the heads' common belief that unified commitment required all members to be willing to subjugate their individual interests for the sake of the team. In this way the SMT would amount to more than a group of individuals, in line with the definition of a team offered by Katzenbach and Smith (Chapter 1) which stressed the importance of commitment to a common approach. About half of the same fifty-six respondents judged their SMT to be effective in carrying out its role, one adding that it was 'good to have supportive colleagues working together towards agreed ends'. This statement highlights the dependence of the head on support that an SMT could offer. A second noted: 'It has developed consultative and informative networks, has given this head a much valued partnership, and given ownership to more staff in developing and meeting the school's needs.' Here the SMT apparently helped ensure overlap between the zone of policy and the zone of practice through facilitating communication between senior managers and other staff. A third pointed to the SMTs' part in involving other staff in management: 'It enables everyone to have a say and keep informed, either through the SMT or line managers.' The head of a school with just over 300 pupils simply stated: 'I cannot imagine running a school of this size without some kind of decision-making senior management team.'

The downside of team approaches was indicated by the quarter of respondents who implied that the team was not fully effective and the small minority who went further and dubbed their SMT as ineffective. Yet there was room for optimism, since one in six headteachers reported that their relatively new SMT was increasing in effectiveness as members developed their ability to work together. The head of a school whose SMT had been created when the school opened two years before commented: 'We are developing our role and still feeling our way. We are finding ourselves becoming more effective as understanding and trust are being built up.'

Where headteachers elaborated on what made for SMT effectiveness or otherwise, clues were offered about their criteria for judgement (listed in Table 3.12). Some were classified as promoting and others as inhibiting effectiveness and, though criteria differed, they were broadly consistent. The importance of reaching out to and being accepted by other staff was expressed by several respondents, one noting that 'we are slowly breaking down the them and us syndrome'. Another mentioned how formal arrangements for SMT meetings could incorporate other staff as appropriate: 'Occasionally other senior members of staff are brought into the team when it is relevant to the subject under discusssion, e.g. SENCO [special needs coordinator].' Yet another underlined the need for two-way communication: 'The SMT must not only assist in making informed decisions but also listen to *all* colleagues so that individuals are valued.' Developing mutual trust was seen as a necessary condition for teamwork, one head implying that SMT members might have mixed ability to become good teamworkers: 'The trust relationship has begun to develop – it's taken two years. Attitude [change] and the leap from class focused to whole school focused is proving difficult – intelligence has to be a large factor in this case.'

Effective teamwork included a shared sense of purpose to which complementary orientations were applied, as expressed by one head: 'All bring different approaches/personalities which provide an effective balance, but all have similar commitment to agreed aims and values and ethos of the school.' Also significant was internal monitoring, including receptivity to staff concerns. A primary school head stated that the SMT was:

Table 3.12 Headteachers' criteria for judging SMT effectiveness

Criteria	No. of times mentioned
Promoting effectiveness	
Strong links between SMT and other staff which win their respect	10
New SMT members 'gel' together and develop mutual trust over time	3
Shared SMT purpose and core values	2
SMT monitoring to ensure continuity and progression	2
Concentration on long-term planning as well as day-to-day organisation	1
Demonstration to other staff that decisions are shared	1
Reduction of headteacher's isolation from staff colleagues	1
Inhibiting effectiveness	
Lack of time for SMT meetings	5
One or more members do not support the majority	4
Individual SMT members' roles not clearly defined	2
SMT too large for ease of meeting and efficient decision making	2
Other staff unwilling to accept a team approach	1

> Very effective in monitoring what goes on in the school. They raise issues
> that staff feel unhappy about and coordinate much of what happens in the
> two [infant and junior] departments, being a positive improvement in
> whole school continuity *and* progression.

Headteachers' view of effective SMTs emerges as one whose members work
together harmoniously towards shared goals within the leadership of the head,
with commitment to a shared culture of teamwork, forging strong links with
other staff and keeping governors informed, while orchestrating the process of
long-term planning and short-term organisation within an overview obtained
by continual monitoring. This view of effectiveness echoes the elements of the
SMT role outlined earlier.

Criteria for judging ineffectiveness included time constraints over meetings,
discussed above, and identifying where there was an odd person out who did not
support other SMT members, suggesting some degree of cultural divergence.
One respondent indicated how teacher members felt their 'loyalties torn',
expected by the head to support the SMT yet also siding with other staff who
were resistant to changes the SMT was attempting to introduce. A second headteacher used the image of a swamp to describe how there were colleagues who
shared her views who were on 'solid ground', dividing the rest into those close to

the shore who were worth working on and those deep in the swamp who were lost causes. It appears that the professional culture among the staff of this school was fragmented, and the head assumed that his or her power was sufficient to shift the cultural allegiance of colleagues only where divergence of beliefs and values was comparatively small. A third alluded to difficulty over defining individual SMT members' roles because of 'a problem with the deputy'. Lack of agreement over role definition was also blamed for ineffective team operation, as was an SMT group which was too large for efficient debate and decision making.

A few respondents indicated how they and their SMT colleagues were attempting to improve their effectiveness as a team. Strategies included changing membership of the SMT by adding staff or cutting back on its size. Two heads expressed the hope that a dissenting member would leave the school because the opportunity would arise only then to appoint senior staff (who would be more likely to share their beliefs and values). These instances show how heads may have limited room to modify SMT membership: the status and associated management responsibility of existing senior staff (especially deputies) alone – whatever their attitude towards teamwork – is likely to be a sufficient qualification for heads to perceive that they must be included in the team. Until such staff leave the school, there is no chance of appointing others to take their place. Several heads were engaged in negotiating individual responsibilities and approaches to teamwork. One pointed to the way the most senior members had held their colleagues back from making a full contribution, and so limited the potential for achieving synergy in the team:

> An issue we need to clarify in more detail is roles and responsibilities. I feel myself and the deputy do not allow the two other members sufficient scope to develop their management skills. Training in September looking at roles and responsibilities may clarify this.

A second head regarded the specification of individual responsibilities and their link with long-term planning and evaluation as a secret of the team's success: 'Job descriptions and job clarification sheets offer yearly targets. The school development plan provides action plans and a built-in evaluation procedure.' Activities designed to promote team development also had a place. One SMT had benefited from management team training with support from the LEA adviser. Two heads had initiated a review of the SMT's effectiveness which extended in one case to seeking feedback from colleagues: 'We have given out questionnaires to staff about how they see the SMT and whether they feel they are getting value for money.'

View from the top

According to the headteachers, most SMTs were a product of the reform period and, where synergy was achieved, they gave heads welcome support with the expanded range of tasks in managing the school for which they were now accountable. Team approaches appeared to be largely an internal affair, offering a structural linkage between the headteacher and staff across the school. There was little hint of any formal team relationship with governors. On the other hand all SMTs, representing a subgroup of the whole staff, were structurally linked with other staff and often at the heart of a matrix of responsibilities spanning the range of school activities. As such, they could provide a means for heads of minimising any gap between the zones of policy and practice, even providing cultural leadership through the exemplary work of individual members and the team as a whole. Adherence to a management hierarchy was expressed in the teams' structure in several ways including the differential salary and status level of staff deemed eligible for membership, the distribution of individual members' responsibilities, and the corporate role as envisaged by the heads. Women were under-represented amongst heads and deputies, the most senior positions in this hierarchy, reflecting wider social conditions affecting the career of women teaching staff.

The account of the working practices of SMTs connected with their part in making major decisions suggested, nevertheless, that hierarchy was not the whole story. There was variation in how far SMT members other than heads and staff outside the team were empowered through some consultative arrangement at least and direct participation in decision making initiated by other staff at most. There seemed to be room, in principle, for heads to express a value placed on equal contribution of colleagues within the bounds of the management hierarchy. The strongly top-down approach allied with managerialism, as advocated by ministers and reflected in official documents, appeared not to have been implemented to the letter in most SMTs, supporting the conclusion from Hall's (1996) research that it may still be possible to survive without acting entirely in the spirit of these reforms.

There were also strong hints that SMTs could bring strain as well as gain for heads, especially where team members did not share educational and managerial beliefs and values, and a fragmented team culture led to internal conflict or withdrawal. The analysis of decision-making procedures suggested that maybe a majority of heads were playing safe by opting for a low-risk approach to teamwork within and beyond the SMT by keeping a tight rein on who was allowed to initiate and participate in making decisions. Others were more open to delegating some of their authority with the proviso that, if they were not comfortable with the way things were going, they could take it back. The story so far has provided a number of insights into the structure and practices of SMTs, but the account is one-sided and short on detail. So, informed by this initial overview, the workings of four SMTs will now be explored in more depth.

Chapter 4

SMTs within the management structure

Members of the four case study SMTs may have shared a stated commitment to a team approach to management, but what they were committed to and the depth of their commitment were far from uniform. The teams each incorporated a response to central government reforms and featured certain structural characteristics, yet there was also diversity in their composition, mode of operation, and centrality as a management strategy. This variety reflected a complex network of factors which were unique in their combination: whether the different parameters for the teams set by the heads; aspects of recent team history such as opportunities for heads to affect appointment of colleague members; the broader institutional history whose legacy included the buildings in which the SMTs had to work; or consequences of the interaction between national primary sector resourcing levels and LEA resourcing decisions for the LMS budget in each school. While heads had some room to manoeuvre within the education system wide dialectic of control to express their individual beliefs and values about team approaches, they were both empowered and constrained by school, national and, to a lesser extent, local factors.

This chapter draws on interview data to begin building up a picture of practices that the SMTs embodied, some of which evolved during the fieldwork period. First, aspects of their context are noted which impinged on the nature of the team approaches adopted. Second, how far the teams were designed as an integral part of the school management structure is considered. Finally, the model of the SMT role developed in the last chapter (Figure 3.3) frames exploration of the part played by each team in managing each school and of contributions of team members to their shared tasks.

SMTs in context

The institutions shared many characteristics: they were LEA maintained; they served the primary age range, attracting a level of funding which determined parameters for allocating promoted posts; and they catered for over 300 pupils. School-level factors affecting the SMTs are compared in Table 4.1. The schools

Table 4.1 Site-level context of case study schools (summer 1996)

Contextual factor	Winton	Pinehill	Kingsrise	Waverley
Pupil age range, school type and governance	3–11, primary (with nursery), county	4–11, primary, county	4–11, primary (with nursery), county	4–11, primary, voluntary controlled
Pupil number, socio-economic status and ethnicity	687, mainly working class, mostly white, 20% Asian and black	586, working class, mostly white	450, working class, mostly Asian	340, working and middle class, mostly white
Gender of teaching staff	25F, 5M	19F, 5M	23F, 3M	12F, 2M
Gender of head, no. of years in present post, past headship experience	F, 3 years, 2nd headship	M, < 1 year, 2nd headship	F 15 years, 2nd headship	M, 13 years, 2nd headship
Location	outer zone of major conurbation	edge of inner city	inner city	urbanised village near city
Site	three 1940s flat-roofed buildings linked by corridors	19th-century and postwar blocks, separated by playground	two 19th-century blocks separated by playground	1970s flat-roofed building, three mobile classrooms
Institutional history affecting SMT	one first and two middle schools on same site merged in 1993	long-term absence of previous head through illness	an infant and a junior school on adjacent sites merged in 1981	rapidly rising number of pupils
Arrangement of pupils in classes	2–3 classes/year	2–3 classes/year (mixed age class)	2 classes/year	1–2 classes/year (mixed age classes)
Impact of inspection	preparation for inspection in spring 1997	preparation for inspection in autumn 1996	anticipating inspection in 1997 or 1998	preparation for and response to inspection in summer 1996

were urban, serving wholly or partly working-class areas. Winton occupied sprawling buildings at one end of a playing field in the outer reaches of a large conurbation. The site was bounded by run-down postwar housing estates, a railway line and an arterial road. Pinehill consisted of two large buildings beside a park and a main road in an outer city area, where housing ranged from Victorian terraces and 1930s council houses to more recent privately owned semi-detached houses and flats. Kingsrise was also close to a busy thoroughfare and situated in two buildings in an inner-city location surrounded on three sides by Victorian terraced housing. Waverley lay in what had once been a village, engulfed by a continually expanding development of mixed housing, mainly privately owned. This school had more cramped accommodation.

The capacity of the schools – with 340 to almost 700 pupils – covered the range of sizes of all but the smallest institutions in the survey sample. Pupil numbers were reflected in the contrasting numbers of teachers, with implications for their representation in the SMT. In all schools, except perhaps Waverley, the size of staff precluded meetings of the entire staff group feasibly constituting the main forum for management activity. Both Winton and Kingsrise included nursery provision, and both catered for a significant number of pupils from minority ethnic groups. At Kingsrise, English was the second language for 70 per cent of children; there was a team of specialist support teachers for English as a second language (ESL) supplied by the LEA, whose leader was an SMT member. Most staff in the four schools were women, consistent with national statistics discussed in Chapter 1. Though the few men were (stereotypically) responsible mainly for older pupils and two were headteachers, women were not under-represented in promoted posts overall. The heads all had first headship experience in smaller schools, but their length of time in this, their second headship, was very different. The head at Pinehill had been recently appointed; his counterparts at Kingsrise and Waverley had been in post for well over a decade.

The layout and quality of school buildings impacted on the work of the SMTs. At Winton there were three large single-storey blocks of classrooms, built in the late 1940s and linked by corridors. Their poor state of repair made them an easy target for vandals. The night before one fieldwork visit, thieves broke through rooflights in the infant department and stole computers, showering glass into two classrooms which could not be used for several days. There had been three major arson attacks in as many years. The flat roofs were prone to leak, buckets strategically placed in rooms and corridors being commonplace. Engineers had failed to identify the source of another kind of water leak – in the mains supply beneath the site – and a special arrangement had been made to waive most of the charge to the LMS budget for the astronomical cost of supplying water. Negotiations were under way to construct a new school building, part financed by selling much of the playing field for housing development, which entailed demolishing the existing buildings. SMT members' shared interest in ensuring that the new building was properly designed and kitted out led them to put great effort into its planning.

The sites at Pinehill and Kingsrise brought their own SMT headaches. In the former, the original Victorian building stood on one side of the concrete playground with a smaller postwar block on the other; whereas at Kingsrise two Victorian buildings, once separate infant and junior schools, faced each other across the playground. SMT members here and at Winton were much exercised with communication across the school, and especially with how to forge a coherent identity and consistent practices among staff who spent the bulk of their working lives in relative isolation from many colleagues. At Waverley, SMT members faced almost the opposite problem. The school roll was rising rapidly due to the influx of children from expanding housing development surrounding the site. The main building, built in the 1970s, was full. The overspill of pupils was housed in three temporary classrooms, and more permanent buildings would soon be required if capacity was to keep up with projected local demand. An unwelcomed task involving the SMT had been to create 'mixed-age' classes spanning two year groups, a move which proved unpopular with parents and required much effort to persuade them to accept the change.

Factors associated with recent institutional history directly affected the SMTs in the three larger schools. Winton was the product of a complex merger less than three years earlier between what were a first and two middle schools, each occupying one of the buildings. A local 'ring fence' policy for staff appointments had meant that the field for all but the most senior posts in the new school had been restricted to staff in the merging institutions. Kingsrise was the product of merging, over a decade earlier, the one-time infant and junior schools on the site, with equally major constraints on staffing decisions at that time. Staff at Pinehill had been through several difficult years connected with the long-term absence of the previous head. The present deputy had been acting head prior to the appointment of the new incumbent, another SMT member had once been an internal candidate for the headship, and all present team members other than the new head had managed the school together prior to his arrival. The learning curve for himself and his other SMT colleagues was steep as they went through a protracted experience of mutual adjustment of the kind that Weindling and Earley (1987) reported in their study of new secondary headteachers.

A national policy with great importance for the SMTs was the first external inspection of their school following reform of the national system for inspection to increase external accountability of state schools. The timing of inspections differed, with the result that the prospect was a background factor at Kingsrise during fieldwork; preparation was under way at Winton; while Pinehill and Waverley were inspected and an action plan drawn up in response to inspectors' criticisms. These inspections placed the quality of managerial work of all SMT members – but especially headteachers as team leaders – under intense scrutiny leading to public judgement.

The fit between SMT and management structure

Formulating a management structure for a large primary school, let alone incorporating an SMT into it, is no simple task. The heads had to design their structure of responsibilities accompanying promoted posts and make incremental adjustments as individual teaching staff moved to posts elsewhere. The head at Pinehill was engaged in adjusting the management structure he inherited on appointment. Possibilities and constraints were posed by many factors, mostly relating to national and school levels, involving a difficult juggling act in attempting to come up with a management structure which was aligned with status levels. These factors included:

- the national system of salary differentials and allowable criteria for their allocation;
- related rules (based on pupil numbers and ages rather than any expectation about management structure) governing the number of appointments at different levels allowable for schools with a particular number of pupils of a certain age;
- the size of the LMS budget (the bulk of which is spent on staffing);
- relative strength of the belief held by heads and governors that promoted posts should carry commensurate management responsibility and of the belief that such posts should be a reward for excellent classroom performance;
- any existing distribution of posts and responsibilities among staff on permanent contracts, and heads' judgements about their competence and potential.

The larger the school, the more promoted posts were possible in principle and at an expanding number of incremental levels – all adding to the complexity of the design task. As Table 4.2 depicts, the four schools had a 3-type matrix consisting of cross-school, department and curriculum coordination management responsibilities, the most complex form of management structure among those reported in the survey institutions. Departments at Pinehill and Kingsrise featured full department leadership responsibility alone, though in both schools there were three departments, each covering two or more year groups of pupils. One teacher at Kingsrise was responsible for a department intended to span the transition from national curriculum key stage one to key stage two. The head hoped to ensure through this arrangement that there was continuity across the key stages and, as the staff concerned worked in both school buildings, to reduce any professional isolation between staff based in each. Waverley – the smallest school – had infant and junior departments and also subdepartmental responsibilities for pairs of adjacent year groups in the junior department. Winton – the largest school – had either one or two subdepartmental management layers within the compass of full departmental leadership, consisting of responsibility for leading a year group of two or three teachers and, in the upper juniors, leading two adjacent year groups.

No management structure exhibited a tidy relationship between types of management responsibility and status, partly because many staff were responsible for more than one area of management. A teacher with three salary increments at Kingsrise shouldered cross-school responsibility for pupil assessment and profiling alongside curriculum coordination responsibility for English; the

Table 4.2 Structure of management responsibilities in case study schools (summer 1996)

Type of management responsibility	Winton	Pinehill	Kingsrise	Waverley
Cross-school	included: **special needs (teacher; 3 increments)** assessment (teacher; 2 increments)	included: **special needs (deputy head) community links (teacher; 3 increments) curriculum leader (teacher; 2 increments)**	included: **in-service training (deputy head) appraisal and assessment (teacher; 3 increments) English as a second language team leadership (teacher; 3 increments)**	included: **assessment and profiling (deputy head)** special needs (teacher; 1 increment)
Departmental	**infant (deputy head) junior (deputy head)**	**early years – reception, Years 1 and 2 (teacher; 3 increments) middle years – Years 3 and 4 (teacher; 3 increments) older years – Years 5 and 6 (teacher; 3 increments)**	**department 1 – nursery and reception (teacher; 2 increments) department 2 – Years 1, 2 and 3 (teacher; 2 increments) department 3 – Years 4, 5 and 6 (teacher; 2 increments)**	**infant (teacher; 2 increments) junior (teacher; 2 increments)**
Sub-departmental	**upper juniors team (teacher; 3 increments)** nursery (teacher; 2 increments) year leader (teacher; 1 increment)			Years 3 and 4 team **(teacher; 2 increments)** Years 5 and 6 team **(deputy head)**
Curriculum coordination	1–2 subjects (teacher; 2 increments)	core subject (teacher; 2 increments) foundation subject (teacher; 0, or 1 increment)	1 subject (teacher; 0, 1, or 3 increments), **deputy**	1–2 subjects (teacher; 0, 1, or **2** increments)

Note: Management responsibilities in bold type were covered by SMT members other than the headteacher. One person might hold more than one type of management responsibility.

deputy, similarly, held a cross-school brief (for managing staff in-service training) and a curriculum coordination brief (for maths). She also experienced a contradiction between two status levels within the management structure. Her class-teaching responsibility lay within the jurisdiction of the relevant department leader (a teacher with two salary increments) who evaluated her classwork planning file, yet her status as deputy meant that technically she held delegated authority over the department leader. At Waverley the deputy experienced a similar structural anomaly, being responsible for assessment and profiling but holding subdepartmental responsibility for the older junior classes. Her work as subdepartmental leader lay within the purview of the junior department leader (also a teacher with two salary increments).

The status level accorded to departmental leadership varied. Winton had two deputies and only here was it possible to divide departmental leadership between the two most senior staff other than the head because they had equivalent status. In the other schools, with only one deputy, departmental responsibilities were allocated to teachers at the same status level as each other in the school but the level differed between institutions. Curriculum coordination responsibility was allocated most commonly to teachers with lower status than departmental leaders, and they dealt with one or two subjects. However, at Pinehill one teacher with two salary increments was responsible for leading curriculum development; she worked closely with all subject coordinators. In the smaller schools the most senior staff other than heads had responsibility for coordinating a core subject within the national curriculum, perhaps reflecting its perceived importance relative to other subjects, coupled with the need to distribute curriculum coordination responsibilities amongst a smaller number of staff than were available in the larger institutions.

How did the SMTs fit into these intricate management structures? Headteachers had overall responsibility for management, but did not shoulder cross-school, departmental or curriculum coordination responsibilities. In Table 4.2, management responsibilities of SMT members other than heads are depicted in heavy type. Apparently, most cross-school and all full departmental responsibilities were deemed substantial enough to be represented in the SMTs, but subdepartmental and curriculum coordination responsibilities were not. The latter were included only when individual staff held these responsibilities in addition to cross-school or departmental responsibilities. Assumptions underpinning the location of SMTs at the hub of the school management structure seemed to be: first, team members other than heads should be positioned to contribute a combination of school-wide specialist knowledge and expertise in areas like assessment or special needs, the managerial workload for which had greatly increased because of reforms; and second, they should have extensive knowledge and leadership experience of groups of classes which, between them, encompassed all the pupils and class teachers in the school. The SMTs fully incorporated two out of the three parts of the schools' matrix management structure, while some curriculum coordination responsibilities were included in the smaller institutions. Links between the SMT and staff outside the team responsible for coordination of most or all subjects would have to be made by means other than SMT members' individual responsibilities (except, perhaps, at Pinehill, where the curriculum leader had joined the team after a lack of linkage had been revealed).

Characteristics of the teams

Key dimensions of SMT membership are summarised in Table 4.3. The survey finding that no relationship existed between school and SMT size is borne out here: the team of four at Winton, the largest school, was the smallest; whereas at Kingsrise, with fewer teaching staff than Winton, the team of seven was the largest. The gender profile in terms of women and men SMT members, indicated in the upper part of Table 4.3, was evenly balanced at Pinehill, with a majority of women at Waverley and all woman teams at Winton and Kingsrise. In the two schools where the headteacher was a man, the deputy was a woman. The majority of the men staff, however, occupied senior promoted posts. In the other two schools, no men had responsibilities attracting more than two increments though in both schools there were higher status posts. At Winton, a man whose post carried two increments for management responsibility had previously been deputy head of one pre-merger school, and had effectively been demoted, on a protected salary, as an outcome of the merger. The national trends discussed in Chapter 3 mask considerable variation at the school level, suggesting that there is some room to manoeuvre if the will to address gender balance is there. The all-women SMTs were in line with one in five of the survey teams, but the combination in Pinehill and Waverley of male head, female deputy and both men and women among other members of the teams was a less common survey result.

The lower part of Table 4.3 shows that there was wide variation over whether SMT members had been appointed to their present post from outside or inside the school. The heads at Winton and Kingsrise had both been heads at a pre-merger school on the present site, so already knew some staff and governors involved in the merger. The table also shows that one or more other SMT members were appointed from within the school in each case, though not necessarily by the present head. The appointments in heavy type are those to which these heads had contributed. Three had been influential in the appointment of all their current SMT colleagues. The mergers at Winton and Kingsrise had afforded their heads considerable scope, though largely from within the pre-merger institutions, and the heads at Kingsrise and Waverley had been in post long enough for past senior colleagues to have moved on, creating vacancies. The head at Pinehill was odd one out, having been recently appointed to a school with a full complement of staff. The SMT here was the only team where all members other than the head had been inherited – not selected – by the new incumbent.

Table 4.3 SMT membership (summer 1996)

Membership factor	Winton	Pinehill	Kingsrise	Waverley
Number of SMT members	4	6	7	5
Gender and status level	F head M 2 deputies 1 teacher (3 increments)	F M head deputy 1 teacher (3 increments) 2 teachers (3 increments) 1 teacher (2 increments)	F head M deputy 2 teachers (3 increments) 3 teachers (2 increments)	F M head deputy 2 teachers (2 increments) 1 teacher (2 increments)
Range of external and internal appointments to present post	*external* **1 deputy** *internal* head **1 deputy** **1 teacher (3 increments)**	*external* head *internal* deputy 1 teacher (3 increments) 2 teachers (3 increments) 1 teacher (2 increments)	*external* — *internal* head deputy **2 teachers (3 increments)** **3 teachers (2 increments)**	*external* head *internal* **deputy** **2 teachers (2 increments)** 1 teacher (2 increments)

Note: Appointments in bold type were made with involvement of the present headteacher.

The composition of each team suggested that heads had assumed the distribution of major individual management responsibilities among SMT members should be aligned with their hierarchically differentiated status – an assumption consistent with belief in a management hierarchy among promoted posts. The main management responsibilities held by SMT members at each status level are set out in Table 4.4. Whereas in the survey the number of status levels found within teams ranged from three to five, here Winton and Waverley featured the fewest with three levels, the other SMTs having four. In the larger schools it had been possible to create one or more posts carrying three salary increments; at Waverley, posts with the maximum number of points possible within nationally set parameters and the school's LMS budget carried two increments. The heads took ultimate responsibility for orchestrating all managerial work inside the school, including operation of the SMT, and for working with the governing body; they also chose to retain sole responsibility for financial management. Deputies at Winton and Waverley had been elected by the staff to represent them as teacher governors, but elsewhere these elected representatives were not SMT members.

Allocation of management responsibilities to deputies and other SMT members reflected the relative importance heads attached to departmental and cross-school responsibilities with, as mentioned above, some individuals in the smaller schools additionally having curriculum coordination responsibility. The impact of reforms was reflected in the content of management responsibilities covered by the SMTs, whether cross-school (like assessment), departmental (to encompass part or all of national curriculum key stages), or curriculum coordination (of core and other national curriculum subjects). There was one instance of a formal element of hierarchical differentiation within the same status level: the deputy at Winton responsible for the junior department received a higher salary than her colleague deputy, who had less experience in this role. The more highly paid deputy was first in line to deputise for the head in her absence. Distribution of SMT members' teaching responsibilities was a corollary of the hierarchical allocation of management responsibilities. The funding level related to school size within the LMS budget also set parameters offering heads variable – but always quite limited – room to manœuvre in freeing up SMT members for managerial work during the school day. The pattern of SMT members' timetabled teaching commitments is depicted in Table 4.5. The headteachers gave priority to keeping themselves clear of a timetabled teaching commitment, avoiding offering such a hostage to fortune, where possible, since they might be called away at any time. While each took some assemblies, the head of Waverley, the smallest institution, was alone in having a moderate regular teaching duty. He took the deputy's class for half a day each week to give her non-contact time.

In only the two largest schools were the deputies freed from responsibility for a class of pupils. Both deputies at Winton did have a substantial teaching commitment, taking assemblies and colleagues' classes to provide them with

Table 4.4 Management responsibilities of SMT members within each status level (summer 1996)

Status level	Winton	Pinehill	Kingsrise	Waverley
Headteacher	overall responsibility, LMS and in-service training budgets, governors	overall responsibility, LMS and in-service training budgets, governors	overall responsibility, LMS and in-service training budgets, governors	overall responsibility, LMS and in-service training budgets, governors
Deputy headteacher	infant department (teacher governor) junior department (teacher governor)	in-service training, appraisal, assessment, special needs, parents, link between head and other staff	in-service training, parents, link between head and other staff, mathematics	assessment, pupil profiling, link between head and other staff, lower junior department, art and display, (teacher governor)
Teacher (3 increments)	special needs, upper juniors team leader	early years department, parents as educators middle years department, classroom management older years department, community links	assessment, pupil profiling, English English as a second language team leader	
Teacher (2 increments)		curriculum management group leader	department 1 department 2 department 3	infant department junior department mathematics, design and technology English, information technology

Table 4.5 Timetabled teaching responsibilities of SMT members within each status level (summer 1996)

Status level	Winton	Pinehill	Kingsrise	Waverley
Headteacher	assemblies	assemblies	assemblies	assemblies, support to provide non-contact time for deputy (10% timetable)
Deputy headteacher	support to provide non-contact time for class teachers, assemblies (65% timetable)	assemblies	class teacher (100% timetable)	class teacher (90% timetable)
Teacher (3 increments)	class teacher, (80% timetable)	class teacher (97% timetable)	ESL support teacher, class teacher (100% timetable)	
Teacher (2 increments)		class teacher (100% timetable)	class teacher (100% timetable)	class teacher (100% timetable)

non-contact time. The deputy at Pinehill, who had been acting head until the present head's appointment and was paid almost the same salary, had no more teaching responsibilities than him, giving her much more scope than her counterparts in the other schools to carry out management work during lesson time. The head had experienced difficulty justifying this arrangement to governors because the size of the LMS budget only just allowed for it. Deputies in Kingsrise and Waverley and all other SMT members in the four schools were responsible for a class (or, in the case of the specialist ESL support team leader at Kingsrise, a full teaching timetable), and most had little or no non-contact time. Almost all their managerial activity had to be undertaken outside lesson time and alongside their class teaching duties like marking pupils' work and seeing parents. Conversely, these SMT members had intimate 'shop floor' knowledge of many pupils and parents, and close contact with the work and concerns of their class-teaching colleagues which gave them a 'teacher's perspective', both of which could inform their work as SMT members.

The composition of each SMT revealed a hierarchy of individual management responsibilities bringing the work of every class teacher into the domain of the team through a combination of heads' overall responsibility and major cross-school and departmental leadership responsibilities of deputies and other staff with the highest status and salary levels. Their location at the heart of the wider management structure of each school suggests that heads intended the teams to bring the domains of policy making and practice firmly into line. So far, how the SMTs constituted a management strategy on paper has been the focus; whether their practice matched up to the potential implied by their pole position in the formal management structure diagram for each school is another matter. A profile of the membership of each SMT, as it stood in the summer of the fieldwork, is offered in Tables 4.6–4.9. (The descriptors which will be used to refer to individual members in the remainder of the text have been entered in bold type.)

Since origins of the profile of SMT members will be discussed in the next chapter, only a summary of key factors is given here. Three SMT members at Winton had been working together prior to the merger, and all four since the launch of their merged school in September 1993. The head had not intended the special needs coordinator to be responsible for a class but, due to a declining LMS budget, this decision had been forced on her. From the beginning of

Table 4.6 Profile of Winton SMT membership (summer 1996)

Status level	Gender	Core management responsibility	Regular teaching responsibility	Number of years in SMT
Headteacher	female	overall responsibility	assemblies	2+
Deputy head	female	**juniors** leader	support, assemblies	2+
Deputy head	female	**infants** leader	support, assemblies	2+
Teacher (3 increments)	female	**special needs coordinator**	Year 6 class	2+

Note: Characteristics in bold type are those used to identify individuals in the text.

Table 4.7 Profile of Pinehill SMT membership (summer 1996)

Status level	Gender	Core management responsibility	Regular teaching responsibility	Number of years in SMT
Headteacher	male	overall responsibility	assemblies	1+
Deputy headteacher	female	headteacher support	assemblies	4+
Teacher (3 increments)	female	**early years leader**	Year 2 class	5+
Teacher (3 increments)	male	**middle years leader**	Year 4 class	3+
Teacher (3 increments)	male	**older years leader**	Year 5 class	6+
Teacher (2 increments)	female	**curriculum leader**	Year 2 class	< 1

Note: Characteristics in bold type are those used to identify individuals in the text.

Table 4.8 Profile of Kingsrise SMT membership (summer 1996)

Status level	Gender	Core management responsibility	Regular teaching responsibility	Number of years in SMT
Headteacher	female	overall responsibility	assemblies	15+
Deputy headteacher	female	support headteacher	class	9+
Teacher (3 increments)	female	**assessment** and appraisal **coordinator**	class	2+
Teacher (3 increments)	female	**ESL team leader**	ESL support	1+
Teacher (2 increments)	female	**department 1 leader**	class	6+
Teacher (2 increments)	female	**department 2 leader**	class	<1
Teacher (2 increments)	female	**department 3 leader**	class	6+

Note: Characteristics in bold type are those used to identify individuals in the text.

Table 4.9 Profile of Waverley SMT membership (summer 1996)

Status level	Gender	Core management responsibility	Regular teaching responsibility	Number of years in SMT
Headteacher	male	overall responsibility	support, assemblies	13+
Deputy headteacher	female	assessment and profiling	Year 5/6 class	5+
Teacher (2 increments)	female	**infants leader**	reception class	1+
Teacher (2 increments	male	**juniors leader**	Year 3/4 class	8+
Teacher (2 increments)	female	**English and IT coordinator**	reception class	<1

Note: Characteristics in bold type are those used to identify individuals in the text.

the 1995/96 academic year the special needs coordinator took over a class of thirty-six pupils in Year 6. The situation at Pinehill was very different. The deputy and the three department leaders had managed the school together prior to appointment of the present head. He had created the present structure of departmental responsibilities to give staff already in receipt of three salary increments a level of management responsibility commensurate with their status, and brought the curriculum leader onto the SMT to strengthen links with staff who had curriculum coordination responsibility. At Kingsrise, the head had favoured an expanding team as the need arose to cover more management areas through individual management responsibilities. Inclusion of the teacher responsible for the ESL support team related to the priority to have SMT representation of this group whose work impinged on that of colleagues across the school. The head at Waverley had also firmed up SMT membership in recent years, covering both key stages and inviting onto the team a teacher with a single salary increment who wished to gain management experience as preparation for possible future promotion. She had subsequently been awarded a second salary increment for coordinating information technology and her team membership, provisional at first, was made permanent.

SMT role and tasks

The stipulative definitions of teams in the first chapter imply that allocating individual management responsibilities to a group within a wider management structure does not in itself comprise a team approach; coordinated and synergistic activity of the group is also required. The analysis draws on the model of the SMT role derived from the headteachers' survey (Figure 3.3). Headteachers' perceptions were complemented with views expressed by other team members, staff outside the teams, and chairs of governors. Accounts varied according to awareness of the teams' operation. Informants outside the teams had less understanding of SMT operation than team members, since they did not attend team meetings. Among staff outside the teams, those with least management responsibility were most likely to perceive the SMT solely in terms of members' own management responsibilities, reflecting their experience of more frequent contact with individual members than with the team. Accounts across the four schools lay within a broad-brush conception of the SMTs' role as *making a strategic contribution to the management of the school, led by the head with the approval of the governing body.* The head at Winton portrayed how the SMT was pivotal in orchestrating management and teaching, bringing coherence and unification to the work of staff in this complex institution. The SMT here was responsible for:

> Organisation, day to day, week to week, year to year . . . the sheer getting the whole thing to hang together smoothly. The school is such an enormous machine, not just because of the numbers but because of the layout, and it is like trying to drive the thing along together without having all the wheels trying to go in different directions at the same time as bumping along. Sometimes we only manage it by the skin of our teeth. Sometimes we have days when we just don't. It's about trying to keep us all going in the same direction, right from the obvious things like when the school photographer comes for it all to go smoothly, to the delivery of the mathematics curriculum. Or the integration of the nursery and reception

so that it then informs development in key stage one and key stage two. The sheer massive task of organisation so that it all looks like a nice, smooth whole.

The model held up at the next level of detail, each element featuring in the operation of the four SMTs:

- the internal *teamwork process* entailed contributing to an overview of the school and its external environment and to a flow of ideas and opinions informed by this overview, while the experience of working together offered individuals a professional learning experience;
- *team tasks* embraced some degree of shared involvement in policy making, planning, ensuring smooth day-to-day running and making a stream of related decisions within the parameters of certain aims or a vision, however far they were articulated and shared;
- proactive and responsive *linkage subtasks* associated in part with individual management responsibilities facilitated a flow of information and opinion between the SMT and other teaching and support staff, governors and parents.

It was at a finer level of detail that significant differences became apparent. When perceptions and practices were unpacked that lay beneath a broadly similar role and the same elements, very different team approaches were revealed. There was diversity over the content, extent and boundaries of team tasks and linkage subtasks; the contribution made by each member to tasks which were variably shared; the form of individual inputs to the teamwork process; the range of individuals' specialist knowledge, skills and attitudes connected with their personalities; and how far such attributes were complementary. Each SMT represented a distinctive team approach to management within the common framework of the model, where members' complementary contributions all included – but could also reach far beyond – their individual management responsibility. Since SMT members at Winton articulated their views of the team role, tasks and process most comprehensively, the fit between their approach and the model will be discussed in full, then contrasts characterising the other SMTs will be explored.

Role of the SMT at Winton

The quotation above indicates how the SMT was at the heart of management, members working together towards coherent longer-term development while trying to keep the show smoothly on the road day by day. There was high mutual awareness of and respect for members' unique contribution to the *teamwork process*, and of the complementarity of their inputs linked with their different personalities. The head was clear about the *support* she received from SMT colleagues:

I am very fortunate because the three people working with me are so capable. We are not dragging anyone along with us, philosophically, work-wise, or anything. We are in tune in that respect. They have got brains in their heads, they have got initiative, they work hard, they deliver the goods.

Her statement suggests members shared a culture of teamwork embracing a similar educational vision and managerial values, respect for each other's competence, and a strong work ethic. She was equally clear about how each personality could be constructive in contributing to synergy within the team:

[The juniors deputy] can be single minded, whereas I tend to be quite a butterfly. They are very good, [the juniors and infants deputies] . . . in keeping things on track because I will do ten things at once, and that's good.

They bring me down to earth and they say, 'Get real!' . . . they make me justify what I'm saying and they tease out the detail to see whether this is just a fantasy or whether it can be translated into something else.

Because of basic personalities, [the infants deputy] is marginally more ready to discuss futures than [the juniors deputy], who is great at planning . . . but in terms of 'This thing might happen, what shall we do?' [the infants deputy] is much more like me in that she will enter into the fantasy of it all, whereas [the juniors deputy] deals in real things . . . but if we all got carried away like I do, what state would the team be in?

The juniors deputy described her tendency in this team to voice caution, but noted how her approach was contingent on the leanings of people with whom she was interacting – here acting as a counterpoint to the head's enthusiasm for new ideas:

If we are planning something, I will look and see where anything could go wrong. I look at the downside of things . . . I always take that approach but would moderate it according to who else I am working with. I find that working with [the head] who is always very open and receptive to anything new, then I tend to be a bit cautious . . . the last thing we need really is yet another person saying, 'Why don't we do this?' and 'Why don't we do that?'!

A third perspective was offered by the infants deputy, conscious that the team combined more talent than any one individual possessed, and that even complementarity did not necessarily mean perfection:

Teams need different skills, and on my own I haven't got them all . . . [the head] is a very good innovator, brings new ideas, wants to set the ball rolling with new things; I would be the main 'keep it plodding along' person; [the juniors deputy] is a completer, she has got a tick list . . . a systematic way of doing things – though we would all recognise that sometimes the completion bit is a bit of a let down.

The distinctive part she played included that of being 'a good listener, quite empathetic with the needs of the staff and the needs of the children in the school'.

The special needs coordinator's perceived unique contribution was consistent with that of the juniors deputy, but linked to her class-teaching responsibility. As the one team member with a class, she felt she had greater empathy with the position of other staff:

> I sometimes feel that maybe I'm the go-between, between the staff and the management team, because I can see both sides of issues. It is very easy when you are not actually class teaching to forget everything that they have to do when you are putting forward some proposal. I think that sometimes I am the voice of reason saying 'Look, hang on a minute.' . . . You have got a more realistic view of what you can expect of people, certainly in terms of meetings after school and at lunchtimes.

The cautionary note she sounded was connected more with implications of SMT initiatives for class teachers' workload than with the concern of the juniors deputy to keep the flow of initiatives within manageable bounds and to ensure implementation, but both team members' contributions counterbalanced the equally valued creativity of their SMT colleagues. Team membership empowered her to champion the interests of class teachers.

Ideas and information were continually exchanged among team members, in SMT meetings, through encounters during the day, and among the deputies and head in particular over the phone during evenings or weekends. While no member could claim a complete *overview* and first-hand knowledge of every aspect of the school, each made a unique contribution based largely on members' cross-school management responsibilities covering, together, the work of all staff. The head noted:

> In terms of input to the meetings, I've got a unique perspective on the finance and budgeting side . . . I deal with the chair of governors, the [school] administrator and the governing body subcommittees . . . What I've got that the others haven't got is a totally global view of key stage one and two.

She gave priority to networking with potentially useful contacts during engagements that took her out of school, and kept her SMT colleagues informed. She was aware how her greater knowledge of the external environment was complemented by the deputies' intimate knowledge of their department and the special needs coordinator's familiarity born of long acquaintance with pupils with special needs, their parents and the supporting work of class teachers. The infants deputy indicated the extent of her departmental working knowledge:

> I like to feel that in the infant department particularly, I am still maintaining a level where I have good knowledge of what's going on in the classrooms, what is going on with particular families. I do have a good rapport with parents, and I know that people come to me as a listener, someone who will help sort out their problems in a non-threatening way.

She also mentioned how she networked with deputies from other local schools and fed ideas and information into the team. She strongly acknowledged the potential of teamworking for *individual professional development*. As the one SMT member who had not worked with the others in a pre-merger school, she perhaps experienced the sharpest learning curve on joining the team:

> I feel I have learned a lot . . . I am always learning from [the head]. [The juniors deputy] as well, I learn things from her – she's very administrative, very organised and sometimes she'll keep me on track . . . Towards the administrative side of my job [the juniors deputy] keeps one step ahead of me and I make sure that I'm not that far behind.

The centrality accorded to the SMT by the head was reflected in the breadth and depth of *tasks* served by the teamwork process. The SMT was responsible for orchestrating the *formulation and implementation of school policies*, including those for each curriculum area. Recent institutional history had imposed a heavy policy-making burden. When the merger took place there was scarcely a policy relating to the new school. A high priority had been to develop the necessary policies, many of which were the responsibility of other staff. With the advent of the opportunity to create a new school building, SMT members became deeply involved in *planning* activity set to continue over several years.

A key *routine organisational* task shared by team members was pupil discipline. Illustrative of the *stream of decisions* confronted by the SMT was the development of a strategy to involve the five most senior staff outside the team, who each enjoyed two salary increments, more fully in managing pupil behaviour. This task had been taking up much of the head's and deputies' time, since they received pupils that teachers sent out of class and ran a detention system. One deputy indicated her belief in graded responsibilities within the management hierarchy by suggesting that there should be an intermediate tier in the arrangement for referral of misbehaving pupils: 'They [the teachers with two increments] were not taking on board the middle management responsibility, and therefore a lot of that falls on us.' The SMT policy and decision-making effort entailed negotiating a change in the management structure to shift the major management responsibility of these staff from developing curriculum and early years policies, since they were now in place, to subdepartmental leadership which would include responsibility for pupil discipline.

The task focus of members other than the head emphasised routine organisation. Both deputies gave importance to day-to-day planning and updating staff on matters like visitors to the school, forthcoming events affecting their classwork, or staff absences. The special needs coordinator noted that, now she had a class, she was involved less with policy making than planning within the policy framework, and she was not able to be party to conversations between other SMT members occurring at odd moments during lesson time: 'The senior management team I feel I have to slip in and out of. Often I am unaware of things that have been discussed during afternoons when I'm teaching, but the other three [team members] are available.' The head was more strategically and future oriented, indicated by her endeavouring to ensure that the prospective new school building would actually happen, and identifying a need for new policies and changes in the management structure.

The variety of *linkage subtasks* relating to other staff was extensive, all members attending and leading regular meetings whose purposes included *consulting* staff on policies, formal decision making to adopt policies and, subsequently, discussing *progress with their implementation*. A daily dissemination exercise embodied shared responsibility for producing a 'day book' for staff, which SMT members completed together by 8.30 a.m. each day. Other staff were expected to visit the staffroom before the start of school to look at the entry in the day book. SMT members attempted to go there for part or all of that time so other staff could raise issues with them. Informal *monitoring* of staff had been undertaken since the school opened, in a recent instance addressing underperformance. One example of the informal approach was keeping tabs on staff punctuality by noticing who did or did not turn up in the staffroom each morning to look at the day book. Another was informing each other about which teachers were sending misbehaving pupils to them. The head and deputies were developing a more formal approach to monitoring classroom performance. The head arranged for a local inspector to train them in the kind of observation undertaken in inspections under the new national framework. She noted how, regretfully, the special needs coordinator was largely excluded from this initiative because of having to take on full class-teaching responsibility, as she would not be as readily available as other members to observe classes during the school day.

Linkage subtasks relating to the *external environment* fell to all members according to their individual management responsibility. The special needs coordinator was frequently involved with external agencies and parents of pupils with special needs. The infants deputy liaised with parents of younger pupils and, in time, was getting to know parents of most pupils in the school.

The juniors deputy got to know many parents in later years, as their children entered key stage two. The head not only knew all the parents, but also put time into networking outside the school, as mentioned above. Structural links between the governing body and the SMT were strong since the deputies were teacher representatives and they and the head each served on a different sub-committee. An example of SMT involvement was gathering staff views on the proposed new school building which were fed into the school development subcommittee. According to the chair of governors, the governing body as a whole rarely initiated changes. Most development was led through sub-committees where staff had a major input through their SMT representative. He perceived the team to be a cohesive entity responsible for the school site, with an overview of the curriculum, provision for pupils with special needs, buildings and health and safety issues. He was aware of the different strengths of the individual members, and of the synergy they achieved:

> Within this team, this is actually one of the most powerful groups of school leaders that we have in the LEA. They have their minor differences within specific areas, but it is resolved within the SMT – very united to the outside world.

The picture emerges of a team approach with intense interaction between members and extensive sharing of their diverse expertise and aptitudes. Despite differentials in status and individual management responsibility, there was strong emphasis on the broadly equal – if both divergent and comple-mentary – contributions of each member.

Role of the SMT at Pinehill

Here, with the arrival of the new headteacher after a long period when senior staff had 'acted up', the new team role had yet to be fully established and its mode of operation to settle down. There was, not surprisingly, less clarity about how SMT members performed as a team than at Winton. The head and deputy alone perceived that they made a unique contribution to the team, and both made a connection with their individual management responsibility rather than to their personality or complementary knowledge or skills. The head couched his leadership of the SMT in terms of his approach to headship:

> I see my role of headteacher as creating an atmosphere that is mutually supportive, that brings out the best in individuals, that is about saying yes more than no but being able to say no when necessary. We've got some very clear school aims which we've developed as a school. My role is keep-ing people on the track, and it is very easy with the day to day nitty gritty of things to forget to look ahead rather than looking down at your feet . . .
> I see my role as getting the school to move along the path. And in order

to do that, it means valuing people, listening to people, taking time with people. It means being a critical friend to people, it means getting people to question their own practice and to develop their own practice. So it's a little bit from behind but also from the front.

Headship therefore entailed leading the SMT, ensuring that *school aims* were articulated and that team tasks were directed towards them. He also alluded to the issue of being uniquely accountable as head for the work of the school and, within it, the SMT, while also being increasingly dependent on colleagues:

> The buck stops with me, when a decision has to be made I will make it and be answerable for it, that's what I'm paid for . . . there's a balance between being a listener, being a decision maker, and actually being fairly firm about which way we go. That reflects back into the management team as being their influence on me for making, in a sense, corporate decisions, but I'm the one who carries the can for the decisions. And I will be the one who is accountable to [inspectors], accountable to the governors, for those decisions.

This view suggests he subscribed to a hierarchical conception of the teamwork process, valuing others' input of ideas. Yet he retained a high level of control over the task of decision making, as he would be held externally accountable for the consequences – facing an inspection within his first year as head. At the same time, he relied heavily on SMT colleagues because he had not been a class teacher since before the reforms:

> I've been out of the full time classroom for twelve years. That means I have never taught the national curriculum – and they have. So they have kept me very much informed about the practicalities of teaching the national curriculum . . . you need to actually do it to appreciate the pluses and minuses of it.

There was further evidence of hierarchy within the team operation expressed through the deputy's contribution to *supporting the head*. She perceived her contribution to teamwork as reflecting her status as deputy:

> You are used as a sounding board by other staff and also by the head. You are in that sort of 'in between' place . . . the other members of the senior management group don't have that as much. With [the head], I know that he would talk with me about things, perhaps before sounding them out with the rest of the senior management group.

When team members other than the head had voiced their concerns over the way the SMT was working, she had attempted to 'ease communication' between them and the headteacher. With such a new team it was perhaps too early for SMT members to feel able to assess how far it had led to individual development, though each member was going through a learning experience as radical as that faced by the infants deputy at Winton. The head acknowledged how working with other members of this team had already contributed very significantly to his *professional development*:

> I have learned a tremendous amount, not only about interpersonal rela-tionships in a very short period of time, but I've also learned an awful lot professionally – some of them in the senior management group are better teachers than I will ever be, so professionally I have grown by listening to them.

This response underlines how individual development is potentially there for all team members – headteachers included.

Compared with the team at Winton, the head at Pinehill put greater em-phasis on day-to-day and routine aspects of the SMT's role in managing the school. The range of *team task content* was more restricted in that, although he had overhauled the management structure soon after taking up his post, over-sight of curriculum development was currently excluded from the SMT brief. Elements of the team role included facilitating short-term *planning* and class-work in each year group; *routine organisation*, described as the 'nitty gritty nuts and bolts bit' such as arranging playground duties; *monitoring staff* with a view to improving teaching quality while minimising potential stress and any per-ceived threat; and developing better *links* with other staff so that all could perceive that they had a say in decision making. The SMT was involved in longer-term *policy making and strategic planning* in areas other than curriculum. The head also looked to other members to help him gain an *overview* of the internal workings of the school. He referred to the importance of 'feedback to me, because with the best will in the world I can't get around to classes as much as I'd like – it's good feedback, communication is really the crucial thing'. The older-years leader noted how he and other department leaders were con-cerned, not only with representing the interests of staff in their department, but also with adopting a broader perspective:

> We're on an equal level, just representing our department. We're repre-senting ourselves as well . . . instead of taking a departmental view or a classroom view of everything, we take an overall view as well of the whole school. Looking at how things are going on . . . how will it affect the whole school?

Linkage subtasks were a major focus for the three department leaders. The older-years leader pointed to the two-way link between his department and the SMT:

What they [teachers in the department] say comes back with me when we meet in the senior management team and conversely what we agree in these meetings I can get back to them . . . I'm a fairly big link in the chain between the people in my [department] team and what's going on in the decision making part of the school.

Linkage through *monitoring* was also a concern of the head, who indicated how he monitored the SMT meetings but also how the team helped him to monitor inside the school:

We are all monitoring in a lot of different ways – at the senior management group meetings one's obviously monitoring the meetings. But the real monitoring is monitoring the decisions that have been made during meetings. Are they actually happening on the ground? Getting feedback from staff about that, getting feedback from the senior management group about that, and seeing the evidence with my own eyes through going round the school.

This SMT was inward looking, having little *external linkage* with governors other than through the head and deputy. She attended full governing body meetings as an observer, and he was primarily responsible for feeding governors' concerns into the SMT and reporting to them on the team's work. It was a team in transition, all of whose members were learning to work together within the new parameters set by the head. He had used his authority to impose a strong element of hierarchy in the way the team played its role.

Role of the SMT at Kingsrise

The head at this school was, by contrast, the longest-serving team member and had hand-picked the other members over the years. The SMT also featured a high degree of internal hierarchy reflected in team members' accounts. The head summarised its role as the 'management, organisation, and general disciplinary policy of the school, but in the job descriptions each one has a slightly different angle that they're coming in from'. Implicitly, therefore, any complementary contributions related to individual management responsibilities. She welcomed the *support* of the team in running a large school spread across two buildings. Yet her personality and beliefs about headship led her to keep a tight hold over her SMT colleagues' contribution:

One of the hardest things in my view is for a primary head to let go and to delegate. We are used to having everything under our control and it is very, very hard to delegate it down and think, 'Are they going to do it the way I want it?' And if they don't get it the way I want it personally, then I know I will have to let them run with it. And if it's effective I must accept it, but if it's not effective, I know that I will have to step in and say, Now look, we have given you your head but do you think this is working?'

The department two leader perceived that members other than the head and deputy were in the team to support them, implying that the head monitored SMT colleagues and offered feedback on their departmental work:

> [The SMT is] a structure within the school, from each of the departments. It's good to have a chance to all come together. [The head] can then tell us things that are working or are not working and we've got a chance to go back and hopefully put it into practice in the department. I think if it was just the action of the headteacher and deputy head trying to do all of that they couldn't do it, so I think hopefully that we make their job a little easier.

The deputy corroborated this view by noting how she helped monitor implementation by department leaders of a newly formulated policy on storage of books in classrooms. She also noted how there was complementarity between herself and the head:

> As headteacher and deputy we complement each other because she's got a great interest in the legal side, she can compartmentalise things. I haven't got that sort of a brain really, but we do complement each other in the way that we work.

The strong head–deputy partnership or coalition apparently constituted a hierarchical team within the team, supervising the work of other members. She noted how the head had a unique *overview* of the school, including all staff: 'The headteacher has a good oversight of the school and of the personnel here as well. She knows them all really well and spots things pretty quickly before other members of staff even see it or are aware of it.' Other members stressed how their contribution to the team related to their hierarchical management responsibility. The assessment coordinator not only took responsibility for the school when the head and deputy were off-site, but also fed in ideas based on her knowledge of staff and their concerns. The department two leader noted how 'even though you are part of the management team, you still feel very much part of the staff – the management team thing is just something else that you do'. Like the special needs coordinator at Winton, the assessment co-ordinator at Kingsrise implied that it was important to include within the SMT senior staff who had a close working relationship with class teachers.

Among SMT members, department leaders alone perceived the team experience to have helped their *individual development*, and they emphasised learning to fulfil their management responsibility. The department two leader also stressed the emotional strength she had gained and her greater interpersonal skills:

At a personal level I think it's developed my confidence a bit, it's made me a stronger person. I think it's also made me look at people differently, look at people more as individuals as well. We are all different, and you have to know the people you're dealing with.

The hierarchical operation of the SMT was reflected in the way *team tasks* were carried out. The department three leader indicated how *policy making* was initiated largely by the head, who sought views of other members about the impact of her proposals on them:

When we have our meetings, [the head] gives us the opportunity, puts forward new ideas, proposals and year plans or whatever. We are given the opportunity to discuss issues and throw up our points of view about where it affects us and our team.

This approach was followed when the school development plan was formulated: priorities put forward by the head and deputy were discussed in the SMT, then the former drew up the final plan. The range of task *content* was broader than at Pinehill in that the SMT remit included curriculum oversight. The ESL team leader described how the team was involved with *routine organisation* and *strategic planning*, topics encompassing:

Who's going to do what – like Christmas concerts, the day to day running of the school, to things like looking at different areas of the curriculum, the staff development plan, the development plan for the school – what are we going to look at next? And ideas for in-service training.

Links with other staff were established. Some related to individual members' management responsibility, as where department leaders disseminated information about SMT decisions. Others were connected with individuals' efforts to stay in touch with other staff, the assessment coordinator noting how 'people can come to me with a complaint or something and I can see that it is valid and I can bring it to senior managers' attention'. *External linkage* with the governing body operated primarily through the headteacher since no other member of the team was a teacher representative. For most SMT members, contact was restricted to the one-off experience of making a presentation to governors to inform them about an area within their management responsibility. The chair of governors perceived that the SMT was responsible inside the school for matters connected with all governing body subcommittees: staffing, buildings, finance, teaching and curriculum. The SMT link was forged via the headteacher's regular report to the governing body and her attendance at all subcommittee meetings.

The head had used her authority to set her stamp on the membership of this SMT and the internal hierarchy of its operation. The universal acceptance of her approach among other SMT members, all of whom had been inducted into the wider staff culture before their promotion into the team, suggested that there was a shared culture of teamwork underpinned by belief in differential positioning within the management hierarchy. The SMT role was strongly orientated towards supporting the head's agenda as top manager, whether as a sounding board for her ideas, a means of extending her ability to monitor other staff and to glean information about their concerns, or a route for disseminating information across the school.

Role of the SMT at Waverley

Here the head was also very well established: the longest serving member of staff. He had given a strong steer to development of the present SMT role with an emphasis on internal hierarchy similar to that at Kingsrise. He indicated how he consulted with SMT members and gained *support* from their *contribution of ideas* related to their closer links with other staff and pupils:

> The most important thing is pupils and learning, so all issues relating to curriculum and setting of priorities are discussed as a team, and then as a whole staff team and then agreed at SMT level . . . staffing issues, though not all staffing issues are taken back to the staff as occasionally those are confidential . . . I do value the input that colleagues can give . . . I do need their input – they're at the sharp end and they do bring a perspective that I may not necessarily have thought of – there isn't much we don't discuss!

As at Kingsrise, the head and deputy held separate meetings on occasion, and the deputy perceived her contribution to the SMT as an intermediary between the head and other staff. She emphasised her relationship with all staff within her individual management responsibility as deputy:

> I'm very much a link between the staff and the head. I find it quite difficult at times, you want to be loyal to everybody, but at times I have to say to [the head], 'I'm sorry but the staff feel quite strongly about this', or the other way round. Very much a link between people.

The infants leader indicated her belief in having a subordinate position in the hierarchy among contributions to the team, claiming: 'There are times when it's appropriate to not be totally equal, and I think that when I'm not, it's appropriate that I'm not.' The English and IT coordinator confirmed the head as the main instigator of the SMT's work, wanting other members to offer views relating to their familiarity with other staff:

> We're a sounding board for ideas coming from the head, and initiatives he's interested in either undertaking or considering for the school, as well

as representing staff views on initiatives. There's some negotiation, feeding information through, and 'rebellious information' has to come through from the shop floor, so to speak. We look at problems that individual colleagues might be experiencing, and general school structures, health and safety issues, and policy changes.

The head's hierarchical approach extended to decision making, and a tendency to withhold from delegating tasks to SMT colleagues. In the words of one, he had used them to

> bounce ideas off the rest of us, discuss ideas with us before going to staff meetings, raise general issues and so on. So, as far as him actually allocating tasks to us, that's been fairly minimal up to now. He's really discussed things with us, asked our opinions on things, we've fed back to him, he's taken that into account, and then he's made decisions or not made decisions.

Yet this SMT member also intimated that the head was receptive to others' ideas, primarily outside the framework of the team. The head, like his counterpart at Kingsrise, experienced a value conflict over delegation but was coming to share responsibility more and beginning to reap some reward:

> I like things done yesterday and often feel I can do things quicker myself. But I have found this is not true. By working as a team, I save time by gradually feeding out responsibilities to colleagues so that they have ownership of decisions as well.

The potential for *individual development* through the team experience was acknowledged by two team members other than the head. The deputy focused strongly on the example the head had provided. She had learned

> interpersonal skills – I feel very much more confident when speaking with other members of the staff, or talking to parents. I've learned an awful lot from [the head] about decision making: when to make a decision and when, perhaps, to hold back. Because it's very easy to open your mouth and then to think, 'I should have waited!' I've learned restraint as well.

A more future-oriented development opportunity had been presented to the English and IT coordinator explicitly so that she could further her chances of promotion to a deputy headship elsewhere.

The *content* of team tasks tackled within the strongly hierarchical approach was as broad as at Winton and Kingsrise. It encompassed involvement in *policy making* (a current issue was expansion of the school), where the juniors leader noted that the head habitually wrote drafts and sought feedback through the SMT. They were involved in a similar way in *strategic planning* (such as identifying priorities for the school development plan). As the head's account above implies, SMT *decision-making* activity typically included ratifying an initial SMT proposal with other staff, followed by his or an SMT decision. Time was also spent on *routine organisation*, like arranging a timetable for using the hall when preparing for concerts.

SMT members stressed the importance of *links* with other staff, partly through ensuring that they all had representation through the individual management responsibility of team members. The infants leader indicated how she worked closely with general assistants, most of whom were allocated to her department, and acted as their link person. Forms of linkage varied, the English and IT coordinator noting how other staff were able to raise issues: 'Staff are able to go to somebody if they have a grievance or a concern and it is taken forward.' Equally, the infants leader pointed to SMT members' responsibility for ensuring implementation of SMT decisions: 'When a policy is made, we are the interim – sort of middle management . . . going away and helping to ensure that it takes effect.' The head took on primary responsibility for monitoring implementation of curriculum policies by observing classes and reviewing pupils' work. As mentioned above, other staff were often involved in ratifying proposals aired first inside the team.

Since the deputy was the elected teacher representative on the governing body both she and the head acted as channels for *external links* between the SMT and governors. As at Kingsrise, contact with the governing body for other members was confined to occasions where they made a presentation connected with their responsibility for coordinating an area of the curriculum. The chair of governors confirmed that he worked with the head, rather than the SMT. He perceived that this arrangement followed from the complementary responsibilities of governors and the SMT and from the approach of the head. Consequently, his awareness of the work of the team came through his formal and informal contact with the head and through the governors' curriculum subcommittee.

Origin and expression of diversity

These four accounts of SMT roles and tasks show how heads did have some room to manœuvre despite national and local contextual constraints and used it in creating a management structure, a team within it, and a role for the team in accordance with their beliefs and values. The broad parameters of the SMT role were common, but the heads used their authority to determine which tasks could be shared and the possibilities and boundaries of other members' contributions to them. The heads were not attempting solely to realise an interest in directive control of the team. Rather, they fostered the kind of support from colleague members that they valued while also delimiting the boundaries of this contribution so that it would remain within their comfort zone. They each acknowledged their need for support in the reform environment, especially that provided by others' ideas, expertise and detailed knowledge which could complement their own. Yet they varied markedly in the degree to which they were ready to take the risk of some loss of control resulting from empowering colleagues through sharing and delegation of tasks.

An element of internal hierarchy was present in all four teams. It was expressed not only in the distribution of individual management responsibilities and content of tasks which heads were willing to place within the team's jurisdiction, but also in the way team tasks were shared differentially among subgroups in the team linked with individuals' formal status and their management and teaching responsibilities. This expression of an internal team hierarchy was counterbalanced by the span of opportunities heads gave colleague members to contribute on a par with themselves. The obverse of the relatively low expression of internal hierarchy at Winton, reflected in the contrasting contributions of the deputies and special needs coordinator, was the high level of equal involvement in a wide range of strategic management tasks. In this team alone were members other than the head preparing to undertake formal monitoring of classroom teaching. The other three teams expressed a greater degree of internal hierarchy, such tasks as heads brought to the team being shared unequally in the sense that the heads generally sought SMT colleagues' feedback on and commitment to implementation of their agenda. In these cases, the head and deputy worked together more closely than with other SMT members. At Kingsrise and Waverley, other members accepted the internal hierarchy, so empowering the heads to operate in this way. SMT members other than the head at Pinehill were still adjusting to a new regime brought in by the present incumbent which had reduced their ability to contribute on an equal basis.

These findings resonate with the notion of a balance between contradictory norms affecting the operation of SMTs introduced earlier. The approach to the role and tasks of Winton's SMT appeared quite strongly egalitarian. The interviews suggested that the pattern of interaction between team members would occupy a position towards the end of the continuum between belief in a management hierarchy and belief in equal contribution which was weighted towards equal contribution, as depicted impressionistically in Figure 4.1. The other three teams were as strongly hierarchical, occupying a position towards the opposite end of the continuum with belief in a management hierarchy in the ascendent. In so far as the heads' approach to leadership within the SMT could be construed as transformational, the head at Winton shared power with other team members most extensively.

The different balance struck by each head did not split neatly along gender lines. The reportedly most egalitarian team was an all-female team whose formal leader had played a major part in selecting her colleague team members. One of the three more hierarchical teams was also an all-female team, whose leader had also 'hand picked' other members of the SMT. Even if, as some writers contend, women headteachers are more likely to share power with colleagues than men (e.g. Jones 1987; Shakeshaft 1989; Jirasinghe and Lyons 1996) it seems likely that such a trend would mask wide variation among individual heads of either gender.

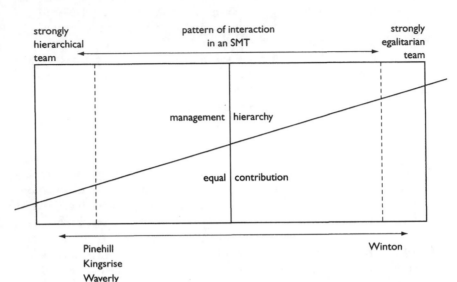

strongly   pattern of interaction   strongly
hierarchical   in an SMT   egalitarian
team   team

management | hierarchy

equal | contribution

Pinehill   Winton
Kingsrise
Waverly

Figure 4.1 Balance of contradictory norms in case study SMTs

The SMTs' structure and role illustrated how the heads looked to team approaches to management as a way of easing their increasingly heavy management burden following from national reforms. School-level factors piled on further pressure to share this burden: all were larger than average institutions; all were housed in buildings which were difficult to manage; and each school embodied management challenges relating to its immediate environment. There were no radical differences in the role of the SMTs in contributing to the internal management of the school according to the heads' leadership. Their role featured the same key elements: some form of complementary contributions to the teamwork process, connected with individuals' expertise within their individual management responsibility and their preferred way of working linked with their personality; some involvement in team tasks of policy making and strategic planning concerned with day-to-day running and longer-term development of the whole school; and linkage subtasks, also largely associated with members' individual management responsibility, to connect the SMT with other staff. Marked differences were apparent within these elements, dependent on the balance each head maintained between empowering colleague members through sharing a wide range of task content on a relatively equal basis, and retaining power by operating hierarchically – restricting the content to be encompassed by other SMT members and their participation in areas that were placed within the team remit. The following chapter examines how these diverse team approaches came about.

Chapter 5

Creating a team in their own image?

Team approaches to management do not happen overnight; teams must be conceived at some point as a new entity, their brief clarified, their membership established and their mode of operation developed. A team may be created from scratch or an existing group may be reconceived as a team. Members and others with whom they interact have to learn to collaborate through an evolutionary process which is never complete and whose course may be unpredictable. The case study SMTs were encountered over a specific period in their team history. Even during this relatively short time, all members experienced some shift in their team practice and perceptions of each other.

The case studies underlined how heads were central in creating and developing team approaches, expressing a transformational aspect of their leadership, since all were bent on developing some form of shared culture of teamwork which did not predate the adoption of a team approach. While their position of authority gave them access to key resources for promoting team development, such as being able to make a major contribution to selecting other members or holding responsibility for the school's in-service training budget, these levers were not enough for teamwork necessarily to follow. Other members also played a crucial part, having recourse to influence over how far they might enter into the spirit of teamwork as advocated by the head, or whether they might offer minimal compliance or even open resistance. So far a largely static picture of the SMTs has been painted, concentrating on their location within the management structure and contrasting emphases in their performance of a similar role. Now the focus shifts towards the dynamics of developing team approaches to management. First, factors are examined which stimulated the heads to opt for a team approach and to set about creating one or, alternatively, to reinterpret evolving practice in terms of teamwork. A different mix of school-level and national influences contributed in each case. An important task for heads was to bring together a group of staff to form the SMT. Various constraints denied heads an unfettered chance to select their 'dream team', though they sought room to manœuvre where possible. The national reform designed to increase the power of governing bodies meant that they now held the balance of authority over selection of staff. A high

premium was therefore placed on heads' ability to use influence with governors. The opportunity to select new team members was a comparatively rare
event in team histories anyway, because these were permanent teams whose
membership related as much to individuals' status and salary levels as to their
management responsibilities. Second, consideration is given to how heads fostered a supportive culture of teamwork that accorded with their beliefs and
values, and how they met with a varied response from other members, depending on elements of their professional culture. Finally, the way team members
learned to work together is explored, whether through planned induction and
development opportunities or everyday experience. Participation in a team
approach to management, as the model of the SMT role suggested, could constitute an individual professional development experience for every member.

The last chapter showed how circumstances prompting the heads to adopt a
team approach in their present post were quite different. Nevertheless, all four
had come more or less gradually to realise that it would be advantageous to
share their management burden beyond the more traditional head–deputy
partnership. This belief emerged as a result of their professional experiences,
against a backdrop of increasing managerial demands associated with national
reforms. It was strongly reinforced for two heads by significant events.

Putting together the SMT at Winton

Experiences in her first headship at one of the schools which merged to
become Winton had brought home to this headteacher the value of teamwork.
At that time she had inherited a deputy with whom she had found it difficult
to work, but when this person left the school, she had been able to appoint a
deputy who shared her professional beliefs and values, and the head–deputy
partnership rapidly became what she described as 'an instant team'. Pupil
numbers in the school grew rapidly as it became more popular with parents
during the 1980s, providing the first opportunity to create a senior post
(carrying the equivalent of two salary increments). The experienced teacher
appointed proved able to work closely with the head and deputy, this three-
some constituting a team 'almost before we knew what a senior management
team was – before it had been invented'. Belief in the notion of an SMT had
here followed practice:

> It was never a conscious decision, 'I am going to have a senior management
> team.' I had two people who were wholly competent and capable who I got
> on well with personally, and it was a natural and normal way of working.
> Therefore when it came to the new school it didn't occur to me to work
> in any other way.

The head's positive account of their working relationship suggests they had
succeeded in developing a strong culture of teamwork. When the school was

scheduled to be merged with two others, the prospect of being interviewed for the headship of what would become Winton presented the head with the occasion to develop her ideas about a management structure which would be effective in that context. When asked at interview how she would ensure good communication in such a large school, she answered in terms of her vision of a management structure which would include an SMT. Her success in securing the post as headteacher-designate of Winton enabled her to use influence with governors over appointing other staff: 'I was in an unusual position in that I had to invent a complete management structure for a new school . . . and then interview for it.' Her deputy from the pre-merger school was appointed as the juniors deputy and her senior teacher was promoted to the post of special needs coordinator, forming the nucleus of the present SMT: a group whose members had already developed a shared culture of teamwork, though based on experience in a relatively small school. The juniors deputy reflected on the contrast between the possibility of the whole staff in the pre-merger school operating as one team and the need for a matrix of teams imposed by the size of the merged institution. She perceived the head to have been preoccupied with the issue of

> how we would make such a large school work. And there was very much an overriding idea of having to have teams because in the past, in a small school, you are a team. You have smaller teams within it, but you are a working team. With so many, we deduced that it would be very difficult to have a whole workable team [of all staff] except on very, very few occasions. So the whole ethos behind it was to have a team approach right through. And obviously people would have dual links with various teams, the idea being that it would then bring everything together. Starting with the senior management team, the curriculum teams, the year group teams and the departmental teams.

This account supports the contention, mentioned in Chapter 2, that increasing size of institutions virtually dictates that management structures must be based on staff subgroups. The pre-merger school had twelve teaching staff, but Winton had two and a half times that number and staff meetings were no longer practical as a setting where all staff views could be aired. It also highlights how the SMT was integral to the design of the complex matrix management structure at Winton. The rationale for including a teacher with the special needs coordination brief in the team was to manage provision for the high proportion of pupils with special educational needs. Her brief brought her into contact with other staff throughout the school, putting her in a good position to contribute to the overview that the head intended to be shared within the team:

> that umbrella view of the school, it really goes right through from nursery to year six. And I wanted that person also to have status within the school.

I didn't want special needs to be shoved into an office somewhere down one of the buildings. Status-wise, I felt it important that it was at a C [carrying three salary increments] and therefore part of the senior management team, to advise within the management functioning of the school.

The spread of individual management responsibilities among SMT members other than the head (see Table 4.2) meant that, between them, they would have extensive knowledge of all pupils and their families. While the head had influenced governors over appointing projected SMT colleagues whom she already knew would share her beliefs and values about teamwork, she also had to operate within significant constraints. First, the LEA's 'ring-fencing' policy for appointing staff other than deputies to the merged school put her under pressure to accept staff whom she would not ideally appoint to management positions. An unexpected opportunity to bring an outsider into the new team was presented when a second deputy appointed from one merging school resigned before taking up post and the head and governors perceived that there was no suitably experienced replacement within the merging institutions. The infants deputy was appointed from a nearby school where she already had deputy headship experience, and the head was satisfied from evidence gathered by visiting her at work and from the interview that she shared key beliefs and values about teamwork, management and education. Second, ring-fencing, coupled with a tight LMS budget, limited the potential for allocating salary increments to staff. The head's preferred team structure would have consisted of five members, including a teacher with three salary increments responsible for the nursery and reception classes. A teacher who already had a similar brief in one pre-merger school, but whose post carried two salary increments, was interviewed but the governors decided not to appoint at the more senior level. While this teacher remained in post, it would not be possible for the head to engineer the intended position, and the SMT was confined to four members:

> Should an appropriate vacancy come up in the infant department in key stage one – because that is where it would have to be to keep the balance – I will still wish for a [post carrying three salary increments] in the early years. That is my dearest wish. But I am frustrated, not so much over finance because I could juggle other staff responsibilities, you can rob Peter to pay Paul, so that's not an issue. It's just the bums on seats, the teachers who are sitting on the seats. And until a [teacher with two salary increments] goes at that level I really can't do anything about it. So I suppose you could say we are running one under par, and have been since we began.

That all members of the SMT turned out to be women had been a side effect of the selection process. Governors (and the present head for posts other than her own), had given top priority to selecting the strongest candidate on professional grounds, gender being much lower on their list of criteria. The chair of governors would have preferred, ideally, to appoint a man to the SMT as he perceived that fathers among the parents might react better to a man. However, he perceived that no male applicants had matched up to those appointed.

The head adopted a strategic stance towards staffing, making contingency plans in case anyone left the school and retaining a mental wish-list of potential replacements whom she might seek to appoint from within the school or to attract from outside. Her conception of the SMT was never static, although its membership had not changed in three years. She balanced commitment to its present form with a vision of possibilities for future development through changes in membership. When a colleague SMT member informed her that she was applying for a job elsewhere, the head already had in mind a person at a nearby school whom she hoped would apply for the vacancy arising if the present incumbent left. She commented: 'It's always the joke in Winton; you never tell [the head] that you are thinking of going, because she has your place filled the next day! You never need to feel bad about going because it is not a problem to her.'

One design consideration for the head had been to have a small team, in line with her belief in a relatively egalitarian mode of operation where all members could take initiatives and engage fully in debate. She wished to avoid the strongly hierarchical approach that she perceived might follow from creating a large one:

> I have always stuck out against a larger team because I couldn't see how I could make it workable on a regular basis. I couldn't imagine how I could have regular and meaningful meetings with seven or eight people. So it didn't just become a token thing – 'We have got a senior management team, we meet once a fortnight, and I bring things to them and say, "This is what I want us to do!", and they rubber stamp it.' I don't think you can have genuine discussions in a group that size.

It is notable that the hierarchical approach she had rejected as 'tokenism', where a head would essentially seek support for his or her agenda, was close to that embraced by other case study heads.

Remodelling the SMT at Pinehill

Applying for a second headship in a school double the size of the one experienced in his first headship was also a major event for the head at Pinehill. His decision to go for a team approach was informed by his positive first headship experience of teamwork and what he witnessed on his pre-interview visit to Pinehill:

> I had developed a team approach to managing my last school and had seen the benefits and successes of it, and so when I applied for this job . . . it jumped

out at me that a team approach was the way forward. Because a school this size can't really function unless there is a structure of some sort, and that structure would seem to be a team structure which actually empowers all the members of the team and that includes all members of staff. That seemed to me something that this school didn't really have properly . . . it was there in name only; it really wasn't working in practice. That was very clear to me on the day before the interview. That night I went home and structured my presentation very much around the need for a team approach.

There is no guarantee that an externally appointed head will find that other staff share her or his beliefs and values about teamwork, and this head perceived he was going into a situation where the staff did not operate according to his conception of a team structure. As senior members they had been in a position, in the absence of the previous head, to express their beliefs and values about their their preferred way of working. It seems likely that they would not fully share the culture of teamwork to which the new head subscribed. The head reiterated the belief he had expressed at interview: 'I was appointed because of my commitment to a management structure which is rational, that empowers people, and encompasses a team approach.' He used his authority to act unilaterally in reallocating staff responsibilities. However, he had much less room to manœuvre than the head at Winton since he inherited the full complement of other staff, and was also constrained by his inability to revise (especially downwards) the status and salary levels which individuals already enjoyed.

If the SMT was to extend beyond the deputy, the assumption that the SMT should represent the most senior staff within the management hierarchy meant that three teachers, each with three salary increments, would be in the running for team membership. These individuals had experienced substantial management responsibility in recent years when, as the head put it: 'They had done their best, basically, to run the school for some time.' At interview, several other members confirmed this account, their view of the team history prior to the arrival of the new head including the enduring story or myth that they had been empowered to operate as equals in managing the school. As he did have authority to change individual management responsibilities, his compromise design solution was to allocate to each senior teacher the responsibility of leading the team of staff in a department. As mentioned in the previous chapter, he had also created the parallel curriculum management team of subject coordinators led by a curriculum leader (with two salary increments). His priority had been to introduce a revised management structure, incorporating a team approach, to give existing staff differential levels of managerial responsibility and workload within the parameters of their current hierarchical levels of salary and status:

There was a clear structure that actually related to the financial side of things and was also seen to be fair, so that more is expected in terms of time and in terms of expertise from a management point of view. There is a debate over whether curriculum management should have a higher profile, and so on, but that [arrangement] is largely historical ... job descriptions were rewritten and redesigned to reflect that structure.

The gender balance was equal among staff whom the head included in the SMT on grounds of their salary and status, which he perceived to be fortuitous because he was concerned not to perpetuate the national shortfall in promoted posts for women:

> In primary schools ... gender is quite an issue, especially in senior management. It's a complete embarrassment ... It's a balance [in this team] that I feel very comfortable with because it is roughly equal and there is certainly a feeling of valuing individuals. Gender, in a sense, is irrelevant to the professionalism that we're looking for.

He was aware of a tension between wishing to achieve equal representation among women and men in senior posts while putting top value on relative individual merit among candidates in specific situations: 'Gender is an issue that we're conscious of; certainly from a management point of view I'm conscious of trying to get that balance right. But the bottom line has to be the best person for the job, whatever the gender.'

A design flaw in the new management structure had soon become apparent: 'The fault at the moment, which I think is becoming fairly clear, is communication between curriculum management and senior management. It is certainly something I would want to develop, how we could improve that communication.' In addition, the head believed that cross-school responsibility for special needs coordination should ideally be incorporated into the SMT. He faced a dilemma over the possible negative consequence of a decision to expand SMT membership to incorporate the curriculum leader and special needs coordinator. There were two constraints. First, as the head stated, 'If you make a management group too big, it becomes unwieldy.' Large size, as the head at Winton had implied, militates against full participation in teamwork during meetings. Further, a financial cost of expansion would be to increase the amount of teacher cover required to enable two more members of staff to attend SMT meetings, which he preferred to hold during lesson time. The alternative of arranging for them to take place outside the school day would have carried a time cost, as he and some other senior staff were already committed to extensive activities after school.

During the year, the head took the plunge by first inviting the curriculum leader onto the SMT, then the special needs coordinator (both of whom were women). The former soon gained promotion to another school and the deputy took over curriculum leadership responsibility, providing a permanent link between the curriculum management group and the SMT. According to the head, the special needs coordinator, who held joint responsibility for this area with the deputy, 'sees herself as a class teacher with an administrative role'. She used influence to relinquish an undesired load by expressing discomfort over the expectation that she shoulder more management responsibility. The deputy took overall responsibility for managing provision, and the special needs coordinator was then released from the team. These instances indicate how the head had, in effect, trialled two changes in team membership and individual responsibility, and how the composition of this SMT was far from settled at its birth. Problems with the team structure, its location within the management structure, and individual responses to team membership prompted the head to make incremental adjustments in the attempt to align its contribution to management more closely with his vision of a team approach. He continued to rely heavily on his coalition with the deputy, a team within the team built firmly into the management structure. After eighteen months in post, the head had retained his vision for the SMT, but had yet to resolve his dilemma over how to promote a more egalitarian way of working while protecting his position at the top of the management hierarchy:

> What we want is a collaborative leadership, and a cooperative leadership . . . but a collaborative and a cooperative leadership can't really be one of equals because that would be unfair – otherwise I would have to be on a C post [with three salary increments]. So I've got to have the overview of that leadership, but I've got to be able to let go a bit.

Evolution of the SMT at Kingsrise

The origin of the two other SMTs was less clear-cut. Their establishment reflected a shift in awareness about team approaches to management and re-labelling of practices that were developing during the years leading up to the recent reforms, reminiscent of the experience recounted above of the head at Winton in her first headship. Experienced staff had worked together, mostly over several years, according to their present division of management and teaching responsibilities. The idea that they constituted members of a team surfaced gradually, rather than the heads consciously choosing a team approach, then assembling its members. The head at Kingsrise had become aware of her increasing dependence on other senior staff some years before the reforms when, in 1981, she was appointed as head of the primary school created by merger of the junior school of which she had hitherto been the head and an adjacent infant school. The head noted how a management structure incorporating staff from both sites 'evolved slowly', the present system of three departments going back to 1992.

The head had been instrumental in both shaping the management structure and selecting staff over the years. An important criterion for selecting senior staff had been to ensure that, between them, they had intimate knowledge of all pupils, their families, and the local community. She viewed the composition of what had come to be conceived as an SMT in terms of her belief in creating a 'balance' of length of service in the school and management experience. The head had stated to the governors when considering the move to three departments shortly after the implementation of LMS:

> Whatever happened to the budget, and whatever other schools were doing, my personal professional view is that any school needs a mixture of age, experience, and youth and vigour and, with my budget – unless it is in dire trouble – that's the balance I would like to see here.

Gender was a potential criterion for selection which she had rejected, and she particularly resented the sexist view relayed by the media that only men could maintain discipline:

> I don't think we should look at gender in terms of positives, although we have ended up with almost completely women in the management structure. That was on merit. I am not a subscriber to the view that we should have special all-women lists. I think it is positively patronising and we don't need it . . . We do have it often quoted on radio by the politicians that they need men to control the discipline. This is regarded as one of the most difficult areas of the city; if I walk into the hall it will go quiet. They [the children] know who's boss.

Governors' approach to filling vacancies for more senior posts had varied, sometimes supporting the head in inviting a teacher to take on a new responsibility, at others advertising a post outside the school. Present team members other than the head had all achieved internal promotion either because they were perceived to be the most suitable person in the school to do a particular job, or because they had beaten external competition. Internal appointments had the advantage for the head that she knew how far those concerned shared her beliefs and values about management. There had been considerable turnover among senior staff as individuals gained promotion elsewhere, their individual success causing difficulty for the head in developing consistent management and teaching practices: 'If the head is the only constant figure over a five-year period, how on earth do you get your management team going, your systems working, and your children responding to continuity and structure?' There had been several selection opportunities in recent years. Involvement of existing SMT members in selecting staff who would join the team was limited, ordered in line with the management hierarchy. Where internal candidates had applied, the head gave them an open reference, consulted the deputy and the assessment coordinator about their view on the suitability of these candidates, and made her recommendations to the governing body. The latter took the final decision after an interview which, according to the chair of governors, was likely to include attention to candidates' ability to contribute as a member of an SMT whose head was a strong personality: 'Their capacity to stand up to the head and express a view that was not the current orthodoxy in the school . . . looking at their capacity to coordinate and lead a team, as well as hold their own within the senior management team.'

The department two leader, the most recently appointed SMT member, noted how criteria for selection were made explicit in the job description and person specification sent to applicants, and how 'they just chose the person, hopefully, who was going to be best at the job and to fit in, and had the expertise'. The notion of 'fitting in' implies that a newcomer to the team should share much of the professional culture of other members. To the extent that fitting in was important for continued smooth operation of the SMT, internal appointments offered the advantage that all involved had worked together in the school, and some mutual adjustment of cultural norms would already have occurred. Certainly, present team members expressed satisfaction with the current composition of the SMT, the deputy commenting: 'The headteacher has got a real knack of choosing people for this school . . . we're all of a kind – we're all a bit mad!'

Indicative of the incremental development of this SMT was the head's decision to invite the ESL team leader to join the team. It emerged from her appraisal that she was not being informed about matters affecting the work of her ESL team. The head had also realised that many issues discussed by the SMT involved the ESL support team but the person responsible for it was not party to relevant decisions. Like the head at Pinehill, she had found that unanticipated consequences of her earlier management structure design decisions had stimulated her iteratively to adjust SMT membership.

Emergence of the SMT at Waverley

The seeds of what became this team were sown in the early 1980s when the present head was appointed. He inherited a rudimentary management structure where posts carrying major management responsibility were restricted to the deputy and head of the infant department (both of whom had since left the school) and there was no tradition of meeting to develop school-wide policy. He wished to impact on other staff according to his vision of good practice, reflected in the restricted form of transformational leadership which culminated in the establishment of the present SMT. His perception that he must involve colleagues in the process of developing the school if they were to come to share his beliefs and values about education and management was symptomatic of his dependence on them. He had used his authority as head to make incremental changes to the management structure which would create conditions fostering a staff professional culture embracing regular debate and shared decision making:

From the day I came, I felt there was a need for it . . . for several reasons. First of all, even in '83 the world was changing – not as rapidly as it has done subsequently. There were not just entrenched attitudes towards management but also quite entrenched attitudes towards curriculum and teaching and learning. I felt the only way to take people with me was to have a structure in place in which they were involved and in which they could make a contribution. If they didn't contribute, I could write all the schemes and policies in the world, and they wouldn't have had the ownership of them.

He had proceeded incrementally, working to gain acceptance for more participation in management across the school. Initially, he had instituted regular staff meetings which he had later made more frequent:

It took about four or five years to start getting it as I wanted it. I inherited a situation where staff meetings weren't a regular feature; I did that on a softly softly basis. I introduced them on a fortnightly basis to begin with, and then as issues arose and the need to move forward in different areas occurred, they were increased to weekly. Gradually the structures you see in place now began to evolve.

A strong partnership was soon forged with the original deputy (and, from 1991, her successor), and he was opportunistic in making external appointments whenever vacancies arose. He established the principle that individuals appointed to senior posts in the management hierarchy would be required to attend regular management meetings of senior staff which had originally comprised just himself and the deputy:

As new colleagues came on board, if they assumed a fairly senior role . . . anybody who was on what was an old 'B' post [carrying two salary increments] was automatically pulled in. It wasn't a question of 'would you like to be — ?'; when interviewed it was made clear that that would be an expectation.

The juniors leader testified to the gradual development of what was now labelled as an SMT. When he had been appointed in 1989, there were meetings of the most senior staff including the juniors and infants leaders, but they were held infrequently when the need arose. SMT meetings had become formalised only in the last two or three years. At his appointment interview, the focus of questions about management had been more concerned with his departmental leadership than membership of a senior staff team. Similarly, the deputy, appointed two years later, noted that her interview had focused on deputy headship responsibilities: 'I don't think the management team was actually mentioned.' The head's concern to share the management load had been given added impetus by his realisation that his curriculum expertise amassed during his class-teaching days was becoming outdated as a consequence of education reforms. His predicament echoes the assertion in Chapter 1 that reforms have increased dependence of primary school headteachers on their colleagues. He could no longer expect to be omnipotent in terms of educational knowledge:

> On the curriculum side, the tremendous overload that has occurred since 1988 and, even more important, the changes it's produced – it would be wrong and impossible for one person to coordinate that so that has certainly contributed towards the need for a more collegiate approach to the planning . . . The two areas I find most difficult, as I'm probably the least expert in the school bar none – including the children – are IT and technology, since I'd left the classroom on a permanent basis . . . I'm basically a luddite, and knowing that you are dependent on the expertise of the others.

The head's criteria for seeking to recruit staff able to contribute to the SMT included extensive 'experience, both on the management side and on the leadership front . . . they've got to have that experience for credibility with colleagues . . . and a range of curriculum expertise and experience'. He was concerned that the credentials of SMT members should be regarded by other staff as appropriate and acceptable. Another criterion was complementarity in the span of SMT members' combined expertise, the head noting how he had unique knowledge about the LMS budget, but looked to colleagues' strengths in curriculum that he could not realistically possess. Involvement of other SMT members in the process of appointing individuals who would join the team had been limited. The deputy had been consulted about candidates but had not served on the interview panel. The strictly hierarchical principle for inclusion in the SMT linked with prior management experience had been relaxed to allow other staff the opportunity to gain some of this experience through team membership. The head perceived that such a move should be made only with the agreement of existing SMT members:

> Since then it's changed, inasmuch as current members, with the exception of the deputy, who I would include anyway, are – not elected – but their attendance is agreed by [SMT] colleagues. If colleagues felt it would be nice to have a change, then we would.

As mentioned in the previous chapter, such a change had been to invite the English and IT coordinator to join the team. He had suggested it might benefit her to join the SMT, subject to colleague members' approval, to gain the management experience she desired to enhance her promotion prospects. Supporting members' individual professional development could also have less positive consequences for building towards a team approach to management. The juniors leader had sought a development opportunity of a different kind which had taken him out of school on secondment for a term, and no other member of staff in the junior department had been willing to stand in for him. The head had become acutely aware of the lack of representation of junior department staff within the SMT during this time. To maintain the juniors leader's sense of involvement in the SMT, the head sent him a copy of SMT meeting minutes throughout his secondment.

Shaping the culture of teamwork

It is evident from the above accounts that reasons why the heads had instigated some form of team approach to management differed according to site-specific circumstances, beliefs and values they brought to their second headship born of previous experience, and what had happened since. Some reasons offered by survey respondents (see Table 3.4) were reflected in the case studies: the heads wished to involve other staff, though they varied in how far they sought to empower colleagues to take initiatives, as at Winton, or sought to empower themselves through harnessing others' support to realise the personal vision they had brought to the post. The reforms had also exerted a diffuse influence, mainly by imposing new management tasks which increasingly fell to members of the teams. Mounting pressure on the teams' agenda was coming from the requirements imposed by forthcoming inspection of the schools. Emphasis on selecting an SMT member specifically to provide a staff development opportunity was confined to Waverley and, even here, it was seen as a preparatory experience rather than one of learning how to contribute to the present SMT.

The contrasting modes of operation of the SMTs were a result of interaction between the heads and the other members they brought into the team, whether by choice or inheritance. The heads' authority to create the team and establish its working practices gave them a strong hand in promoting a culture of teamwork to which colleague members would subscribe, whether leaning towards the egalitarian or the hierarchical. In three teams, the head had played a major part in selecting other members and most or all of the present SMT members had worked together for several years. A large measure of satisfaction was expressed among members with the composition of the team and the ability of the group to engage in fruitful teamwork. Observation of team meetings confirmed that interaction within them was largely harmonious and complementary, indicating that members had internalised sufficient shared beliefs and values about teamwork to conduct the business of the SMT as they conceived it. The impact of the heads in forging a cohesive culture of teamwork was indicated as much by what did not happen as what did. As will be discussed in the following chapter, such arrangements for managing the meeting process as setting the agenda, chairing, turn taking, dealing with interruptions, keeping to task, keeping a record of discussions or reaching decisions were universally accepted within these teams and so went unremarked and unchallenged.

A shared culture of teamwork was not so well established at Pinehill, where the arrival of the new head and his use of authority to make unilateral moves to change individual members' responsibilities and the working practices of the SMT had impacted on a team culture already fragmented by past lack of formal leadership. Here, interviews with SMT members revealed some dissatisfaction with the composition and operation of the team among the three department leaders. Observation suggested that, at first, there was not universal acceptance about some aspects of the head's view of 'the way we do or don't do things around here', both inside the team and in relation to other staff. Arrangements for meetings were not contentious, possibly because they were consistent with others' previous practice. One department leader, however, reportedly felt undervalued by the new head because he had unilaterally drawn tighter boundaries around individual management responsibilities, stating when interviewed that: 'It used to be a totally equal team, no matter what the [individual salary and status] positions were ... I used to feel equally valued as everyone else in the group. And I think the new management structure's more top down.' The new head and the deputy were perceived to have formed a hierarchically dominant group within the team.

The initial level of fragmentation did not last; during the next year there was evidence of transition as individuals made mutual adjustments, beginning the process of cementing a more widely shared culture of teamwork. Reflecting back on the first year of his present appointment, the headteacher commented on a shift in his belief about involving colleagues in developing practice as a result of his experience:

> If I have learned anything since I have been at Pinehill, I am learning to shut up. Sometimes you have to know when to keep quiet and let other people have their head. This is hard; I have a very clear vision of where we ought to go and what we should end up looking like, but we are not going to get there if I impose it all the time – it's got to be a shared vision.

Like the head at Waverley, he had wished to implement his vision through other staff, but had attempted to introduce it much more rapidly. He had since slowed the pace, and was now working towards a more widely shared vision by empowering colleagues to make a greater input. One department leader had noted this shift with approval, suggesting that the team was on the way towards greater cultural accord: 'We are on the right road. I feel that people are valuing what other people say, that we're not being lectured at so much; I think what is going to happen now is more corporate management.'

Another potentially potent means of team culture building for heads – extensive involvement of existing SMT members in selecting their future team colleagues – was not employed in Kingsrise and Waverley where the opportunity had been presented. Even informal consultation here did not appear to reach beyond the deputy, consistent with the hierarchical orientation of the heads and reinforced by the formal authority of governors to make appointments. In so far as other members indicated that they perceived themselves to occupy a subordinate position in the management hierarchy, they would not have expected to be involved. Indeed, it was reported above how the deputy at Kingsrise approved of the head's unique part in selecting staff.

Structured and unstructured team development

Members of each team were learning to work together productively through a process of team development which was almost entirely subliminal and fortuitous, an outcome of shared experience in doing the job where they focused on management tasks rather than team development itself. Little use had been made of *structured development activities* like teambuilding exercises for the whole SMT (see Wallace 1991a). Such heavy reliance on learning through job experience alone related to factors affecting some or all teams: limited awareness of possibilities for structured development; paucity of external provision; priority given to developing individuals' ability to lead teams of other staff over their ability to be an effective SMT member; the low priority for team members of making time for team development activities when they were already very busy; and an assumption that, when individuals were appointed to the SMT, they should already be competent to fulfil the requirements of the job description, including their contribution to the team.

Existing members had received no formal induction where they joined an established team. The head might introduce externally appointed staff to the school, but not more specifically to the team and its operation. When the SMT at Winton was formed, induction was deemed unnecessary as three members had previously worked together. The head had planned to provide a day's induction for the externally appointed infants deputy, but her attempts had been overtaken by events as she and her SMT colleagues were heavily stretched with getting the new school up and running. The infants deputy commented that she had managed without an induction and, more importantly for her, that her team colleagues had been sensitive to her early concerns about being accepted in the team:

> We had a standing joke, the first few weeks of being here, of when was this induction going to take place? It was like, 'have roller skates, will take on this deputy headship'. I just seemed to be running around from one building to another . . . I had feared that I wouldn't perhaps fit in, or I was going to be the new person and feel that I'd be left out at some point, or that I wouldn't be involved as much, but that hasn't been the case at all. Because I think they [other SMT members] also realised that was a potential difficulty . . . we gelled very much as a group.

The head at Pinehill was the newest member of his team, and all members of the SMT at Kingsrise had been internally appointed, so were familiar with the school. The head made a point of having an occasional 'chat' with new team members: 'Talking with them and guiding them in what I think the role should be and them feeding back how they think it's working, what they feel comfortable doing and what they are not yet confident enough to do with their own colleagues.' The focus of these discussions apparently lay primarily on colleagues' performance of their individual management responsibility rather than their contribution as members of the SMT. A need for induction support was expressed by the department one leader, who had just been promoted to this position. She had found the transition from class teacher to department leader difficult at first, being 'used to managing children but not grown-ups'. It was taking time to win department colleagues' acceptance of her as their leader, having had equal status with them until now: 'People are used to you being on one level and then suddenly you're doing something else. If a person comes from outside the school into the management team, then staff are only used to that person being one thing – a manager.' At Waverley there was no tradition of formal induction; in the words of one member, 'It's literally come in, sit down, get on with it!' The recent external appointment of the infants leader and other teachers had highlighted the lack of documentary information available for new staff. The issue had been discussed in the SMT and it had been decided to formulate a staff handbook.

Management training had also played little part in development of the teams. Most consisted of off-site courses provided by the LEA for individuals in their own role, not shared opportunities for the team as an entity. Both deputies at Winton attended a management course designed for deputies, but it had not dealt with teamwork or team-building. The head and deputies, however, had been together on an LEA course more directly focused on head–deputy partnerships. The juniors deputy reflected: 'Anything that is on offer now . . . I think that we are beyond. So I think that now we are at the point of developing ourselves.' A more directly relevant activity for the whole SMT had been organised by the head in collaboration with the heads of five other local schools. They had been away with other members of their teams on a residential weekend programme, where there had been opportunities for each SMT to do team-building activities as a group, complemented by sessions where everyone at the same salary and status level across the six SMTs could exchange with each other.

Several members of the SMT at Pinehill had experienced some kind of management training but, ironically, not together. The head had completed a master's degree programme at a higher education institution, and two department leaders reported having done team-building activities led by a consultant in school during the days of the previous incumbent. The present head looked to LEA management courses to meet needs of individuals identified through staff development interviews, and to the opportunity for each SMT member to develop management skills during the regular non-contact time awarded to staff. Team members received non-contact time at different points in the week. It seems probable that individuals focused more on their individual responsibility within the management structure for leading other staff than on their contribution as a member of the SMT. Team members at Kingsrise had least involvement in structured development support. No member had received any management training. The head stated that the only LEA management course available was for deputies, the focus of which was confined to managing the curriculum. It is noteworthy that all members of this team conceived of training solely in terms of external courses for individuals. In contrast, every SMT member at Waverley had completed or was currently taking an external management course. The link with teamwork was indirect, however. Each course was for individuals, ranging from a 'one-term training opportunity' that the head had experienced in the late 1980s to short LEA courses on 'management skills' attended separately by the head, deputy, and English and IT coordinator. The head was looking to his local 'cluster group' of schools set up by the LEA to introduce shared training activities.

An informal but nevertheless structured development activity of a very different kind featured only at Winton, where SMT members occasionally met up for a semi-social occasion intended both as part of team development and as a means of doing uninterrupted SMT business. Commitment to a team approach here extended to ceremonial occasions which helped to bond team members while working on their agenda. According to the head: 'The social side is part and parcel of teams because we are usually doing school business, but there isn't necessarily an agenda, or it is a very loose agenda like [discussing ideas for building of] the new school over an Italian meal.' In the other case study schools, SMT members did not deliberately mix their shared business with shared pleasure in a relaxed setting away from the school.

Since structured activities had been little used in most SMTs, members' ability to work together was very largely (and for Kingsrise entirely) a product of *unstructured development*. The different levels of complementarity among contributions achieved in the SMTs grew with experience of mutual support among heads and their team colleagues. The passage of sufficient time for mutual adjustment was a critical factor, as demonstrated by the earlier account of cultural fragmentation and slow transition at Pinehill. Development of trust was gradual, resting on consistent experience of support and colleagues' effective fulfilment of their individual responsibility and contribution to teamwork in the SMT. Almost a year since the arrival of the new head at Pinehill, a department leader reflected that:

> If you don't trust the responses of others within the team, you are unlikely to say what you think. We are still in the process of learning to trust one another and I don't feel completely comfortable with the situation we find ourselves in. It will take time to counteract and get rid of that feeling.

More experienced team members could provide newcomers with a positive or negative role model whose managerial practice they might emulate or reject. As described in the previous chapter, the infants deputy at Winton had set out to learn from aspects of SMT colleagues' practice which accorded with her professional beliefs and values, working to assimilate the professional culture which she perceived them to express through their work; the deputy at Waverley had also learned by observing the head's performance. For the majority of senior staff other than deputies and heads at Kingsrise and Waverley, their present post carrying membership of the SMT was the first experience of substantial responsibility outside the classroom. The department one leader at Kingsrise had enjoyed the 'confidence building' opportunity that SMT membership had given her, and commented: 'I'm learning all the time; we've got a lot to offer each other.' The infants leader at Waverley had also benefited in the short time since her appointment: 'I gain confidence when something we deal with goes well, which then helps me to tackle the next thing. And I gain job satisfaction from seeing the relationships between the people build up and improve.' Development of individual members' capacity to contribute effectively to teamwork through the experience of being in the SMT could also apply to heads. It was reported earlier how the head at Pinehill had learned that he needed to foster a more equal contribution from other SMT members. His counterpart at Winton perceived that she had reaped the benefit of empowering colleagues: 'It has made me less bossy . . . less autocratic, more democratic – it doesn't come easily to me!'

These accounts illustrate how an important component of team development is connected with individuals' emotions, such as a sense of being valued or of confidence in contributing to the team, or even of learning to subjugate an impulse to control. Shared humour, though not necessary for team performance, could help SMT members to form a bond, rendering teamwork an intrinsically valuable experience and fostering a positive attitude towards working together. Humour featured in all the teams, and particularly strongly at Winton. Observation of SMT meetings confirming the head's view that members had developed a close but informal working relationship underpinned by shared commitment to teamwork: 'It is a team with skills, knowledge, good attitude, commitment, conscientiousness and loyalty and support. The loyalty is incredible, the support is second to none, and we have lots of laughs.' Reflecting on an all day off-site SMT meeting she noted how, not only had team members worked hard, but 'we did enjoy ourselves'. Jokes often turned on irony, making light of serious issues while taking them seriously. The head and special needs coordinator had turned up late to one such meeting because of having to deal with a break-in at the school overnight when the head's computer had been stolen from her desk. The special needs coordinator announced to other members the good news that: '[The head's] desk has been cleared.'

Unique to Winton was non-work-related social contact between team members. At the other schools, socialising was confined to a few individuals who had become friends outside their work context, or to formal occasions for the whole staff as at Pinehill, where staff had an evening meal out together twice a term. The purpose of this form of socialising was simply to enjoy each other's company, but there was a spin-off for SMT members at Winton that these occasions furthered the bonding which had come to underpin their close and mutually supportive working relationship. The infants deputy testified to the value of socialising soon after her appointment for team development, having been on holiday with the head and juniors deputy and their families:

> The fact that we went on holiday together and fate gelled us together as a group of people who could be quite open with each other and laugh about things. Even though some situations are tricky, the work is hard, the days are long, we can trigger each other off and keep each other going. And to me that's better than having a really formal induction process.

Multiple images of development

The last chapter depicted how heads had used their authority as top manager to design a management structure into which individual responsibilities of SMT members were located, and to set parameters for the team role according to the relative strength of their allegiance to belief in a management hierarchy and in the equal contribution of its members. This chapter has shown how the heads variably employed their power of decision to embark on a team approach to management, subject to promises to governors that might have been made at interview, or to reinterpret evolving management practice as embodying an SMT. Yet, within the dialectic of control among team members, influence held greater sway than authority over developing the shared culture of teamwork required to undergird the capacity to work together productively. Heads could count on their ability to establish structures and give the group of senior managers a team label. They certainly could not guarantee development of close collaboration through complementary contributions of team members, whether on a relatively equal or more hierarchical basis, since they were dependent on colleagues' willingness to work together in this way.

The strong cultural accord characteristic of three teams was a product both of selecting like-minded members who would stand a good chance of sharing the management and educational beliefs and values of the head, and of nurturing a way of operating which suited all members, largely through unstructured development experiences. Selection opportunities narrowed the parameters for transformational leadership in respect of SMTs in that, where colleagues shared key beliefs and values, it was unnecessary to transform this culture. The difficulty over developing a shared culture of teamwork at Pinehill highlights just how significant opportunities to select members can be for heads seeking to develop their preferred version of teamwork. Equally, the cultural gulf between the initially hierarchical approach adopted by the head and the belief among department leaders that they should be treated more as equals illustrates how incompatible images of team approaches pursued by different members may inhibit team development.

The variable but, in all cases, limited use of structured team development activities indicates that they are not vital for teamwork to develop and flourish in favourable circumstances. On the other hand, those that involve all team members getting together to focus on improving their ability to work as a team may provide a setting for opening up intractable issues like the disjunction between expectations of the head and colleague SMT members at Pinehill. Such concerns may not otherwise be easy for members other than heads to voice, especially where heads operate with a strong hierarchical emphasis. Evidence from elsewhere, as discussed in the first chapter, implies that such activities have potential to speed the development of a team. The constraint imposed by limited availability or affordability of such support for all four teams was bolstered in three cases by the shared belief that training meant traditional off-site courses for individuals. In contrast to Winton, there was little evidence of initiatives in the other SMTs to engage in structured whole team development work.

The contrast discussed in Chapter 4 between the relatively egalitarian approach at Winton and the strongly hierarchical approach in the other case study schools is further sharpened by differences between the heads' strategies for promoting development of a team approach. Forms of unstructured and structured development at Winton were more wide ranging, reaching beyond the professional arena. This breadth of development effort was, arguably, linked to the more equal and therefore more extensive commitment to teamwork sought by this head in comparison with the other three. For strongly hierarchical operation reflecting a restricted form of transformational leadership, they required less of their colleagues: to accept a subordinate position in line with the management hierarchy; to support the heads' initiatives to meet their agenda; and to carry out their individual management responsibility. This distinction between the teams was also reflected in the balance of individual contributions to fulfilling the role of the SMT and the structure, content and process of their core shared activity – regular team meetings – to which attention will now turn.

Chapter 6

Talking shop

Coordination of team members' work through regular meetings was a feature of the case study SMTs. Their operation as a team rested substantially on communication between all members, rather than solely on a hierarchical management structure where main lines of communication would run between heads and colleagues according to their individual management responsibility. Not only were meetings central to carrying out the shared role of the SMT, but they were also the core ritual through which the culture of teamwork was fostered and sustained. Much SMT business was done through interaction between members in this private arena where, in their different ways, SMT members tackled the team tasks of policy making and strategic planning for their school. This chapter draws on observations of SMT meetings and interviews with team members to examine in more detail how they worked together, concentrating on the major contrast between the relatively egalitarian operation at Winton and the more hierarchical approach in the other schools.

First, the pattern is examined of meetings involving all SMT members or a subgroup within the team. There was diversity in commitment of time to meetings and the extent to which an internal hierarchy was built into their structure, consistent with the emphasis on differential contribution according to the management hierarchy or on equal contribution among SMT members. Second, *individual team roles* are discussed: two patterns of behaviour identified among contributions to teamwork which were expressed very differently in the SMTs, preferred individual team roles not necessarily being associated simply with particular team members or with their salary and status level within the management hierarchy. Through examples it is portrayed how team members had developed individual team roles which enabled them to offer complementary contributions to fulfilling the role of the SMT as a whole; how teams were led; and how members could use power to work towards synergy. More SMT meetings were observed at Winton than elsewhere. Similarities between the other three schools revealed by this more limited observation, however, supported by accounts from interviews with team members, enable a composite picture of two forms of complementarity among individual team roles to be put forward. Third, the meeting process is summarised, showing how similar elements were incorporated in the four SMTs but with variation in the extent to which heads shared responsibility for each part, and the way team meetings addressed team tasks is briefly explored. Finally, consideration is given to how members of each team habitually approached their contribution to decision making according to the balance of individual team roles and their willingness to make compromises in pursuit of consensus.

The structure of team meetings

The pattern of SMT meetings depicted in Table 6.1 was revealing. Winton had the most differentiated arrangement with three kinds of meeting connected with the wide range of shared team tasks. The purpose of daily and weekly meetings was generally restricted to short-term planning and routine organisation, supplemented by the infrequent and much longer meetings (lasting from one and three days) where more strategic and long-term issues were explored in depth. The strength of mutual commitment to a team approach to management was indicated by the way members not only met daily before lessons began but also spent around five hours per week in meeting together, occasionally eating into their time at half terms and weekends. The findings of the headteachers' survey suggest that such commitment of time was exceptional.

Time spent in team meetings in the other teams was considerably lower, the smaller and less equal contribution the heads sought from their SMT colleagues apparently requiring less face-to-face interaction for coordination of individual members' work. The two-hour weekly meeting at Pinehill, though under half the time occupied by Winton team meetings, was still greater than the majority of SMTs in the survey. It provided a less frequent opportunity for whole team updating than the Winton team's daily sessions, and the team tasks were less extensive (this was the one SMT whose brief did not include curriculum issues). Nevertheless, members had a quite frequent and substantial period to devote to team tasks, and were able to meet during the school day, in contrast to most survey SMTs. The team at Kingsrise spent least time in SMT meetings, amounting to around three-quarters of an hour per week overall, in line with a minority of SMTs in the survey. Members came together weekly, the opportunity for extended discussion of longer-term issues being restricted to the fortnightly after-school meeting which alternated with the fortnightly meeting before school. The team at Waverley, committed to an after-school meeting of an hour or so each week, was more typical of the survey SMTs. Here the one type of meeting covered day-to-day and longer-term issues. Taken alone, time commitment to meeting is a very crude indicator of commitment to a team approach. No allowance is made for how effectively this time is used, nor for other forms of joint work. This finding is, nevertheless, consistent with evidence cited in earlier chapters that commitment to a team approach was greatest at Winton, though it is equally clear that members of the other teams

Table 6.1 Pattern of SMT meetings

Formal SMT meetings	Winton			Pinehill	Kingsrise		Waverley
Frequency	daily	weekly	approximately termly	weekly	fortnightly	fortnightly	weekly
Timing	before school	Thursday or Friday afternoon inside lesson time	school days and weekends	Friday afternoon inside lesson time	Monday before school	Monday after school	Monday after school
Duration	half an hour	one and a half hours	one to three days	two hours	half an hour	one hour	at least one hour
Purpose	organisation for the day	organisation for the next week	strategic planning	administration and pastoral issues	updating, organisation for the fortnight	planning and routine organisation	planning and routine organisation
Approximate time commitment per week	five hours			two hours	three quarters of an hour		one hour

were also making a sustained effort to coordinate their contributions to the management role of the SMT.

There were meetings of subgroups centring on the head in each team, summarised in Table 6.2. The head and deputy or deputies met informally when necessary to deal with management issues arising during the school day. At Winton, this arrangement had become more common after the special needs coordinator had taken responsibility for a class. A similar arrangement existed in the other three schools, sometimes extending to the assessment coordinator at Kingsrise but, at Pinehill, it was complemented by a regular meeting between the head and deputy intended mainly for short-term planning, but where some decisions were also made and others were discussed before taking proposals to the full SMT. The timetabling of a meeting for these purposes reflected how the head–deputy partnership constituted an inner cabinet in this SMT. Here curriculum management was addressed through a weekly formal meeting between the head, deputy and curriculum leader. Apart from this instance, the SMT subgroup in the four schools consisted of the most senior team members in the management hierarchy, suggesting that heads and deputies shouldered the main burden of responding to the day-to-day issues that arose.

Complementarity between individual team roles

The patterns of behaviour tentatively identified as intrinsic to teamwork were *leadership of the team* and *team membership*. There are two parts to leadership of the team, incorporating elements of the definition of leadership offered by Louis and Miles (1990) introduced in the first chapter. Giving direction to the SMT, whether to maintain current operation or to instigate change, involves *setting parameters for teamwork by orchestrating team members' contribution*. Orchestration entails strategic planning, especially in the early days of developing a team approach, such as determining a vision of a shared role, selecting team members, establishing the structure of meetings, and developing the team's brief and procedures. It also encompasses creating conditions favourable for others to act, whether by encouraging or directing other members to contribute through the approach to chairing meetings, or by leading through example. Parameters for teamwork embody both possibilities and their boundaries. Especially for heads, because they are externally accountable for the SMT, *ensuring that teamwork follows these parameters by scrutinising their boundaries* is the flipside of creating possibilities. It may involve monitoring team progress and taking action if boundaries are overstepped by team members, ranging from directing other SMT members' work to protecting their ability to operate inside the parameters set. Conversely, the parameters for teamwork may be adjusted in the light of monitoring and feedback.

There are three components of the team membership role which dovetail with leadership of the team. First, individuals may offer *leadership within the*

Table 6.2 Pattern of meetings of subgroups within SMTs

SMT subgroup meetings	Winton	Pinehill			Kingsrise	Waverley
Participants	headteacher and deputies (when special needs coordinator not available)	headteacher and deputy	headteacher and deputy	headteacher, deputy and curriculum leader	headteacher, deputy and sometimes assessment coordinator	headteacher and deputy
Frequency	*ad hoc*, occasional	weekly	*ad hoc*, daily	weekly	*ad hoc*, daily	*ad hoc*, daily
Timing	inside lesson time	Monday morning inside lesson time	outside and inside lesson time	Friday morning, inside lesson time	outside and inside lesson time	outside and inside lesson time
Duration	variable	one hour	variable	one hour	variable	variable
Purpose	management issues arising	organisation for the week	management issues arising	curriculum management issues	management issues arising	management issues arising

team by setting the course for action on items from the team agenda, by lead-ing on issues concerning individual management responsibilities or taking on new tasks as issues arise. Second, they may *contribute as equals* with other mem-bers to joint work, including the teamwork processes of sustaining an overview and pooling ideas and the team task of decision making. Third, they may express *followership within the team*, facilitating leadership of the team and team membership by accepting parameters for teamwork and respecting their boundaries – whether by working within the groundrules for chairing and turn taking, supporting whoever may be leading within the team, or facilitating the efforts of others to contribute. They may also attempt to persuade colleagues to express leadership of the team or team membership by withholding from making a contribution.

The heads employed their authority according to their beliefs and values about teamwork to delimit how and by whom leadership of the team and team membership were carried out. They retained leadership of the team largely for themselves, except when temporarily delegating the role to the deputy (or senior deputy) in their absence, but set different parameters for colleagues' contribution, especially the degree to which they encouraged other members to express aspects of the team membership role. The latter were, however, empowered to exercise delegated authority or influence in electing whether to take up opportunities on offer. Heads were more or less exclusive leaders of their teams partly because other members believed that they should be and, through followership behaviour, helped empower them to fulfil this role. Chapter 2 discussed how power is shared within the dialectic of control between all parties to interaction, whatever individuals' position in a status hierarchy. The heads could develop their preferred version of a team approach to school management only if other members used their delegated authority and influence to work in the same direction, so building up the mutual em-powerment that synergy implies. Expression of the three components of team membership behaviour in each SMT rested on the strength of commitment among all members, reflected in the extent to which they shared the culture of teamwork nurtured by heads. While both individual team roles were integral to all four SMTs, there were clear differences in content between the team at Winton and the other three teams, giving rise to relatively egalitarian or more hierarchical versions of complementarity.

Leadership of the team at Winton

This team role was mainly the headteacher's prerogative though, consistent with team members' reflections on their contributions reported in Chapter 4, the juniors deputy was observed to ensure that team members moved through the agenda and completed tasks. When collating documentary information about LEA provision of in-service training courses to be disseminated to other staff, she checked that all information had been matched to the staff for whom it was relevant. She also chaired meetings if the head was unable to attend or was called away. The head's managerial beliefs and values were expressed in her very informal style of interaction in the team, and in the way she encouraged all SMT members to collaborate on many shared tasks. Her entrepreneurial approach to management was reflected in her proactive effort to make contacts which would benefit the school, reporting back to her team colleagues. Her initiative to build a new school on the site had been a major achievement.

The head's effort to *set parameters* for a team approach to management had begun with *strategic planning* which had made full use of the opportunity presented by the merger, and she continued to consider both the short- and longer-term agenda for the team. An early post-merger priority was to set staff with posts carrying two salary increments the task of developing policies for the areas of the curriculum for which they were responsible. This work was nearing completion, and the head was actively looking ahead to see how they might take on new responsibilities now the new institution was well established. Other strategic priorities included preparing for the school inspection. She orchestrated SMT meetings by *creating conditions* which would maximise space for her colleagues to contribute through a low-key approach to chairing, allowing proceedings to move at an unhurried pace despite heavy pressures faced by SMT members leading to frequent interruptions. She encouraged all members to contribute to the team agenda (often set by the deputies alone) clarifying both what needed to be discussed and how to deal with each item, and she initiated extended meetings for more strategic issues. The degree to which a shared culture of teamwork had been internalised was indicated by the way the deputies would start meetings by checking that day-to-day organisational matters had been covered, without mention of any agenda.

The head encouraged other members to lead on issues inside and outside their individual management responsibility, ensuring that the team experience could be a professional development opportunity. All members were equally entitled to place items on the team agenda and to call meetings. She regarded her colleagues in the team as her 'representatives in many ways' with other staff, and gave them latitude to lead groups of staff on behalf of the SMT. Each deputy had been given delegated authority to chair her own department meetings, the head noting, 'I like that, not always – just because I am the head – having to be in charge.' The head used her authority to empower her colleagues through delegating and giving them the autonomy necessary to do the job. Regular meetings for both infant and junior departments were held at the same time, enabling the head to attend for any item which involved her directly in either meeting. Conversely, the head was empowered through being able to trust other SMT members' competence to deputise for her and run the school in her absence. As head, her unique contribution to the team included a strong orientation to the external environment, as noted above, and she continually sought to use her entrepreneurial skills in 'doing deals' to benefit the school. Recently, despite all SMT members being exceptionally busy, she had attended a meeting as a member of the education broadcasting council of the British Broadcasting Corporation (BBC) because she wanted to capitalise on the opportunity to make contacts which might contribute to equipping the planned new school:

> I was torn because I needed to be back in [school], because I could see that there would be all kinds of things at school level that I needed to do, but on the other hand I was torn because I know my job is also to make things happen.

During the course of this meeting, she had access to the head of a national organisation promoting educational technology who was interested in information technology in schools. She had broached the possibility that the BBC might fund provision of television monitors in every classroom. 'I got three really meaty bits of business done but all the time I was feeling bad about it, though it didn't make me come back!' On her return to school, she updated her SMT colleagues on contacts she had made and how she hoped to take her initiative forward.

She nurtured a hard-working and harmonious team through *cultural leadership*, modelling behaviour that symbolised the culture of teamwork she worked to develop and sustain. Such actions included:

- demanding as much of herself as she expected of others – she was normally the first staff member to arrive in school (at around 6.45 a.m.) and often the last to leave, committing whatever time she perceived the team agenda to require, and frequently working at home in the evenings and weekends to prepare documents for discussion;
- adopting a style of interaction marked by informality and interest in colleagues' lives beyond the workplace – all members were on first name terms and talked freely about aspects of their lives outside school;
- being open to suggestions that challenged her ideas – when she had advocated that the task of cataloguing all audio-visual aid equipment in the school was delegated to ancillary staff, she had acquiesced to the argument of the juniors deputy that the deputies should tackle it to ensure it was done thoroughly;
- staying on task, which extended to continuing with debate or finding something else constructive to do when interruptions led to a team member temporarily leaving the meeting;
- participating equally in the ritual of making tea and coffee for the SMT and bringing in treats, as when she provided cakes on her birthday;
- socialising with any team member who wished to reciprocate – individuals often visited her at home;
- expressing her sense of humour and enjoying colleagues' banter – while SMT members were reviewing the pupils' standard assessment test results

and considering why they were not up to the national average, the infants deputy picked up a glove puppet of a furry bear and put it on her hand. The head asked her what the glove puppet thought the answer was.

She was self-aware, taking into account the possibility that she might inadvertently contribute to difficulties and, if so, modifying her behaviour. The juniors deputy had consistently responded coolly when the head had launched new ideas during team meetings before school. She had initially responded angrily, but had come to a realisation that she had been acting out of turn:

> What I was doing was that I was having brainwaves overnight, because I'm that kind of person, and coming in with this great idea . . . and I know it was the wrong way to do it . . . I just stood up and said, 'I am fed up with everything being so negative in the mornings!' And I took myself for a walk. They got on with the business, I came back, apologised, and we just got on with it – no problems . . . that made me really look at what the purpose of these early morning meetings is. It's not to move school policies forward, it is just to get the day sorted out.

Her *scrutiny of the boundaries* of team operation was rarely observable because she trusted other SMT members to stay within the parameters for teamwork they had established together. Other members' contributions to meetings fed into her continually updated overview of their work on shared tasks and their individual management responsibilities. Her close *self-monitoring* led her to realise on occasion that she had transgressed these boundaries and needed to avoid compromising the very full contribution she had encouraged her team colleagues to make. The deputies were responsible, before school started, for completing the 'day book' for staff and depositing it in the staffroom to inform other staff about organisational matters of the day. The head had taken to completing the day book before other SMT members arrived, then presenting it to them at the early morning team meeting. She had found that she sometimes got information wrong and, perceiving her well-intentioned actions were counterproductive and irritating the deputies, she decided to leave their task to them. She monitored the workload of team members and had used her authority to *protect* the operation of the SMT by expanding parameters for teamwork to include the occasional extended meetings mentioned earlier – taking place off-site where possible to minimise interruptions.

Team membership at Winton

The cohesive culture of teamwork in this team was reflected in the way the head's part in providing leadership of the team was complemented through the contribution she and her colleagues made to team membership. On particular issues, any member might take the *lead within the team*. The special needs coordinator led least frequently, on topics connected with her cross-school responsibility for pupils with special educational needs. Responsibility for a class had left her with less time for management tasks and she felt over-stretched in trying to fulfil her class teaching, special needs and SMT respon-sibilities. Both deputies took on a variety of initiatives, not necessarily connected with their individual management responsibility. The infants deputy led on creating a 'school file' where all administrative procedures would be set out, with a view to inducting new staff, while the juniors deputy led on reviewing audio-visual aid equipment and piloting a new approach to pupil behaviour management. They often shared leadership equally, as where they both worked on implementing a computerised registration system, each taking responsibility for her department. The head led on a range of tasks, from strategic planning issues like creating the school development plan, through major policy changes such as the proposal to add a new tier of departmental management, to school-wide administrative matters like deciding on dates for future staff in-service training days. While leading within the team was expressed by all members, there was some element of hierarchy in the kind of issues on which they led: the head moved forward most major policy and planning matters, while other SMT members took initiatives with a narrower compass and more often linked with day-to-day management.

For most of the time during SMT meetings, team members other than the colleague taking the lead *contributed as equals*. All members were observed to put forward ideas connected with particular agenda items and to contribute to the shared overview of the team, drawing on their complementary experience and responsibilities, which included:

- teaching responsibility – the special needs coordinator, who taught a Year 6 class, championed the interests of Year 6 in a debate about creating a specialist music room;
- experience in other schools – the infants deputy suggested giving staff with two salary increments a new departmental responsibility reminiscent of the 'floor manager' posts she had witnessed elsewhere;
- management responsibility – the juniors deputy informed colleagues about arrangements for Christmas parties for older pupils;
- contact with individual staff – the head informed other members that a cleaner had complained to her about the mess that teachers had left, allow-ing flour to be trodden into classroom carpets.

Support for the head was provided through attending to her agenda along-side items put forward by others, but also at an emotional level. The head arrived late for one off-site meeting, having dealt with the latest stage in a difficult child-protection case going to court that day. The child had been brought to school by a social worker, and was deeply upset at the prospect of 'having a new mum and dad'. The head stated that she was 'feeling mangled' by the experience, and her colleagues immediately offered her reassurance.

Every SMT member generally contributed as an equal to any team task, whether at the routine organisational end of the range, as in completing the day book, or the strategic policy development end, as when working towards greater involvement of staff with two salary increments in pupil behaviour management. This initial concern resulted in a proposal to incorporate pupil behaviour management responsibility within a wider proposal to give teachers with two salary increments substantial departmental responsibility. The debate on the issue was observed; it was open ended, beginning with a review of present responsibilities. Each team member offered one or more ideas, and the policy as formulated reflected some aspect of the input from each person. Overall, the touch of hierarchy over who led most within the team, noted above, was matched by the relative proportion of ideas contributed by different SMT members connected with different kinds of team task. Observation of team meetings when all members were present suggested that the head offered more ideas than any other team member on more strategic issues, but her colleagues tended to put forward more ideas on most routine matters.

Followership behaviour was expressed by all members, indicating their *acceptance* of parameters for teamwork set by the head through entering into the spirit of this approach and engaging with team tasks to hand. Members also made efforts to *facilitate* teamwork, usually unasked, and occasionally in response to a request from a colleague. Instances were as follows:

- self-censoring – the juniors deputy told an anecdote and signalled that the group should not stray further off task by saying, 'But I digress.';
- recording ideas emerging from discussion – the infants deputy summarised points on a flipchart;
- informing colleagues about the content of discussion they had missed – the head updated the special needs coordinator when she returned from playground duty;
- seeing to whatever needed doing – the special needs coordinator collated documents about in-service training opportunities for distribution to other staff;
- turn taking – the juniors deputy checked with a colleague that she had finished elaborating her idea before stating her own thoughts;
- making tea and coffee and bringing in treats – even the observer was included in the juniors deputy's gift of Christmas pudding chocolates!

A key form of followership behaviour, highly significant for this team's operation, was the way members other than the head helped when necessary to ensure their actions stayed within the head's comfort zone. They appeared to switch from the belief in equal contribution that underpinned so much of

their interaction by briefly expressing their belief in the management hierarchy, so empowering the head to delimit their contribution if she saw fit.
They would check voluntarily that she was willing to go along with a course of
action they were advocating. After one SMT meeting, a Year 6 teacher came
into the head's office and she and the special needs coordinator discussed an
informal initiative proposed by the juniors deputy to pilot a new approach to
pupil behaviour management in Year 6 classes. The juniors deputy turned
to the head and asked if it would be OK to go ahead 'without you knowing the
detail at this stage', to which the head agreed.

The solid foundation for the SMT provided by the culture of teamwork was
demonstrated when the head was not present. She frequently withdrew from
meetings to deal with distractions, and other SMT members would either continue with the team task or, congruent with her example mentioned earlier,
find something else constructive to do until she returned. During one meeting,
the head noticed a man walking past the office window who had been investigating leakage of water from pipes under the school. She left to speak with
him, handing the juniors deputy a piece of paper where she had been noting
down a summary of the current debate, saying, 'You lot finish off.' Other
members completed the task, the juniors deputy writing down suggestions,
checking her colleagues agreed with what she had stated. She said, 'I'll run that
by [the head] when she gets back.' This statement reflected her concern
that the head should be informed about what they had done and be given the
opportunity, as team leader, to approve it.

As the more senior of the two deputies in the management hierarchy, the
juniors deputy would routinely express followership behaviour in this way,
temporarily taking on the role of leading the team, but stopping short of making decisions in the team leader's absence, and handing back leadership as soon
as she returned. When the head was late for an off-site meeting, the juniors
deputy led the other members in first deciding what agenda items they could
start on before she arrived, then working together, writing down their recommendations, and presenting them to the head on her arrival. The juniors
deputy offered close support to the head in other ways, on one occasion
demonstrating how she was more aware of the head's diary commitments than
the head. When the latter stated her intention to talk to staff on the following Tuesday, the juniors deputy immediately responded, saying, 'You can't.'
She pointed to the head's prior engagement already written in the diary.
Complementarity among individual team roles as expressed in this relatively
egalitarian SMT rested on the mix of behaviours summarised in the third column of Table 6.3. The head set parameters which other team members
accepted. These parameters fostered sharing opportunities among all members
to lead within the team and maximising the potential for all members to contribute as equals to debate, with all individuals' opinions carrying equal
weight. Followership among members other than the head was sophisticated,
including reverting contingently from acting in accordance with the dominant

Table 6.3 Complementary expression of individual team roles

Individual team role	Component	Winton	Pinehill, Kingsrise, Waverley
Leadership of the team	setting parameters	head fosters support for her agenda and extensive contribution as equals, including shaping agenda and taking initiatives	heads foster support for their agenda and restricted contribution as equals which largely excludes shaping agenda and taking initiatives
	scrutinising boundaries	head monitors self and others and adjusts parameters for teamwork, largely implicit as other members accept them	heads variably monitor self and others and adjust parameters for teamwork, largely implicit where other members accept them
Team membership	leadership within the team	all members frequently lead on particular issues, weak hierarchical ordering of leadership	heads most frequently lead on particular issues, strong hierarchical ordering of leadership by other members
	equal contribution	very strong emphasis on all members contributing as equals to agenda set by head and others	moderate emphasis on members contributing as equals to agenda set by head, with small input from others
	followership	acceptance and facilitating behaviour among all members other than head	acceptance behaviour among all members other than heads, facilitative behaviour hierarchically ordered

belief in equal contribution to the contradictory belief in a management hierarchy, so as to stay within the head's parameters.

Leadership of the team at Pinehill, Kingsrise and Waverley

Complementarity in the more hierarchical SMTs was based on contrasting expression of individual team roles, summarised in the final column of Table 6.3. The balance between team roles appeared similar in these teams. Leadership of the team fell even more exclusively to these heads than to the head at Winton, with the exception of the deputy substituting temporarily in their absence. Earlier chapters showed how their *strategic planning* in very different circumstances had led to remodelling an existing SMT along more hierarchical lines at Pinehill and gradually developing what became conceived of as a team structure, shared role and membership designed to empower the heads at Kingsrise and Waverley. A more formal approach to interaction reflected these heads' managerial beliefs and values, symbolised at Kingsrise by the way other SMT members addressed the head and referred to her by her surname, whereas she always used their first name. Though their priorities varied, the three heads were deeply affected by reforms. At Kingsrise the school development plan was a focus of SMT attention during the time of fieldwork, whereas the agenda in the other two teams was increasingly dominated by preparing for and making changes in response to inspection of the school. The heads habitually set the SMTs' agenda according to their priorities and, though opportunities were made available for other staff to feed in their concerns and for other SMT members to add items, the heads reportedly supplied the great majority of items, especially those relating to more strategic issues.

They orchestrated SMT meetings through *creating conditions* fostering their team colleagues' contribution to this agenda, shaping debate by providing the agenda and chairing in a manner which was often directive, depending on the issue at hand. The head at Pinehill had consciously encouraged his colleagues to participate more after his initial directive stance, and one department leader noted how individual team members were increasingly putting forward matters which were discussed. To a greater or lesser degree the three heads controlled the parameters of colleagues' contributions through bounded debate: inviting comments on proposals they put forward, sometimes after initial discussion with the deputy (rather than all members pooling ideas as a first step). There was little evidence of other team members taking initiatives beyond those associated with their individual management responsibility, and even here they were closely supervised.

The heads expressed *cultural leadership* by making explicit their expectations about how SMT colleagues should 'do things around here', through the documentation of job descriptions, or what they said or symbolised through their behaviour. When discussing the formulation of a marking policy, the head at Pinehill advised other members that they must be careful in working out criteria for when to bin a child's work as this practice was inconsistent with the principle of valuing a child's effort to which he subscribed. The head at Kingsrise, on coming into an SMT meeting which had started without her, had expressed approval that the discussion seemed to be going well, so encouraging colleagues to keep, in her absence, to a task she had set. The head at Waverley spoke most at SMT meetings, habitually preparing proposals for which he sought a response before completing their formulation himself. Speculatively, this behaviour may have symbolised the head's superior position in the management hierarchy, perhaps helping to reinforce the view expressed by other members that he wanted their support primarily for his agenda.

As at Winton, heads' *scrutiny of the boundaries* of parameters they had set for teamwork was not observable in so far as other members accepted their part and acted within these parameters. The head at Kingsrise did, however, call an SMT meeting to decide how to improve the relationship between the team and other staff because of a breakdown in communication between them. She and other team members had become aware of the problem through feedback that individual teachers did not know about information which she thought had been disseminated through the SMT. She had realised there was sometimes a considerable time lag between an SMT meeting where information was announced and the next department meeting, since the latter were held monthly. All three heads monitored individual members' performance as teachers along with other staff. During the SMT meeting at Pinehill to discuss a marking policy mentioned earlier, the early years leader divulged that she threw away pupils' work which was below their normal standard (as when they were feeling unwell). The head replied that he had thought she was going to say she would put a line though substandard work, and he had been about to 'admonish' her. The head at Kingsrise informed other SMT members that she had noticed certain areas of work had not been completed in some year groups. In an SMT meeting focusing on preparation for inspection, the head at Waverley unilaterally evaluated, in turn, the work on all display boards throughout the school, judging which were of high quality, which needed 'tidying up presentation-wise' and which must be replaced. Colleagues apparently accepted his judgements without question, responding by offering suggestions for improving the displays which he had found wanting.

There was evidence that the heads *self-monitored*, variably acknowledging where they had transgressed boundaries governing SMT operation. It was recounted earlier how the head at Pinehill had realised how his directiveness had brought him into conflict with other SMT members. His actions had overstepped the boundaries of acceptability to them and he had worked since to foster greater participation, adjusting his leadership of the team to meet their preferred parameters for teamwork half way. The other two heads were aware of their internal conflict over delegating and allowing other SMT members to participate fully, and the head at Waverley was attempting to modify his behaviour to bring himself into line with his belief that he ought to involve his SMT colleagues more. He had begun to write minutes during team meetings to stop himself dominating:

> I try – but I'm very bad at this because I'm a head, aren't I? – not to say too much, but it is a fault, I do drive things. I think a lot of heads do. What I've started doing, I now minute the SMT meetings; now if you're minuting you can't do all the talking as well. I do find if I act as minuting secretary, although I'm the chair, I can't be writing down and contributing all the time. So that way, colleagues make a major contribution – but they aren't people who are afraid to make a contribution anyway.

Team membership at Pinehill, Kingsrise and Waverley

A key to complementarity among individual team roles in these SMTs was a culture of teamwork featuring acceptance among team members that contributions to teamwork might legitimately be ordered hierarchically, in line with differential status, salaries and management responsibilities. The heads most frequently *led within the team*, especially on major issues they had placed on the team agenda. Interviews with members of the three teams suggested that, after the heads, those in the upper echelons of the management hierarchy (deputies and senior teachers with major cross-school management responsibilities) led within the team more often than their colleagues with lower status, and that the latter would lead on day-to-day rather than school-wide policy issues. To fill out the picture of leadership within the team, instances are summarised from each school.

The head at Pinehill had initiated the process of allocating pupils to classes for the coming year through bounded debate, first formulating criteria for their placement on which he sought SMT colleagues' agreement. He and the deputy, as the inner cabinet, then made up provisional class lists according to the agreed critiera which they put forward for comment at a second SMT meeting, modified in the light of suggestions, and presented at a full staff meeting for further adjustment. At each stage, the head took the final decision on whether to accept suggested changes. Within the SMT, therefore, differences in the amount of participation by members other than the head directly paralleled their status differentials, with department leaders being less involved than the deputy. On another occasion, the deputy led the process of gaining feedback from SMT members on the outcome of consultation meetings with cross-phase groups of staff. The early years leader, informally, took the lead on giving feedback, suggesting that flipcharts produced by the team member allocated to each cross-phase meeting should be used as the basis for discussion.

At Kingsrise, the head had instructed the deputy to gather views of staff in each department on priorities for the school development plan, calling an SMT meeting to discuss targets to be included in it. There the deputy led within the team on reporting back by going through a summary of staff views on particular curriculum areas. The head not only chaired the meeting, so creating conditions for teamwork as the team leader, but she led within the team on the content of priorities and targets for the school development plan. After the deputy had reported on a curriculum area, the head tended to be first to respond, making an evaluatory comment and offering ideas about what should be done. Several times she directed other members to take action, as where she stated that the SMT must agree a means of evaluating lesson plans. When the deputy reported on the need for teachers in the nursery department to bring their approach to lesson planning into line with that of the other staff, the head – rather than the department one leader whose responsibility it was – replied by stating how far lesson planning should be adapted by being less formally structured. The assessment coordinator, whose management responsibility included the process of evaluating lesson plans, also contributed on points of procedure. Other members listened, but made little input. At another meeting, the assessment coordinator led a discussion on standardising weekly lesson plans.

The head at Waverley convened an SMT meeting to discuss an action plan for the school in the light of the inspection, adopting a strategy of bounded debate. He distributed his draft action plan for religious education, drew colleagues' attention to particular points, sought their advice on improving what he had written, and asked them to identify any omissions. The deputy volunteered, on another occasion, to lead a staff meeting on behalf of the SMT to discuss the school policy on countering bullying. When preparing for the inspection, the English and IT coordinator had offered to tidy up the school library – for which she had management responsibility – and to consult other staff about improvements.

There was room for all team members to *contribute as equals* to debate, though more restricted than at Winton, lying principally within the agenda set by the heads and being expressed mostly by members other than heads because the latter so often led within the team. During discussion of the marking policy at Pinehill, contributions by members other than the head, which drew on their experience and responsibilities, included:

- teaching responsibility – the early years leader championed the perceived interests of teachers in suggesting that the policy document should be short because busy teachers would be more likely to read and implement it;
- curriculum coordination responsibility – the middle years leader argued that it was sometimes appropriate to throw away pupils' work in mathematics when they had been practising skills and were not concerned with presentation;
- management responsibility as an SMT member – the curriculum leader reported the views expressed by staff in the cross-phase group she had facilitated;
- overview of school policies – the older years leader suggested that the marking policy should take into account current procedures for editing pupils' work;
- knowledge of parents – the deputy asserted that parents should be made aware of the marking policy so that they would know why some mistakes in their child's work would not be corrected.

The head, who chaired this meeting, also offered ideas which other members could take up or challenge, such as suggesting it was less important that marking symbols were standardised than that pupils understood whatever symbols their teacher was using.

A comparable pattern of interaction was observed at Kingsrise, exemplified in the negotiation of terminology for the weekly curriculum planning sheet to be adopted throughout the school. Within the head's initiative on lesson planning, the assessment coordinator led the team via bounded debate. She circulated her draft planning sheet in the SMT meeting and asked colleagues for their comments. The deputy queried the heading of 'topic maths' as she was unsure what the term 'topic' meant, and the assessment coordinator responded by suggesting that the term 'maths' alone would suffice along with a brief heading summarising work to be covered. Alternatives for wording were offered by the department one and department three leaders and the head. The assessment coordinator reiterated that she was open to any suggestion which would improve on her draft, and the head, as chair, moved the discussion on by arguing that the planning sheet be tried out as it stood and the heading re-examined if it proved problematic. So too, at Waverley, team members could contribute as equals in their response to the head's proposals. They also contributed as equals to the SMT overview, as witnessed by exchange of information between team members during one meeting. The infants leader advised the head on whether a parent of a child in her class was suitable for appointment as a school meals supervisory assistant; the deputy reported that the bell system outside a newly built classroom was not working; and the juniors leader reminded colleagues of the school policy on not wearing jewellery during physical education lessons.

Followership was largely represented by *acceptance* of parameters set by the heads and contributing from within them. Few instances of *facilitative* behaviour were observed, which, speculatively, may have resulted in part from heads giving such a strong lead that other members did not expect to take initiatives to help the teamwork process along. The deputy and assessment coordinator at Kingsrise, the most senior staff in the management hierarchy apart from the head, did start off an SMT meeting in her absence. The deputy answered the telephone, deputising for the head, and the assessment coordinator made a point of summarising the debate so far after she joined the meeting to update her on what she had missed. There were limits to followership: at Waverley the deputy rejected the head's suggestion that she take a school assembly on the Friday before the inspection because she was already scheduled to take one during it.

In sum, at Pinehill, Kingsrise and Waverley, the heads' quite strongly hierarchical approach to leadership of the teams and propensity to take the lead within them left other SMT members with moderate scope for leading within the team and contributing as equals to debate. They generally took up the opportunities for contributing to teamwork that were on offer, so there was complementarity in the balance of individual team roles. Here it rested on members other than heads using influence to empower the team leader by being ready to acquiesce to his or her exclusive leadership in setting narrow parameters for teamwork and initiating most of the content addressed by the team. Willingness to support the head in this way rested, in turn, on a strong belief in the management hierarchy as a framework for action which seemingly outweighed belief in equal contribution.

The SMT meeting process

The setting for team meetings was partly determined by the size of the SMT and facilities available for private discussion during the school day. On-site SMT meetings at Winton and all SMT meetings in the other three schools were normally held in the headteacher's office. The room at Winton was large enough to incorporate both a set of low chairs around a coffee table and a large table and upright chairs. Meetings were held at the large table where members could lay out documents and diaries and take notes comfortably. In the other schools, team members sat in a circle in low chairs away from the head's desk. Individuals took any chair, spaces next to the head being occupied by whoever arrived first, except at Kingsrise. Here the management hierarchy was symbolised through the way the head, deputy and assessment coordinator elected to sit together. At Kingsrise and Waverley, the heads' offices were only just large enough to accommodate all team members, prompting a move to the staffroom for some meetings observed. The problem of cramped accommodation was acute at Waverley, where one observed meeting was held in the head's room with members making notes while balancing their agendas and coffee cups on their laps. The other meeting observed took place inside half of the staffroom, partitioned by a flimsy screen. When a teacher who was not a member of the SMT came into the other half, it became obvious that SMT members could be overheard, causing the head to stop talking because the issue being discussed – the possibility that staff relationships could deteriorate if the inspection went badly – was sensitive. The teacher needed to collect an item from the part of the room occupied by the SMT, so the head defused the situation through humour, calling out, 'Come in, we've stopped talking about you!'

SMT meetings in school were variably subject to interruption, secretaries in all cases shielding team members from telephone calls except where they were unable to deal with an enquiry or problem. Such meetings were frequently disrupted only at Winton, where phone calls were supplemented by staff or pupils knocking on the door. This situation was one stimulus for reviewing management responsibilities of staff with two salary increments with a view to them taking on most pupil discipline and pastoral care work, a major cause of these interruptions.

It was discussed above how heads set parameters for contributions to the SMT agenda as leaders of their teams. Their approach to agenda setting varied, the head at Winton giving most space for colleagues to participate. The agenda was partly fixed, allowing all members to contribute within the regular focus without prior consultation. Early morning meetings centred on exchange of information about routine organisation for the day; the first item for weekly meetings was organisation for the following week. The head added other items for this meeting, sometimes in response to colleagues' requests (having learned, as recounted earlier, that the agenda for the early morning meetings was best restricted to arrangements for the day). The agenda for extended meetings was constructed through discussion during the prior weekly meeting and reviewed at the beginning of the extended session.

The other heads set the agenda for all meetings, sometimes in consultation with the deputy, with the proviso that other members could suggest an item to the head beforehand. At the beginning of SMT meetings the head at Kingsrise handed out copies of an agenda she had prepared and proceeded to work through it, determining the order in which items were addressed. Her counterpart at Waverley was observed to distribute copies of documents he had drafted, and to draw colleagues' attention to passages where he sought their comments. A team member at Pinehill reflected that heavy reliance by the head on identifying items could mean that important areas were not considered regularly in the SMT, an issue he had begun to address by opening up the agenda to department leaders. At Kingsrise and Waverley, members other than the head could bring up issues during the final 'any other business' agenda item, though this arrangement inhibited discussion in any depth, not least because members did not wish the meeting to overrun. Consequently, observation suggested that the opportunity to bring items up at the end of meetings was little used other than to inform colleagues about matters connected with their management responsibility. Where heads both set the agenda and gave notice about its content at the beginning of a meeting, other members' contribution could be inhibited because of the limited time they had to consider their view. One team member at Waverley noted how the head used the SMT to 'air his thoughts out loud', seeking feedback from colleagues, but

> A lot of the best thinking in SMT meetings, as far as I'm concerned, probably occurs after the meeting. Now that could be [the head's] fault because he doesn't usually provide you with an agenda, so we don't really know what's going to come up until we actually get there . . . a lot of information is flung at you in a short space of time, it's coming at the end of a busy day when you've been involved with children all day long. It becomes, then, increasingly difficult to focus, to concentrate, to give him really valuable feedback. Probably in the couple of days which come afterwards, thoughts occur to me. You've had a chance to chew it over in your mind, and you think: 'Well, I don't think that's such a good idea after all. I wouldn't do that, [head], if I were you.'

The four heads included chairing SMT meetings within their contribution to leadership of the team, the light touch of the head at Winton contrasting with the more directive approach of the other heads. They covered the same processual matters, but with more emphasis on steering the meeting in line with their position as top manager. The head at Winton characteristically orchestrated the meeting process by seeking colleagues' view on how to proceed. She was observed, first, to combine her ideas for the agenda with consulting other team members. On one occasion she wrote a draft agenda and asked for additional items at the start of the meeting. On another she invited all members to draw up the agenda together. Second, she often put forward 'process decisions' about when and how to tackle items, and sought her colleagues' opinion on her proposals. She produced a written agenda for one meeting and suggested that they deal with three complex items by working out how to address them in forthcoming meetings, asking other members if they agreed to this idea. Another time, the juniors deputy took the initiative to lead the meeting by raising the issue of how to respond when parents stated that the surname of their child had changed, suggesting, 'We need a policy on this.' The head responded, 'Shall we write it down?' Third, she habitually questioned individuals to check their views or concerns. During the review of management responsibilities of staff with two salary increments, the head noticed that the infants deputy was thumbing through the job descriptions document they were discussing and asked her what the issue was.

The head was also assertive, requesting colleagues to undertake tasks like writing down outcomes of discussion. Their commitment to the culture of teamwork meant that, often, they would perform such tasks unasked, or in response to no more than a general statement from the head, as when she commented that they would need a flipchart and the infants deputy immediately brought the flipchart over to where everyone could see it. The head took responsibility for timekeeping, being ready to initiate closure on items and to propose how outcomes should be taken forward. While no formal minutes were taken, she ensured that either she or another team member recorded whatever was deemed necessary to progress the issues at hand.

The content of SMT meeting agendas supported the role of the teams in managing the school, items covering principally that part of the teamwork process connected with pooling ideas and contributing to an overview, and the team tasks of policy making and strategic planning. The range of items reflected the balance sought by each head (and, at Winton, other SMT members to a lesser extent) between sustaining an overview, monitoring inside and outside the school, consulting staff during the development of school policies, making policy decisions and ensuring smooth routine organisation. While only a few SMT meetings were observed, the overlap between categories identified in the teams suggests that their members were all involved in contributing to the SMT role through agendas spanning day-to-day school-wide administration and some longer-term policy making. It should be noted that the range of content within each category almost certainly under-represents the full diversity in any SMT. Nevertheless, the pattern discernible of agenda items in these meetings suggests that the categories may have been the most common ones in use. Table 6.4 summarises categories of agenda item identified by analysing the focus of SMT meetings observed at Winton, their

Table 6.4 Types of agenda item for SMT meetings at Winton

Category of agenda item	Contribution to SMT role	Range of content	Examples
Check/routine organisation	decisions on routine organisation and process decisions related to policy making, contributing to overview informing these decisions	preparation immediately before events	checking events and arrangements for the day and coming week
		timetabling of regular events	checking head's staff meetings list for next term, disseminating information
		implementation of routine procedures	special needs coordinator updated other SMT members on pupils with special needs
		preparation for meetings between SMT and other staff	juniors deputy to remind music specialist about presenting draft music policy at staff meeting
Shared awareness	mainly contributing to overview, a few decisions	information from outside school	head informed other members about LEA development plan
		information from inside school	head reported that assembly with local police officer showed many children play outisde un-supervised late in the evening
Policy making	policy decisions and related process decisions, contributing to overview informing these decisions	initial consideration of issue	head announced she wished to review work of staff with two salary increments
			special needs coordinator and head announced they had discussed system for allocating special needs support
		process decisions for managing issues	deciding when and how to conduct review of staff with two salary increments
		SMT proposed decision	staff with two salary increments to become department leaders
		ratification of proposed decision	head to meet staff with two salary increments to present consultation paper
			response of other SMT members sought to proposed allocation of special needs support
		making final decision and preparing for dissemination	*SMT members agreed allocation of special needs support, special needs coordinator to disseminate*
Staffing	mainly contributing to overview	staff complement	head announced that a new reception class teacher would be needed next term

contribution to the SMT role, the range of content within each category, and one or two examples of each item. The *check/routine organisation* category reflects attention paid to ensuring that day-to-day arrangements were made and staff notified, entailing many decisions about routine matters and, occasionally, process decisions about how to handle aspects of policy making involving staff outside the team. The exchange of information embodied in this category contributed to the shared overview of SMT members. They spent a small proportion of meeting time updating each other about information relevant to their team tasks, but not directly connected with current decisions. The *shared awareness* category covers such items, serving also to broaden SMT members' overview. Some information originated outside the school, coming mostly from the head, some from inside, often linked with individual management responsibilities. The exchange of information under these first two categories formed part of the linkage subtask of monitoring other staff and key players in the local community including governors and parents.

Policy making was a major category, the range of content embracing some stages in decision-making procedures revealed in the headteachers' survey, together with process decisions to manage the sometimes long drawn out decision-making procedure (which were not mentioned in the survey returns). In the table, stages in the decision to change the responsibilities of staff with two salary increments are depicted in normal type, and those connected with the decision to adopt a new system for allocating special needs support are depicted in italics. Occasionally, *staffing* matters were raised, especially by the head, as in the case of new appointments. There was overlap between most categories at the other three schools and Winton, as Table 6.5 portrays, consistent with their similar role in managing the school. The additional agenda item category of *external accountability* related to school inspection. The examples reflect the greater incidence of heads taking the lead on any item than at Winton according to their more hierarchical approach to team-work. The range of check/routine organisation items extends to monitoring by heads of colleague members' work as departmental managers responsible for curriculum coverage in classes under their jurisdiction. The variety of issues each SMT was observed or reported to address during the academic year 1995/96 demonstrates that, though the degree to which heads involved other SMT members in management did vary, all four engaged team colleagues in some way in a substantial range of school-wide management issues. They included work on management of pupil behaviour, staff development and in-service training, and developing and assessing the curriculum. Preparation for inspection and action planning afterwards dominated team meetings at Pinehill and Waverley for several months; a major element of the management structure was reviewed and modified at Winton, Pinehill and Kingsrise; and planning new accommodation took up team members' time at Winton and Waverley.

Table 6.5 Types of agenda item for SMT meetings at Pinehill, Kingsrise and Waverley

Category of agenda item	Contribution to SMT role	Range of content	Examples
Check/routine organisation	decisions on routine organisation and process decisions related to policy making, contributing to overview informing these decisions	preparation immediately before events timetabling of regular events implementation of routine procedures	head announced arrangements for visit of school photographer (Waverley) head checked arrangements for Christmas celebrations (Kingsrise) head instructed SMT members to ask teachers in their department to prepare class lists for next year with suggestions for changes to minimise behaviour problems (Kingsrise)
		monitoring SMT members' management work	head enquired why some classes had not completed some science topics (Kingsrise)
Shared awareness	mainly contributing to overview, a few decisions	information from outside school information from inside school	head informed SMT colleagues that governors were controlling plans for expanding accommodation (Waverley) head stated amount of money in school fund (Kingsrise)
Policy making	policy decisions and related process decisions, contributing to overview informing these decisions	consultation with other staff on issue making final decision and preparing for dissemination	feedback from SMT members on outcome of consultation meetings they had chaired (Pinehill) deciding on format of standardised weekly curriculum planning sheet and arrangements for trialling with other staff (Kingsrise)
Staffing	mainly contributing to overview	staff complement	head informed SMT colleagues about progress with appointing a maths specialist (Waverley)
External accountability	presenting school to external agencies	reporting to external inspectors	head consulted SMT colleagues on his report for inspectors (Waverley)

Contribution of SMT meetings to decision making

Making school-wide decisions involved staff inside and outside the SMT, but part of the process took place in the privacy of SMT meetings. Members across the teams subscribed to the norm within their culture of teamwork that decisions must normally be made by reaching a working consensus on outcomes, consistent with the belief that each member had an equal contribution to make to this core team task. Seeking consensus implied allegiance to the related norm that individuals should be ready to compromise their view if there was disagreement. Going with the flow of opinion facilitated formulation of proposals for action that all parties could accept, favouring the unified commitment required for synergistic effort to implement decisions. Belief in the management hierarchy complicated this picture because the ultimate authority to make decisions and accountability for them rested with heads. Other team members were well aware that the head had authority to withdraw any decision from the SMT and make it unilaterally, despite their ability to employ influence in resisting or minimally complying with directives (as happened when the head at Pinehill imposed the new management structure). Given the disparity between heads' authority and concomitant accountability for making SMT decisions according to the management hierarchy, and their dependence on other members coupled with the belief in some degree of equal contribution to decisions, who should compromise first? The answer seemed contingent on how far heads held hard to a particular decision outcome. Where they did, other members would be expected to make any compromise in their direction, with the back-up sanction that the heads ultimately possessed authority to impose their preferred decision anyway.

There was divergence on how consensus was achieved in the teams, reflecting the alternative forms of complementarity in the balance of individual team roles. It has been described how, at Winton, all members readily contributed ideas and occasionally challenged each other's views, including those expressed by the head. Consequently, disagreements could occur and the head would typically respond, as chair, by calling a halt and making time to revisit the debate after a cooling off period:

> It can get quite heated. We never argue, we don't fall out or do bitchy things or storm around . . . more often than not it is me that will say: 'Let's just leave this.' We will do something else, then we will come back another time. And we do usually resolve it.

The variety of ideas actually expressed by each member was, however, delimited by individuals' 'self-censoring' (and unobservable) compromise behaviour serving the interest of achieving consensus. They had become familiar with colleagues' professional beliefs and values and would often withhold from expressing a view that was likely to clash with theirs. The juniors deputy commented:

> If there is something we know we are going to discuss, you can almost mentally predict what the other person's approach is going to be and therefore have dealt with it in your own mind before you put your point of view. So, for instance, I would not put a point of view which – unless of course I felt very strongly – I knew would be in complete contradiction to theirs, because I know we would all be starting from a complete standstill

at that stage. You have almost weighed up what you think they are going to say before you say what you are going to say.

Another form of compromise for members other than the head entailed the temporary switch from adherence to belief in equal contribution to belief in the management hierarchy highlighted earlier, where disagreement could be resolved by handing the decision back to the head. These contradictory beliefs and values could both be held by SMT members without engendering conflict because they were able to switch between them in unison. In the words of the juniors deputy, on rare occasions 'It will be things which we have to say either verbally or in your own head: "Well, at the end of the day you are the head, therefore the decision is yours."' The head, in turn, took comfort from being able to depend on her colleagues' willingness to give way to enable her to keep a decision within her comfort zone:

> There's often a casting vote type of situation, and they will accept that and acknowledge that there are some times when we are not all going to agree, and we will have gone backwards and forwards but in the final analysis I will just have to say: 'This is the way it is.' I think it works quite well because we know we would never move forward on a lot of issues if we didn't have that unspoken arrangement.

The culture of teamwork shared throughout this SMT appeared to include the norm that the head had not merely a right but a duty to pull rank as team leader to ensure progress, though only where equal contribution did not result in consensus. The implicit nature of the temporary handover arrangement could prove counterproductive where other members were unclear how closely the head wished to adhere to a particular course of action. The special needs coordinator noted how sometimes she sensed late in the day that the head had a particular outcome in mind, despite the appearance of open debate, where:

> The discussion hasn't been fruitful because we have a discussion but, prior to the discussion, the actual decision had almost been made. It would have taken a very major point to have challenged the final decision . . . [the head] has got a clear idea of the way she wants things to go, [the juniors deputy] sometimes has a different idea, we will have a lot of discussion, then I think usually the bottom line is it goes the way the boss would like it to. And in fact that's what she gets paid for. The bottom line is: if the decision isn't to her liking, she still has to carry the can for it.

This account implies that the special needs coordinator subscribed, nevertheless, to the belief that the unique level of accountability accompanying the head's position as top manager legitimated her setting parameters for her colleagues' contribution and reverting to a hierarchical mode of operation where necessary to keep a decision within these parameters. The emphasis on equal contribution in this team was contingent, circumscribed by the management hierarchy which mostly figured only as a backdrop for interaction within the SMT. Where there was disagreement over decisions, voluntarily handing them back to the head pre-empted her from more explicitly pulling rank. The special needs coordinator noted how the head had overruled other members on only a few decisions concerned with routine organisation, never on major policy changes.

Consensual decision making in the other teams reflected the more hierarchical form of complementarity between individual team roles, emphasising heads' extensive leadership within the team and other members' followership which enabled them to operate in this way. Compared with the head at Winton, they supplied a higher proportion of the ideas on which SMT decision making was based and relied more on bounded debate, so reducing the scope for disagreement. This form of team culture appeared to express more strongly the norm that subordinates within the management hierarchy should be ready to compromise in the direction of heads' preferred decision outcomes. Avoidance of disagreement, or its straightforward resolution within heads' comfort zone, depended on members other than the head subscribing to the relatively hierarchical culture of teamwork they fostered. Earlier it was discussed how conflict arose within the Pinehill SMT soon after the head's arrival because other members were not ready to accept his authority as head to overrule them over the decision to establish the management structure. He noted how in this situation he was 'doing a dictator's job', but that it was becoming more rare as he and his colleagues adapted to each other. It was also noted how the head reportedly tended to consult the deputy first, then present proposed decisions to the full SMT, so giving them the opportunity to put forward ideas but mainly in response to his. Where disagreement had emerged that could not be resolved by prolonged discussion, as when he put forward a new arrangement for pupils coming into school from the playground, the head had used his power of veto to put his preferred option in place. A department leader observed that the likelihood of disagreement sparking off deeper conflict depended on how far each individual was willing to compromise: 'It's making moves about who's going to give way.' Here, norms about the give and take of compromise necessary to yield a working consensus in the face of disagreement were only now being established.

Characteristic of SMT members' hierarchically differentiated contributions to decision making at Kingsrise was the rarity of disagreement between the head and her team colleagues, indicating how the ease with which consensual decision making was achieved was due to the hierarchically oriented culture of teamwork being shared throughout the SMT. No member could recall a major conflict of views within the team, the assessment coordinator commenting that agreed priorities within the school development plan framed the aims for

much of the team's work. Members other than the head accepted her entitlement to override them if there was strong disagreement on the grounds that
she had ultimate responsibility for SMT decisions, but also noted how they
were ready to compromise. The department three leader expressed her willingness to go with the majority view (so helping to empower colleagues to
reach consensus), while the department one leader reported how potential conflict was avoided because, where members 'disagreed professionally, then they
agreed to disagree professionally', keeping the disagreement on a professional
– not personal – level. Other strategies mentioned included talking through
issues at length, seeking common ground between members with differing
views, leaving them till another occasion, and trying out the outcome of a decision with the proviso that it would subsequently be reviewed. The head was
observed to advocate this course of action over the decision to trial the new
weekly curriculum lesson planning sheet discussed above. One member was,
however, concerned that SMT members other than the head might be overly
self-censoring, compromise being achieved at the expense of airing the full
range of views: 'I feel as a senior management team we're not always honest
with each other. People could give a bit more and say more of what they feel
so that we could, as a group, thrash issues out.' The situation at Waverley was
similar to Kingsrise, also featuring a hierarchically oriented culture of teamwork shared among all team members, providing the foundation for making
compromises to achieve consensus. It was accepted that the head would
override other members and make the final decision if there was lasting
disagreement.

Forms of complementarity and levels of synergy

It has been stressed how a hallmark of teamwork is what team members do
together in their quest for the synergy between each member's contributions
which makes a team more than a group of individuals. The findings presented
in this chapter underline how central the heads were in empowering their SMT
colleagues to coordinate their contributions to the joint work of each team
through meetings while simultaneously setting boundaries which delimited the
extent of this contribution. They set the course for teamwork in SMT meetings through establishing the frequency and timing of regular SMT and subgroup meetings; they chose how extensively they would lead within the team
on particular items and how far to encourage their colleagues to make an equal
contribution to debate; they controlled the degree to which other members
could contribute to the team agenda; they orchestrated meetings through their
preferred approach to chairing; they fostered consensual decision making; and
they decided under what circumstances to use their authority to withdraw
decisions from the SMT and make them unilaterally.

  In short, the heads controlled parameters for joint work through team meetings affecting the potential for synergistic interaction: whether, at Winton, to

create conditions favouring maximal input of ideas and initiatives among all team members on a wide range of issues with school-wide implications; or whether, in the other schools, to establish a more narrowly bounded framework for team meetings whereby they retained tighter control over the process and content of the teams' contribution to management. The former head had expressed quite extensive transformational leadership; the latter heads a more restricted form. Yet the experience at Pinehill portrayed here and in earlier chapters demonstrated how controlling parameters did not automatically mean that the potential level of synergy they sought within these parameters would be achieved. A shared team culture was a prerequisite, as illustrated by the other three teams where heads had been able to appoint their team colleagues. The heads depended on other SMT members to buy into the form of culture of teamwork to which they subscribed if they were to make full use of the authority delegated to them in working towards the same educational and managerial aims.

Where team members other than heads had responded positively to their overtures and a shared culture of teamwork had been established, two forms of complementarity among individuals' preferred team roles were apparent. Relatively egalitarian complementarity at Winton, with strong emphasis on sharing leadership within the team and contributing as equals to debate and decision making, appeared to realise the high potential for synergy following from the scope enjoyed by all members to contribute their ideas and initiatives. More hierarchical complementarity at the other three schools (in so far as it was achieved at Pinehill), emphasising leadership by the head and followership by other members, also appeared to realise its potential for synergy. With progressively less room for members further down the management hierarchy to bring ideas and initiatives of their own, which might challenge those of the heads, it appears that the ceiling of this potential remained lower than within the more egalitarian approach.

Team meetings may have been at the heart of teamwork, but the linkage subtasks through which SMT members sought to impact on other staff and external agents, including governors, were also integral to the shared role of the SMT. To complete the story of the four teams' operation these relationships, which gave SMT meetings a significance beyond their worth as a talking shop for their members, will be discussed next.

Chapter 7

Them and us

The SMTs were instrumental to the headteachers' quest for synergy extending to every area of the work of professional and support staff. Just as heads depended on support of their team colleagues, so all SMT members depended on the work of other staff if the role of the SMT was to be fulfilled. In Chapter 1 it was argued that what synergy across the school might mean had become overtly loaded in terms of central government politics through the national reforms, dictating that the focus of synergistic effort must be directed to lie within parameters set by central government interests. Heads, as ever, promoted a form of school-wide synergy where staff pulled together in a direction consistent with heads' educational and managerial beliefs and values. In the new, more hostile environment, however, these beliefs and values now included the priority of ensuring that the staff combined effort lay also within the bounds of acceptability to governors, parents and inspectors. The extent to which this form of school-wide synergy could be achieved depended on the relationship established between the SMT and other staff. The possibility of SMTs facilitating transformational leadership which extended beyond the team to a substantial input from staff across the school was bounded by these environmental factors. The previous three chapters have concentrated on the inside story of the teamwork process and team tasks in contributing to the SMTs' shared role. Now it is time to broaden the focus to explore how SMT members conducted their business through their linkage subtasks with other staff, under the supervision of governors, and on behalf of parents.

Since the SMTs were concerned primarily with professional and support staff, the analysis will focus mainly on this relationship. First, factors are discussed which rendered interaction between the SMT and other staff complex and potentially uncontrollable in a directive sense, despite the clear superordinate–subordinate structural relationship that existed – on paper at least – in each school. Second, a summary is offered of the structure of meetings, complemented by less formal means of communicating, through which SMT members carried out linkage subtasks. Third, SMT decision making is revisited, extending the discussion in the previous chapter to reviewing participation of other staff and the varying balance between top-down and bottom-up orientations for different kinds of decision in each school. How far the relatively egalitarian or hierarchical approach of the heads was reflected in the range of involvement among other staff is considered. Fourth, characteristics are investigated of the demarcation between the inner world of the SMT and the outer world of other staff. Efforts were made by SMT members – not always successfully – to pre-empt the development of a 'them and us' perception among staff in these large schools through their performance in public. Finally, the more distant relationship between the SMT, governors and parents is considered.

SMT plus or *versus* the rest?

Several factors contributed to the complexity of the relationship between SMTs and other staff which reflected, but also belied, the hierarchical distribution of management responsibilities in the schools. First, bringing the zones of school-wide policy making and practice together required not only formal stuctures and mandates, but also the acquiescence and support of other staff. They may have been placed in a subordinate relationship to the SMT members who had line management responsibility for aspects of their work within the matrix management structures, but the distribution of power within the dialectic of control between members of staff and the associated pattern of cultural allegiances within each school cut across these formal lines. While SMT members enjoyed authority delegated by the heads, other staff also had delegated authority for their management and teaching responsibilities and had recourse to influence which could be used to facilitate or block attempts to shape their work. They could resist passively or more actively. The head at Pinehill, when taking up his present post, had unilaterally introduced a curriculum-planning pack he had designed for staff, but they had found it unworkable. Staff inside and outside the SMT had confronted him at a staff meeting, where he acknowledged the force of their argument and not only withdrew the pack but also initiated a more consultative approach to major decisions affecting other staff.

Second, like the SMT culture of teamwork, the staff professional culture also featured contradictory beliefs and values. Hierarchical control was strongly favoured by the universal belief in the management hierarchy which helped empower the SMT. No informant from outside the teams implied that the SMT should not be, as one teacher at Winton put it, 'involved in everything that a school is'. Indeed, several teachers wanted the SMT to manage on their behalf so they could concentrate on realising their priority class-teaching interests. One at Kingsrise commented: 'The role of teaching is such a demanding one that often staff are happy that somebody else should be doing things that they need not necessarily be involved in.' A colleague looked to the SMT for protection from external intervention connected with national reforms: 'The SMT are becoming a bigger buffer between us and everything that's expected of the school.' At the same time, different beliefs could temper readiness of other staff to accept SMT management activity and so empower team members to promote school-wide synergy. Two key beliefs reflecting the history of primary schooling were discussed in Chapter 1. Individuals widely assumed that they should be allowed some autonomy as class teachers and managers which SMT decisions and monitoring activity could transgress. They should also be entitled to participate in management decisions affecting their work, a belief surfacing when heads and their SMT colleagues were perceived as having failed to consult on such matters (as illustrated by the incident at Pinehill mentioned above). One teacher at Winton resented the way a detention system for misbehaving pupils had been introduced without consulting staff outside the SMT. Another at Kingsrise, with ideas on how to reorganise the way pupils lined up in the playground, noted with regret how an ostensibly SMT decision on this issue had actually been made by the head without airing staff views inside or outside the team. A teacher at Waverley noted approvingly how support staff were now consulted more by the infants leader, who enabled them to raise issues by passing their concerns back to her SMT colleagues. The infants leader noted: 'It's early days, but hopefully it will have the effect that they feel more valued and more part of decision making in the sort of things that affect them.'

Third, the potential for mutual empowerment of SMTs and other staff depended on their shared commitment to finding mutually acceptable compromises between the mainly school-wide interests pursued by the SMT and the diverse and often incompatible sectional interests pursued by individuals and groups of staff. The predominant means of approaching their reconciliation were overt: through directives from heads, largely accepted because of belief in their entitlement to do so as top managers in the management hierarchy; and through debate between SMT and other staff. An alternative was covert, but could be legitimated for SMT members by their belief in the greater good of avoiding a potential conflict over compromises which other staff would find difficult to make. There was an acute shortfall in the LMS budget at Winton, leaving very little money for the annual allocation of curriculum resources. SMT members had excluded other staff this year from consultation over what had become solely a team decision about how much money each subject should receive. The outcome of this decision had not been disseminated outside the SMT except to individuals who indicated they had a need to know. The juniors deputy summed up the position:

> At the moment we are working on a chicken and egg situation. I know that all the money within the curriculum headings is not enough . . . it really is down to the very last penny; there is no leeway at all. So those [subject coordinators] who have asked, 'How much money have I got?' to buy this, that or the other, have been told. This is not a deliberate ploy as such but it's the way it's worked out. Those who haven't [asked], haven't

necessarily been told. We got to the stage when [the infants deputy] and I discussed whether or not we should go ahead and tell everybody how much they had. But things were very tight. One of the views I take is that if you tell some people that there is so much to spend, they'll spend it. Whereas if you don't say there is and they need it, they'll come and ask for it. So although it's not necessarily a good policy, that's the way we are operating at present. We need to review that; it is certainly not the way we intended it to work.

The definition of manipulation in Chapter 2 implies that, from SMT members' perspective, this action was not manipulative because of the legitimation offered by lack of finance. (It seems likely, however, that these grounds for legitimacy would have been challenged had other staff become aware of the SMT strategy.)

Fourth, SMT members with class teaching responsibility (all but the four heads, and the deputies at Winton and Pinehill) faced potential role conflict arising from their dual cultural allegiance. There was evidence that a minority of individuals experienced tension between the expectation of heads and deputies that they should subscribe to the SMT culture of teamwork and put school-wide interests first and their continuing allegiance to the staff professional culture, pulling them towards giving priority to the sectional interests of their pupils and of colleague class teachers. The special needs coordinator at Winton had been on both sides of the cultural divide, not having a class until this year. Her situation gave rise to a dilemma about the confidential information she received from SMT colleagues and from other staff, which she resolved by utilising her power to withhold from action:

> In staff gossip I need to make sure that management things which are confidential aren't discussed but, by the same token, I have to do exactly the same thing with things that are told to me in confidence by [other] staff which they don't want to be for the senior management team. It's not my place, I don't feel – whether it is for the good of the management team to know them or not – to tell them.

By refraining from feeding certain information from other staff into the SMT, she ruled out its potential contribution to the SMT linkage subtask of monitoring because she believed in respecting confidences of her class teacher colleagues. By refraining from divulging confidential SMT information to other staff, she operated in accordance with the SMT culture of teamwork which demanded unity over disseminating or withholding information generated behind the closed doors of SMT meetings.

It was earlier discussed how heads in the other three schools reported that SMT members with departmental responsibility were reticent to monitor performance of other staff in their department. Speculatively, for them to have done so would run counter to the belief within the staff professional culture that they were entitled to some classroom autonomy and should be trusted to use it responsibly, meaning that classwork should not be monitored for accountability purposes by colleagues other than, perhaps, the headteacher (who was not responsible for a class). Newly qualified teachers in the four schools, however, believed SMT members should visit their classroom more than they did – not for accountability reasons, but to provide constructive feedback which would serve the priority interest of beginning teachers in their own professional development. This perception, surfacing because they did not get enough of what they wanted, was typified by one at Winton: 'What would be nice is if you had them [SMT members] popping in on a support level that you don't particularly get.' Another at Pinehill complained:

> I feel isolated from what the senior management team do – not just from what they do but also, do they know what I do? I realise it's a big school but no one has come to see what I've been doing or knows anything about me. I feel I'm a kind of satellite, just going my own little way.

The head at Winton was aware of teachers' wish that she should visit them but, compared with her pre-merger school, the present institution was too large and staff too thinly spread:

> My staff have now accepted TLC [tender loving care] is not for me any more because that's not the environment in which we can work. They get professional support, obviously . . . but I don't generally go round every day dispensing love and affection. I can't do it any more.

Fifth, there was a gap between insider and outsider information on SMT operation. Other staff had little first-hand experience of how SMT members carried out their shared role. Teachers responsible for an area of management were clearer about the part played by the SMT than colleagues with no brief beyond the classroom because they tended to have dealings with SMT members connected with their management area. SMT activity did impinge on everyday work of all other staff and they were impressionistically aware of the variable degree of hierarchy expressed within the teams discussed in earlier chapters. The special needs coordinator at Winton was less visibly on a par with other SMT members now she had a class; the head and deputy partnership at Pinehill was widely seen as the source of most major decisions; the head at Kingsrise was singled out as the forceful leader of her team, few other members being thought to raise any issues; and the head at Waverley was regarded as the driving force, actively supported by his SMT colleagues.

Other staff had never seen how SMT members contributed to major decisions during their meetings, so could not be sure how far views they had expressed during consultation or ratification had affected decisions. A minority of teachers in three schools questioned what might be taking place in SMT meetings. One (at Pinehill) reflected on the possibility of bias in reporting of SMT decision making by the department leader: 'They [SMT members] may have a meeting together but, by the time it's brought to us, it's only individual perception we get.' A second (at Kingsrise) claimed that recommendations from other staff were reinterpreted:

> We can have a discussion and we can reach a decision which we thought had been reached by consensus, but when it is committed to paper or implemented, it will be given a slant by the person at the top, so that what comes out is some sort of 'bastardised monster' of what went in. Only the general features of the joint decision can be discerned, not the nitty gritty, so that the decision then becomes the person in charge's opinion of what she thought staff had intended.

A third (at Waverley) reported simply: 'We are fed back decisions but we are not given much detail about how decisions are reached.' Staff outside the SMT at Winton were clearer, though conscious in the light of their involvement in consultation on policies needed for the newly merged school, that they had little room to contribute to the SMT agenda.

Sixth, a corollary of pursuing mainly sectional interests outside the SMT and school wide interests inside was a disparity between the overview held variably among members within the team and the less comprehensive knowledge of school-wide issues which informed views expressed by other staff. Their responsibility as class teachers and less extensive management responsibility than that held by SMT members tended to reinforce the gap between breadths of perspective. Conversely, other staff had more detailed knowledge than SMT members of their own area of teaching and management. At Winton, one teacher perceived that SMT members had failed to capitalise on the expertise of other staff through sufficient consultation or encouragement to raise issues because of their priority to make so many major policy decisions:

> With the amalgamation it was very difficult. A lot of the members were feeling very much a 'them and us' syndrome. It was, like, the senior management team and then everybody else . . . I think a lot of the decisions are made with the senior management team to suit themselves and to suit their own needs. Then everyone else is told what to do and how we are going to do it. And I just look at the experience and the wealth of knowledge we have got from other members of staff in the school, who perhaps are not members of middle management but who are very experienced classroom teachers. Teachers with something more to offer, and that expertise isn't being used.

Seventh, other staff had most contact with their immediate colleagues, the SMT member responsible for their department, or other individual team members according to their management responsibility. Face-to-face interaction with the full team was restricted to public occasions like staff meetings and in-service training days, so other staff had limited exposure to the SMT culture of teamwork. That they, nevertheless, shared beliefs within the staff professional culture about how SMT members should 'do things around here' in public was revealed when team members at Pinehill failed to live up to their expectations, temporarily forfeiting credibility as a team capable of management. The deputy had announced new assessment procedures, developed without consultation, at a staff meeting. SMT colleagues with departmental responsibility had strongly criticised her in this very public forum. Other staff reportedly disapproved of departmental leaders being allowed by the head, who chaired the meeting, in effect to wash dirty SMT linen in public. One staff member hinted at the beliefs held by other staff about SMT public behaviour in these terms: 'The team needs to present a more united front at times. Conflict is not good for the health of the organisation and it has affected other members of staff, especially those who are sensitive to atmosphere.'

This incident suggests that other staff accepted their SMT on sufferance. Their continued compliance, even in these unprecedented circumstances at Pinehill, rested on inertia built up through their underlying belief in the management hierarchy. More active support for the SMT (necessary for achieving school-wide synergy) was contingent on team members acting in a manner which other staff perceived as befitting an SMT. Other staff in the four schools may not have liked the way SMT decision making excluded them at times, but it was widely viewed as the way things could be done within a management hierarchy. Playing out an SMT conflict in public overstepped the parameters of acceptable SMT behaviour for other staff. Such overtly expressed conflict was very rare, and the observations and interviews confirmed that here, as in the other SMTs, the team generally operated within the bounds of acceptability to colleagues outside the team.

Interaction between SMTs and other staff

Meetings were an important setting for SMT members to carry out linkage subtasks with other staff on behalf of the team. In these large schools, with their complex matrix management structures, many meetings involved one or more SMT members according to their management responsibility and other staff for whose work they were responsible (see Table 7.1). The most highly differentiated arrangements were at Winton, reflecting both the size of the school and its stage of development after the merger. Meetings for promoting curriculum development and planning covered each layer of the matrix management structure. They enabled SMT members to orchestrate curriculum development and implementation, giving extensive opportunities for the

Table 7.1 Pattern of meetings between SMT members, according to individual management responsibility, and other staff

Management meetings with other staff	Winton				Pinehill		Kingsrise	Waverley
Type of meeting	curriculum policy development	curriculum implementation	year leaders	subject coordinators	curriculum management group	department	department, ESL team	department
Participants: SMT members	all SMT members	deputy responsible for department	head and deputies	head and deputies	head and deputy (occasionally), curriculum leader	leader of department	leader of department, ESL team	leader of department
Other staff	one subject coordinator, year leaders	teachers in one year group within department	year leaders	subject coordinators	subject coordinators	other teachers in department	other teachers in department	other teachers in department
Frequency	one per subject	half-termly	three weekly	termly	weekly	three weekly	monthly	monthly
Timing	Tuesday, after school	variable day, after school	Tuesday, after school	Tuesday, after school	Thursday, after school	Monday, after school	Monday, inside lesson time	variable day, after school
Duration	three-quarters of an hour	one hour	one hour	one hour	one hour	one hour	half an hour	one hour
Purpose	subject coordinator presents final draft of subject policy	teachers present curriculum plans	year leaders present long-term plans	curriculum development	curriculum management	routine organisation and pastoral issues	curriculum, routine organisation and pastoral issues	curriculum, issues and schemes of work

linkage subtasks of consultation and ratification and of monitoring, along with dissemination of SMT expectations and response to issues raised by other staff with curriculum coordination responsibility.

Subject coordinators met together occasionally with the head and deputies, and also had their final draft of the subject policy they had developed in consultation with colleagues ratified at a meeting with the SMT and year leaders. The latter had responsibility for implementation in their year group, assisted and monitored through meetings with the deputy responsible for the department. Year leaders also met regularly with the head and deputies in another SMT monitoring exercise. Here they presented curriculum plans for their year groups which were expected to indicate how subject policies were being implemented. At Pinehill, structural links between the SMT and subject coordinators were very different. Here the curriculum leader held regular curriculum management team meetings with subject coordinators, which were occasionally attended by the head and deputy. She had become the main SMT link-person as a member newly invited into the team, positioned to carry out linkage subtasks connected with curriculum development. Most linkage with other staff for matters other than the curriculum operated through the system of department meetings, each led by an SMT member. Department meetings were also the main linkage structure at Kingsrise and Waverley, but here their purposes included curriculum development.

In addition to linkage meetings connected with SMT members' individual management responsibility, there were meetings designed to facilitate two-way communication with a wider group of other staff, summarised in Table 7.2. The four schools featured a regular staff meeting, but reliance was placed on it as a form for discussion at Waverley alone (the smallest institution). In the other schools, more work of dissemination, consultation and ratification, and giving opportunities for raising issues was done through parallel meetings of subgroups of the whole staff. It was noted above how they featured department meetings. The head at Pinehill was experimenting with five cross-phase group meetings, each consisting of staff drawn from across the three departments and one or two SMT members, as a means of extending the level of consultation with other staff in the policy-making process prior to SMT decisions being made. In three schools temporary working parties of volunteers had been set up which included one or more SMT members. Their brief was to develop proposals connected with a particular policy, from scratch or in the light of consultation, which would be taken to the rest of the staff to be ratified. Meetings could be for other purposes: at Winton school meals supervisory assistants met with each deputy to report on the lunchtime behaviour of pupils from their department; at Kingsrise the whole staff met regularly for staff development work.

Meetings created conditions for fulfilling SMT linkage subtasks but did not necessarily serve so well the sectional interests of other staff who did not share the overview of school-wide issues which led to SMT priorities. The urgency

Table 7.2 Pattern of general meetings between SMT members and other staff

General meetings with other staff	Winton			Pinehill			Kingsrise		Waverley	
Type of meeting	staff	school meals supervisory assistants	working party	staff	cross-phase group	working party	staff	staff development	staff	working party
SMT members involved	all SMT members	deputy for the head, juniors department	deputy	all SMT members	one SMT member per group	one SMT member	all SMT members	all SMT members	all SMT members	headteacher, deputy
Other staff involved	all other teachers	school meals supervisory assistants	group of three teachers	all other teachers	teachers from all three departments	group of other teachers	all other teachers	all other teachers	all other teachers and support staff	group of other teachers
Frequency	monthly	daily	irregular	half-termly	half-termly	fortnightly	half-termly	weekly	weekly	weekly
Timing	Tuesday, after school	lunchtime	after school	Monday, after school	Monday, after school	after school	Monday, after school	Thursday, after school	Wednesday, after school	after school
Duration	one and a half hours	quarter of an hour	one hour	one hour	one hour	one hour	one hour	one hour	one hour	one hour
Purpose	consulting and disseminating, subject teams consult on draft policy	pupil discipline	drawing up school aims after consulting teaching staff	consulting and disseminating	consulting on policy issues	formulating school development plan	consulting and disseminating	consulting and staff development activities	consulting and disseminating	developing a staff development policy

Note: All schools had five annual in-service training days attended by staff.

of putting a complete set of school policies into place after the merger at Winton had led to other staff being heavily involved in meetings for consultation and ratification. During the period of policy development, the head had reduced the number of meetings with subject coordinators and with year leaders, leaving little meeting space for them or their colleague teachers to raise issues. This arrangement transgressed the belief prevalent within the staff professional culture that other staff should be entitled to contribute part of the agenda addressed through the various meetings, engendering a sense of divorce between the interests of other staff (us) and the SMT (them). One teacher surmised:

> At times you feel they don't really want to know your opinion, it's more – I hesitate to use the word authoritarian, but its more – 'we need to impart this knowledge', or 'this is it'. And sometimes you feel it is not open to discussion, but fortunately there are some very vocal members of staff who won't tolerate that; they might raise issues that other people wouldn't, but want to.

Restoring a greater voice to other staff became perceived as an important issue which was raised with the SMT. Team members faced a dilemma over how far to pursue strategic school-wide priorities which were of less importance to other staff and how far to create meeting time empowering other staff to raise issues of less importance to team members, while avoiding adding to what one teacher described as the 'surfeit of meetings'. The juniors deputy commented:

> We have been aware that this has left us with a gap. But it's very difficult getting this balance between having too many meetings and keeping everything going. On the one hand, we are aware of it; on the other hand, staff are saying, 'Look, we don't think we are as well informed as we ought to be.' At the same time, they don't want to have more meetings, so it's just a case of balancing it really.

The SMT compromise was to increase time in staff meetings given over to raising issues, while attempting to keep up momentum with development of policies.

Face-to-face interaction between SMT members and other staff in meetings was complemented by multifarious informal encounters between individuals where information and opinion could be exchanged and SMT members could observe how other staff were operating in relation to team concerns. In terms of SMT linkage subtasks, this form of interaction gave other staff opportunities to raise issues which could be fed into the team agenda. Additionally, it enabled SMT members to disseminate information and monitor colleagues outside the team within the realm of their individual management responsibility.

SMT departmental responsibility was pivotal to SMT links with other staff in the four schools, as the latter most frequently sought attention of the team member responsible for managing their department. On occasion other SMT members, especially heads, were also approached. Most teachers and support staff were based in the same place during the school day, limiting their range of contact with colleagues. Two factors affected their level of access to the department manager. First, some SMT members encouraged informal contact more than others. Most were reportedly very approachable, though two, in different schools, were perceived as less receptive to overtures of staff in their department than colleague SMT members (so missing out on a source of information which could contribute to the SMT overview). Second, the proximity varied between department members' base and wherever SMT members with departmental responsibility habitually worked. Informal contact with departmental colleagues was less straightforward at Winton than in the other schools because the deputies were not class based and, though each had an office in their department, they spent little time there. Here, as at Pinehill and Kingsrise, the nature of the site meant that certain classrooms were located some distance from the base of the SMT member responsible for the department. One teacher in department two at Kingsrise pointed to how access to the department two leader 'around a class door' was restricted because their classrooms were in different buildings.

Reaching beyond responsiveness to initiating colleagues' participation in departmental management issues could empower SMT members as a form of cultural leadership, promoting school-wide synergy by encouraging other staff to work together towards established school aims. One teacher in the infant department at Winton spoke approvingly of the consultative style of the infants deputy:

> Wherever possible, [the infants deputy] will always come to me and discuss issues with me. And that makes me feel good about the job that I am doing as well, but it makes me feel that I have more responsibility within the school so I am more part of what is going on, and she always gives you the impression that she really respects your opinions.

Chance encounters in the staffroom were rare because most SMT members did not visit it regularly when other staff were present. Whether to do so appeared to be left to individuals: the special needs coordinator was the only member of the Winton SMT observed to spend lunchtime in the staffroom; the deputy at Pinehill made a point of visiting it.

Written forms of one-way communication were a feature of SMT interaction with other staff, mainly for the linkage subtask of disseminating information. They included minutes of SMT meetings at Pinehill and Waverley, posted up on the staffroom noticeboard. Most other staff interviewed confessed to being too busy to read them, possibly reflecting their priority sectional interest in their sphere of work. The head at Kingsrise wrote minutes which she placed in a file to which all staff had access. Staff outside the SMTs in the four schools reported that they gleaned information about matters they assumed had been discussed at SMT meetings through reports at staff or department meetings. The day book at Winton mentioned in earlier chapters, a notice sheet circulated to staff at the beginning of each week at Waverley, and a whiteboard in the staffroom of the four schools enabled SMT members to convey messages, having set the norm that other staff were responsible for reading them.

Contribution of other staff to making major decisions

The previous chapter examined how heads set different parameters for other SMT members to contribute to major decisions. Here the picture is completed by incorporating the contribution that other staff were empowered to make to particular stages in procedures set up by the heads, with reference to the account of such procedures in the survey. The analysis is tentative since observations and interviews were confined to a small sample of decisions. It appeared to confirm that whether and how staff outside the SMT were involved in decision making was contingent on a limited range of options. There was less diversity between SMTs in the pattern of involvement or exclusion of other staff than the internal contrast highlighted earlier between Winton and the other teams over heads' involvement of their SMT colleagues in decision making. In other words, the extent to which heads empowered colleague SMT members to contribute to transformational leadership, though variable, was still greater than such empowerment as they attempted to offer other staff. Any transformation of the staff professional culture promoted by heads, with and through the SMTs, was in the direction of ensuring that their practice lay within the heads' comfort zone which encompassed conforming to the boundaries of acceptability to governors, parents and inspectors.

Though procedures within the SMT at Winton were more egalitarian compared with the other teams, involvement of other staff featured only slightly less hierarchical ordering than at Pinehill, Kingsrise and Waverley. Consistent with their belief in a management hierarchy, the heads retained within the SMT the delegated authority to participate in – rather than advise on – making the bulk of final decisions. Analysis of procedures indicated that they featured similar stages to those identified in the accounts of survey respondents, though activities entailed in any stage were more complex and diverse than survey responses had indicated. Where other staff had some part to play, their involvement was very largely confined to consultation, formulation of proposals where related to their management responsibility, and ratification; only rarely did they have a hand in the initiation of major decisions. Their contribution to transformational leadership therefore differed in only a small degree, being more or less tightly restricted.

Several factors affected the contingent nature of decision-making pro-cedures. First, the national reforms constituted a pincer movement, squeezing room to manœuvre at school level over the range and content of decisions. They set the curriculum agenda and ensured it was followed through inspec-tion and publication of national tests. Much of the decision-making agenda was linked with central government requirements, while boundaries for alter-native courses of action were quite tightly prescribed. As the survey responses hinted, deciding *whether* to do things like compiling a school development plan or writing a policy for each area of the curriculum was not, realistically, an option. Parameters for decision making were restricted to *how* to implement them through making process decisions about the procedure to adopt and deciding on detailed content. So although heads were the immediate initiators of most major decisions, they were increasingly (though certainly not entirely) dancing to a central government tune.

Second, the site-level context and recent institutional history affected the need for particular decisions and the means of involving other staff in mak-ing them. It was documented earlier how the merger at Winton had spawned the priority of developing all policies for the newly created school, whereas most policies were in place in the other, longer-established institu-tions. Size of school, and therefore size of the staff, was equally significant for choice of procedures. The structures of meetings discussed above con-stituted, in part, strategies for intermediaries to represent the views of groups of other staff because it was impractical for all individuals to repre-sent themselves in the same forum. Consequently, some other staff could find themselves involved by proxy, or by their written submission, rather than face to face.

Third, heads' managerial beliefs and values about the appropriate level of involvement among other staff were of paramount importance because of their authority over decision-making procedures. Two implicit principles appeared to be variably adopted by heads. One was to involve other staff whose work would be most affected by the outcome of a major decision; another was to foster involvement of other staff according to how far they were perceived to have greater experience and expertise than SMT members. Except, perhaps, for department leaders at Pinehill, where the full SMT was not involved in curriculum decision making, heads generally allowed other team members more say in a wider range of major decisions than other staff. All four heads encouraged extensive involvement for certain kinds of decision.

Fourth, inclusion of particular stages in decision-making procedures varied according to which team tasks within the shared role of the SMT any deci-sion was most centrally related. Table 7.3 summarises one decision in each category identified in the case study schools where other staff were involved in some way. Most observed or mentioned in interviews fell into the three categories of:

Table 7.3 Categories and examples of major decisions addressed in each school

Category of major decision	Winton	Pinehill	Kingsrise	Waverley
Policy making	curriculum subject	marking	early years curriculum	dealing with bullying
Strategic planning	compiling school development plan	compiling school development plan	compiling school development plan	formulating post-inspection action plan
Routine organisation	pupil detention system	—	staff communication procedures	pupil record keeping
Management structure	middle management responsibilities	—	—	job descriptions for support staff

- formulating major *policies* affecting all or a subgroup of staff;
- creating formal, *strategic plans* affecting school-wide priorities for development;
- creating and modifying arrangements for school-wide *routine organisation*.

In addition, heads of two schools engaged both SMT members and other staff in decisions about modifying or clarifying *staff responsibilities within the management structure*. The requirement to include presenting a decision to governors for ratification in the decision-making procedure was also connected with these categories. Major policies and formal strategic plans were taken to the governing body after professional staff had completed their contribution.

A final factor affecting the contingent nature of decision making was whether staff outside the SMT were willing to accept the procedure proffered by senior staff and decision outcomes. In a small minority of instances, other staff had rejected a proposed SMT decision presented for ratification, result-ing in revision of the procedure to extend their involvement.

These factors shaped how particular decisions were made. Greatest involve-ment of other staff was built into the procedures for *formulating major policies* which shared many similarities (see Table 7.4). A background stimulus for initiation was knowledge that, whenever the school's turn to be inspected came, documentation on a prescribed range of policies and their impact on practice would be scrutinised. Consequently the heads were drivers of policy development. The member of teaching staff with management responsibility for the policy area led a process of consultation with some or all other staff, culminating in formulation of the proposed policy. One or more activities

Table 7.4 Involvement of staff outside the SMT in policy decision making

Stage in decision-making procedure	Winton (subject policies)	Pinehill (marking policy)	Kingsrise (early years)	Waverley (anti-bullying)
Initiation	SMT	head and deputy	head	head and deputy
Consultation	subject coordinator led subject team in drafting policy	discussion of head's and deputy's initial paper in cross-phase groups led by SMT member ↓ SMT members fed back at SMT meeting	department one leader led discussion in department of draft policy	discussion of deputy's initial questions at staff meeting led by deputy, staff divided into infant and junior groups
Proposal	subject coordinator wrote draft policy	deputy wrote draft policy	department one leader wrote draft policy	deputy collated comments and wrote draft policy
Ratification	draft policy discussed at staff meeting ↓ discussed in year group teams ↓ year leaders fed back year team views to subject coordinator ↓ subject coordinator amended draft	draft policy discussed in cross phase groups led by SMT member ↓ SMT members fed back comments at SMT meeting	department one leader presented draft policy at staff meeting	deputy presented draft policy at staff meeting
Final decision	subject coordinator presented policy to year leaders and SMT ↓ policy submitted to governors for approval	deputy amended draft in writing policy ↓ policy submitted to governors for approval	SMT member amended draft in writing policy ↓ policy submitted to governors for approval	deputy amended draft in writing policy ↓ policy submitted to governors for approval

concerned with ratifying the proposal gave all staff a chance to offer opinions on detailed elements of the proposal. The final decision was essentially made by the policy writer where he or she was a member of the SMT in the light of comments made at ratification. No SMT member at Winton had curriculum coordination responsiblity, the final decision being formally taken when the subject coordinator presented the amended policy to year leaders and the SMT. The procedure in this school alone empowered staff outside the SMT to participate in making the final decision though, even here, a proposal would not go through without SMT backing. In Table 7.4, the entries in italic type are those stages in each procedure where one or more SMT members participated, indicating how sometimes they included particular members, while at others, they involved the whole team. In each school, SMT members were empowered to monitor the procedure and shape the policy; in three schools one or more team members participated in each activity at every stage.

The procedure at Winton was also the only one where an SMT member did not take the lead. It was designed to maximise the use of expertise and curriculum coordination responsibility (delegated outside the SMT); to offer all teaching staff an input; to minimise time commitment of most staff, as several policies were being developed at once; and to ensure SMT members and year leaders participated at the end of the ratification stage of policies they would be responsible for implementing. The policies being developed in the other three schools happened to be ones where delegated responsibility fell to a member of the SMT, so here a team member was positioned to steer the procedure and play a major part from the outset in determining the content. Most extensive involvement of all staff was at Pinehill, where the head had introduced the framework of cross-phase groups for consultation and ratification in response to staff complaints about lack of opportunity to participate in previous decisions. Observation of these group meetings showed that the quality of the inputs made and fed into the next stage depended on the leadership of the SMT member responsible for chairing and recording views expressed. The head used a flipchart for recording, frequently checking what he was writing with the person whose comment it was. A department leader was observed to hurry colleagues through the meeting, stating at the beginning that 'this shouldn't take long', so constraining their opportunity to contribute, and writing notes without checking that what contributors had meant had been accurately recorded. These notes formed the basis of this group's input into the next part of the procedure, reported by the department leader in the SMT meeting that followed. The deputy produced a draft set of principles as a framework for other elements of the marking policy in the light of the consultation activities. She presented it to her cross-phase group so that they could ratify it but several members found it confusing. Concentration on the framework drew attention away from considering detailed proposals for marking procedures.

At Kingsrise, time commitment of staff was greatest for those responsible for and affected by the policy concerned. The department one leader steered the consultation stage for the early years curriculum policy. Staff involvement was confined to her colleagues in the department consistent with the principle that those with most expertise in the policy area, who would also be

responsible for its implementation, should be given the opportunity to contribute. All staff participated in ratifying the draft policy at a staff meeting.
The policy for counteracting bullying being developed at Waverley affected all
staff, who were both consulted and given the chance to ratify the draft policy
document. The consultation stage was led by the deputy, who would write the
policy, at a staff meeting where she set boundaries for debate by asking staff in
each department to respond to broad questions she had set.

Heads in each school were engaged in generating a form of *strategic plan*
required as a result of national reforms. In three cases, where the school development plan was being compiled, they had engineered process decisions to
allow some or all teaching staff outside the SMT to participate in a formal consultation exercise to identify development priorities and targets. Teaching staff
at Kingsrise each completed a form during a department meeting, and the
deputy had collated responses and reported them at a subsequent SMT meeting, as mentioned in the last chapter. Here SMT members could add their comments on the summative views of other staff, and discuss ways of working on
widely identified priorities. SMT members at Winton also organised a major
consultative exercise, distributing a questionnaire to other staff. They collated
the responses and drafted the plan together during SMT meetings. The consultative procedure at Pinehill operated through the curriculum management
team, giving primacy to the expertise of subject coordinators who fed in their
views on the subject for which they were responsible during a curriculum management team meeting. Within the SMT, therefore, the head, deputy and curriculum leader were centrally involved in this area of school-wide decision
making but department leaders were not. The head at Waverley also restricted
involvement of colleagues in producing the mandatory action plan for
improvement following the school inspection. It was recounted in the previous
chapter how he sought SMT members' comments on aspects of his draft plan,
a form of ratification, before it went to governors for approval. While staff
outside the team would be affected by its content, the head did not elect to
involve them directly, relying on their representation by SMT members
responsible for their department.

Where decisions on major policies reflected the principle of consulting
widely, those on matters of *routine organisation* in three schools reflected more
closely the principle of restricting involvement of staff outside the SMT in
decision making to those responsible for the area or whose work was most
affected. SMT members at Winton had devised the pupil detention system
which they would run without supervisory support from other staff, and
decided to trial it without consulting staff outside the team first. The SMT
decision at Kingsrise about improving procedures for disseminating information from the team to other staff was initiated by the head in response to feedback from staff about a problem with the design of the meetings' structure.
Apart from helping to identify the problem, staff outside the SMT were
not consulted about the solution. It seems likely that responsibility for

dissemination was seen as exclusively part of the shared SMT role, team members having a duty to revise the means of dissemination.

The experience of creating a unified system for keeping pupil records at Waverley was one instance where staff outside the SMT were empowered, through using influence, to reject an SMT proposal they found unacceptable. They triggered an SMT process decision to arrange for extensive consultation and ratification stages involving all staff outside the SMT who would be expected to implement the revised record-keeping system. The deputy had put forward a proposal for colleagues to ratify, to which they objected. The SMT response was to consult further, inviting staff to put forward their ideas. Several options were supported by different groups. Ratification was undertaken by trialling each proposal throughout the school for three weeks so that staff could evaluate all three, one receiving strong approval from most staff. This and the second most popular system were adapted to make them as similar as possible, and infants staff used one while juniors staff used the other. As the deputy observed: 'It takes a long time, but that way nobody feels that their idea is devalued.' Through their protest, staff outside the SMT had won a greater say through additional stages in the decision-making procedure which extended to participating in the final decision. The SMT process decision to rethink the procedure underlines how power is distributed: team members – and ultimately the head – depended on other staff being willing to work synergistically with them for the decision to be fully implemented.

Decisions to firm up or alter *staff responsibilities within the management structure* expressed the principle of involving solely the staff whose jobs would be affected and any colleagues with management responsibility for their work. The head at Waverley instigated the construction of job descriptions for support staff, enlisting the help of members of the 'staff professional-development policy' working party which he chaired. The group of three SMT members – himself, the deputy and the infants leader (most support staff worked in her department) was supplemented by a general assistant who represented the support staff. The head proceeded, characteristically, by seeking to ratify the relevant section in the policy document he had prepared. He then worked through individual support staff job descriptions with the general assistant and infants leader.

The decision to alter the management responsibilities of teachers with two salary increments at Winton took the same principle a step further by including all these members of staff in face-to-face discussion with the head. The sequence of activities in the various stages is summarised in Table 7.5 below. The proposal grew out of concern expressed by the deputies over lack of any intermediate tier of staff with management responsibility for dealing with disruptive pupil behaviour. The head was equally concerned that the emphasis of curriculum policy development responsibilities shouldered by staff with two salary increments was declining as policies were put in place. Consultation took place entirely within the SMT: the issue was debated at an off-site

Table 7.5 Stages in decision to alter management responsibilities at Winton

Stage in decision-making procedure	Decision-making activity
Initiation	within SMT – deputies voiced concern over responsibilities of teachers with two salary increments in SMT meeting
Consultation	within SMT – SMT-meeting agenda item to develop proposal for changing responsibilities
Proposal	SMT proposal to create middle management departmental responsibilities, head wrote consultation document
Ratification	head discussed proposal and document at meeting with staff with two salary increments ↓ head interviewed each teacher with two salary increments to review individual job description
Final decision	head revised proposal and job descriptions ↓ revised proposal and job descriptions submitted to governors for approval

extended SMT meeting and the head then wrote a proposal in the form of a consultation document. She suggested to her SMT colleagues the process decision that she meet staff with two salary increments alone, because she perceived that they might feel intimidated in expressing their views if all SMT members were present: 'I accept that the women in the team [SMT] are four strong women and that staff could say, "There's a wall, there are four of them; you try and get past that."' She noted how she had adopted a contingency approach to ratification. The full SMT would be paraded for other decisions where it suited her interest for other staff to perceive that the SMT had made a decision which they would not be invited to ratify. (This strategy was not made explicit to other staff, but was legitimate within the head's beliefs and values and so, for her, not manipulative within the definition adopted in Chapter 2.) She introduced the proposal at this meeting and followed it up by meeting with each individual to examine the implications for her or his job description, securing a favourable response which enabled her to put forward a revised proposal and job descriptions for approval by governors.

Analysis of SMT decision making in the case study schools supports the account of two-fifths of the survey respondents that procedures were contingent within limits. It points to key factors affecting the process decisions that heads were uniquely placed within the management hierarchy to make over parameters and boundaries for involving SMT colleagues and other staff, determining which stages to include and who could participate in them. The procedures explored in this chapter did not match exactly those identified in the survey (see Table 3.10), mainly because more detail was discernible than survey responses specified. It was possible to make a comparison between the case study schools, however, according to which, if any, members of staff these heads involved in the stages which had differentiated the types of procedure in the survey. These types referred only to those decisions where survey respondents did involve the rest of the SMT in some way. It was discussed in previous chapters how the case study school heads varied in the range of decisions they took unilaterally or with the deputy, the head at Winton allowing a wider range of decisions to fall within the remit of the SMT and empowering her team colleagues to make a more equal contribution than the others. It also appears that, though other staff were clearly able to make a less equal contribution than members of the SMT, the head nevertheless empowered other staff responsible for and affected by particular decisions to make a slightly greater contribution compared with their counterparts in the other schools. It extended, with curriculum policies, to participating in making the final decision. The range of procedures lay between an approximation to type C in Table 3.10 (where involvement in deciding on the introduction of the detention system was confined to SMT members) to an approximation to type G (where other staff were both consulted and some participated in making the final decision on curriculum policies).

The other case study heads made more decisions unilaterally and, at Pinehill, in conjunction with the deputy. These decisions were more top-down in orientation than the most hierarchical in the survey (beyond type A where full SMT involvement was confined to the consultation stage). Of those where all SMT members were involved, procedures ranged from an approximation to type A (as where the head at Waverley consulted other SMT members on the post-inspection action plan) to type F (where other staff in the three schools were involved in the consultation and ratification of policies but the final decision was retained within the SMT). An exception was the decision on record keeping at Waverley, which became closer to type G after staff had rejected the original proposal. They were then able to trial different approaches and participate in the final decision.

These few examples show how, in line with the survey results, different balances were struck in the procedures adopted between a top-down orientation consistent with heads' belief in a management hierarchy and a bottom-up dimension reflecting a belief that all staff had potential to make an equal contribution (see Figure 3.4). The speculation made in Chapter 3 was confirmed that heads set norms for the procedure to be used in different circumstances (except where the objection of other staff persuaded them to change their mind). The range of procedures did appear to vary with the relative strength of their belief in a management hierarchy and in equal contribution of colleagues inside and outside the SMT, and this variation did lie within limits. The head at Winton followed norms that other SMT members should participate equally in almost all decisions. Other staff should be consulted and involved in ratifying or even participating in making final decisions in the area of their expertise and which directly affected their responsibilities and their everyday work. The balance between the top-down and bottom-up orientations of the other heads gave more emphasis to the top-down, following the norm that they should take a larger range of decisions alone (or, especially at Pinehill, with the deputy). Where other SMT members were to be involved, it was appropriate for their contribution to be hierarchically ordered (exemplified by the propensity of heads to confine colleagues' involvement to ratifying their proposals). Other staff should be consulted on and should ratify only decisions where they had expertise and which directly affected their responsibilities and their work. The fact that decision-making procedures at Winton appeared to lie between types C and G and those elsewhere from outside type A (where they were unilateral) to type F (except where other staff successfully protested), suggests that, despite the external pressure from national reforms, significant room to manœuvre remained for heads over the balance they adopted between a top-down and bottom-up approach to decision making.

Demarcation and SMT credibility

Staff outside the teams variably conveyed their sense of a hierarchical demarcation between senior staff and themselves in terms of their relative involvement in managing the school. It was expressed through comments about 'them' or 'the management' who were centrally involved in managing and 'us' or 'the staff', more concerned with teaching their class and dependent on senior staff for management information. This comment from a teacher at Kingsrise captures the sense of demarcation:

> Sometimes issues are discussed that we are unaware of, and we find out later about issues that we would have liked to have known about sooner. This can create a bit of an 'us and them' situation where the senior management know everything and occasional snippets are passed to the ones at the bottom.

Differences within the SMTs were highlighted earlier between the relatively equal contributions made by team members at Winton and the more hierarchical order of contributions in the other three schools. A strong demarcation *inside* the SMT was perceived in the latter. Demarcation lines inside the teams and between them and other staff coincided with the distinction between professional staff who had responsibility for a class and those who did not, as Figure 7.1 depicts. The most senior staff without a class were managers first and foremost; staff outside the SMT were class teachers, some of whom did a bit of management on the side; while SMT members with a class had to juggle substantial management responsibility and their class-teaching load.

There was a single, almost clear cut demarcation between the SMT and

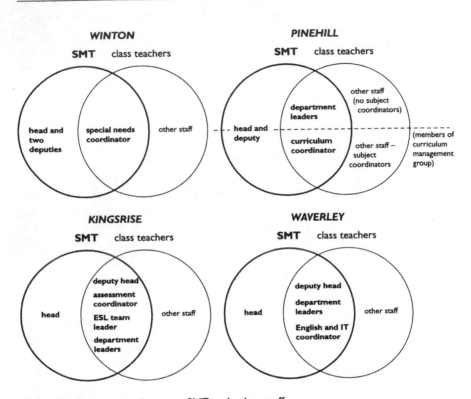

Figure 7.1 Demarcation between SMT and other staff

other staff at Winton, the special needs coordinator alone having a foot in both camps. The situation at Pinehill was complicated by exclusion of the full SMT from curriculum management. When the curriculum leader left the school and the deputy took over formal responsibility for leading the curriculum management team, this shift of responsibilities reinforced the internal demarcation between the head–deputy partnership and department leaders. There was greater overlap between staff who were class teachers and SMT members in Kingsrise and Waverley, the smallest schools.

The extensive sharing of management tasks and strong cohesion within the team at Winton had the unintended consequence of helping to foster the perception among other staff of one in-group (the SMT) with themselves as the out-group, commonly including the special needs coordinator on their side of the demarcation line. Elsewhere, the more hierarchical approach created the perception of a demarcation within the SMT as well as between it and other staff, and so blurred the in-group/out-group distinction because it was based on multiple demarcation lines. The potential for school-wide synergy could be inhibited because of the consequence of any group of staff developing a shared belief that they were an out-group and disadvantaged by another group. Such a focus could stimulate establishment of a dissident subculture whose adherents could form a coalition, using influence to undermine efforts of the perceived 'in-group'. Ironically, the single and almost clear-cut distinction between the SMT and other staff at Winton provided conditions favouring such a perception among all staff outside the team, uniting them around one shared sectional interest. The multiple demarcations in the other, more hierarchically managed schools provided conditions for more disparate subcultures, each shared by a smaller number of SMT members and other staff with a more narrowly defined sectional interest. Arguably, the risk of antagonistic polarisation between the SMT and other staff was greatest at Winton, whereas the multiplicity of groupings elsewhere could be conceived as having a 'divide and rule' effect, lowering the risk of an antagonistic subculture emerging around a single 'SMT versus the rest' axis. For other staff at Winton, 'them' always meant the SMT, though the special needs coordinator was often left out of the reckoning; elsewhere it might mean the entire SMT or the head and deputy. Rather than on 'them', perceptions of where the principal demarcation lay frequently referred to 'him' or 'her' – to the head alone.

Whatever the pattern of demarcation, the incident of public conflict within the SMT at Pinehill reported above showed how there was potential for the credibility of the SMT with other staff to come under threat. The support of staff outside the SMT, on which team members depended if school-wide synergy was to be achieved, was conditional on their perception that SMT members were doing an acceptable job as a team. The possibility of a credibility gap arose for the teams because much of their joint work was done in private, other staff having to trust that they were not being manipulated when, say, consulted prior to a final decision being made within the team. That part of the teams' performance which was public was open to scrutiny of other staff, SMT credibility depending on team members behaving in a way which other staff found acceptable. Consequently, heads were particularly concerned to promote a culture of teamwork that would ensure the SMT had good 'street-cred' with other staff. They very largely succeeded, helped by the strength of the belief of other staff in the management hierarchy such that a loss of credibility was much more likely to fuel quiet cynicism than overt antipathy, and minimal compliance rather than revolution. Several areas of SMT activity or inactivity could help to bolster or undermine the credibility of the team.

First, as already discussed, approaches to decision making gave staff outside the teams a hierarchically subordinate part to play. Their participation in ratifying proposals enabled them to see more directly whether their contributions were reflected in the final decision and helped avoid situations where they might perceive their views did not count. Heads and deputies without a class-teaching responsibility were particularly vulnerable to the perception among other staff that they were out of touch with members on the shop floor;

consultation – as long as it was considered genuine – had the symbolic value of demonstrating an SMT concern to learn from those who perceived that they knew best what it was really like in classrooms.

Second, it was equally important to create conditions for two-way communication through linkage subtasks between SMT and other staff which were seen to work. It was noted how failure to disseminate information at Kingsrise had brought critical feedback precipitating the SMT decision about improving communication with other staff. At Winton, individual staff outside the SMT indicated their resentment where they had received mixed messages from team members, exemplified where they were informed about changes at the last moment which they believed team members could have disseminated earlier:

> There is sometimes a case of, 'Well, does it matter?' [coming from SMT members] – when it does matter to the class teacher. We are told to plan in advance and plan on a weekly basis, and then we are told we have to be flexible.

Here it was implied that SMT members did not always practise what they preached. A high value was placed on planning in the kind of staff professional culture that team members sought to inculcate. Yet it was apparently contradicted where they did not seem to other staff to have planned ahead themselves. Equally, consistency of SMT messages was viewed as a characteristic of effective teamwork, reflecting beliefs and values within the staff professional culture about obligations of the SMT:

> There were earlier contradictions which did not reflect a team approach at all. Obviously, that was more to do with a lack of communication and finding out what they needed to impart to people, and that needs to be consistent. It was that lack of consistency and contradiction that stopped them being a team really, and generally I think they are a more coherent team than they have been in the past.

Approachability of any team member was strongly valued and conversely, as mentioned earlier, being perceived as unapproachable cost individual SMT members dear in terms of lost opportunities to carry out linkage subtasks and the goodwill and respect of other staff on which synergy could be built. Even being ready to bend the general rule that teachers should speak first to their department leader on management issues, to suit the personal interests of other staff, could foster a perception that SMT members were supportive of colleagues outside the team. The four heads and, more variably, the deputies were reported as being willing to respond to the request of other staff to see them about their concerns, so bypassing their department leader. At Winton, one teacher indicated that it was possible to use influence to manipulate the

SMT: 'Although they do work closely as a team, I suppose it is a bit of working the system, they work very much as a team but you can work on them individually.' If money was needed to buy resources, this teacher would go to the head, rather than to a deputy, because she was seen as a softer touch. Other staff could use influence to divide and rule the SMT on such minor matters.

Third, team members presenting a united front on final decisions taken within the SMT was important to other staff, a teacher at Winton reflecting: 'They are very together and support each other in decisions that are made. There is no "Well, such a person decided on this but we don't agree." They are as one when decisions are made.' It was also appreciated where individual team members were honest about what had taken place in the private arena. According to another teacher at Winton, SMT members were ready to admit where there had been a difference of views within the team but also expressed cabinet responsibility for SMT decisions, by stating: 'That isn't my view, but the decision has been made and that is how we have to work.'

Fourth, SMT members were expected to offer cultural leadership when visible to other staff. Beginning teachers, as recounted earlier, did not see as much of SMT members as they would like. Visits to classrooms would constitute cultural leadership through symbolising team members' interest in colleagues' work. A teacher at Winton pointed to the consequences of the team seeming remote in this very large school: 'I think there is a feeling that some people have that you only get direct contact when things go wrong. In a management of people way you don't feel they are looking after you.' As other staff rarely saw SMT members together, on such occasions their behaviour as a group could symbolise how far the SMT was an entity with a unified purpose. SMT members at Winton arranged a major consultation exercise for the entire teaching staff on ideas to be incorporated in the design of the new school building. A coach trip was organised to visit a newly built school during an in-service training day. Team members were observed to act in unison throughout the visit to give colleagues the fullest possible opportunity to see round the school. They demonstrated that they both cared about the comfort of other staff and genuinely wished to gather their views by:

- providing staff with a set of questions prepared by the head to help frame their deliberations on design issues;
- making tea and coffee and arranging lunch;
- inviting each year group team of teachers to tour the school and come up with suggestions;
- walking round individually, discussing points and listening to opinions expressed by their colleagues;
- responding to a request from two teachers to change the order of activities so that all staff could ask questions of the SMT before having a second and more focused look round.

The deputies and special needs coordinator fed opinions expressed to them during the day back to the head, so that they would be taken into account. The head indicated to other staff that she was working in their interests with others responsible for designing their new school to ensure classrooms were large enough and teachers would have sufficient storage provision, her endeavour symbolising her support for their concerns.

In sum, SMT credibility could never be assured while a private SMT arena was retained, but it could be fostered and situations avoided which might open up a credibility gap. Other staff were unlikely to rebel if the SMT did lose credibility, but their active support needed by the heads and their SMT colleagues to promote school-wide synergy depended on the perception of other staff that the behaviour of all team members was exemplary and that the SMT was a synergistic whole working with and for them rather than against them.

Unequal partnership with parents and governors

Parental involvement is characteristic of primary schools, whether working there, fund raising, attending school productions and other public events or, for those escorting younger children to and from school, having daily contact. Most parents in the case study schools interacted with the SMTs only in so far as they had contact with individuals according to their management and teaching responsibilities, who might report back to team colleagues. Occasionally, an issue might arise where representations made by parents led to substantial management activity involving the SMT. Parents at Waverley expressed misgivings about the prospect of mixed age classes being introduced, prompting extensive consultation and negotiation which culminated in the head making the final decision to go ahead.

The other major channel for voicing parental concerns was through their representatives on the governing body. Even here, as noted in Chapter 4, external linkages between the SMT and governors, including the parent representatives, were routed through the heads and, in three schools, the deputy or deputies. Heads and other SMT members were accountable to the governing body, designed by legislation to cut across the management hierarchy through teacher representatives elected by the staff. SMT members other than heads who had regular contact with governors had either teacher governor status, or – for the deputy at Pinehill – observer status. Staff representation, together with that of parents, the local community and the LEA, provided a formal check on the activities of heads. Yet the odds of influencing professional practice in school were stacked in heads' favour.

First, the profile of governors elected by staff to represent them was weighted in two schools towards the most senior staff. At Winton, all staff governors were SMT members; at Waverley, the head and deputy outnumbered the other teacher governor; at Pinehill, the head was supported by the deputy; and only at Kingsrise was the head the sole representative from the SMT attending governors' meetings. Second, the authority of heads over everyday management empowered them to delimit information presented to the governing body. They wrote the regular headteacher's report, they had a hand in setting the governing body agenda within the framework set by LEAs, and could set the norm that communication initiated by governors from outside the staff should be channelled, in the first instance, through them. Third, they were empowered through a shared interpretation of the balance of authority for management among senior staff and chairs of governors to lead on professional matters, but within a framework of budgetary, staffing and premises decisions in which governing bodies were more fully involved. Policies connected with curriculum and teaching were developed by the professionals, but had to be justified before receiving formal approval. Chairs of governors were primarily concerned to support the staff, who were the main source of initiatives.

The sense of a clear demarcation between the province of staff and governors was made explicit by the chair at Waverley: 'I perceive it's the head and senior management's role to manage the school, and it's not for me to stick my nose in and to keep asking: "What are you doing and how are you doing it?"' This demarcation was permeable to the extent that heads and other professional staff were prepared to inform the governing body and the latter sought this kind of information, supplemented by anything gleaned from other sources such as individual parents. The complex relationship of distinctive and overlapping zones of policy and of practice between governing bodies, the SMTs and other staff is depicted in Figure 7.2. Permeability of the demarcation between professional staff and governors is represented by the central area of triple overlap: that part of the SMT and other staff arenas made public to the governing body. The SMTs retained a private arena, which could expand or shrink depending on what individual members divulged: the internal SMT conflict at Pinehill spilled over into the area that was public to other staff (the permeable area of demarcation between the SMT and other staff arenas indicated in the lowest area of overlap in the diagram). Governors who were not employed in the school had become aware through various sources, though the issue was never discussed in any governors' forum.

As with internal linkages, meetings were the main forum for communication, largely determined by legislation. They enabled heads and other staff representatives to carry out their external linkage subtasks of monitoring other governors' concerns and, selectively, informing them. Alongside full governing body meetings were subcommittees which heads and, at Winton and Waverley, deputies who were teacher governors might also attend. Formal presentations by SMT members other than the head related to their management responsibility were a means of informing governors at three schools. Other contact was through meetings supplemented by telephone contact between the head and

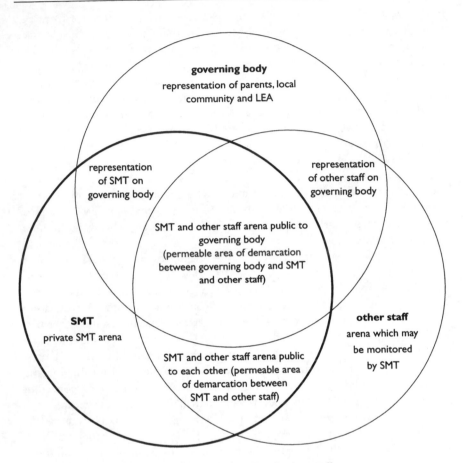

Figure 7.2 Relationship between governors, SMT and other staff

chair of governors, which took place very frequently in three schools, but less often at Kingsrise (see Table 7.6).

This pattern of meetings, when compared with the much more frequent meetings held within SMTs and between them and other staff, underlines how the SMTs were mainly concerned with internal management. Linkage with governors was hierarchically differentiated among team members: only those with highest formal status – heads and, in three schools, the deputies – had much to do with the contribution of the governing body to managing the school. Heads' authority within the governance structure may have been confined to their responsibility for everyday management, but they retained a leading position in the orchestration of school development. They used influence to steer the flow of information into the arena public to the governing body, variably supported by other SMT members, and assisted by the belief among chairs of governors that this should indeed be their role.

Table 7.6 Pattern of meetings between SMT members and governors

Type of meeting	Winton	Pinehill	Kingsrise	Waverley
Governing body	headteacher (governor) deputies (teacher governors)	headteacher (governor) deputy (observer status) individual SMT members occasionally make presentations	headteacher (governor) individual SMT members occasionally make presentations	headteacher (not governor) deputy (teacher governor) individual SMT members occasionally make presentations
Governing body subcommittees	headteacher (finance and personnel) juniors deputy (premises) infants deputy (curriculum)	headteacher attends all subcommittee meetings	headteacher attends all subcommittee meetings	headteacher attends all subcommittee meetings deputy (staffing and finance)
Chair of governors	chair and headteacher meet monthly, telephone contact weekly	chair and headteacher meet weekly	chair and headteacher or deputy occasionally have informal discussion	chair and headteacher meet weekly, interim telephone contact

Achieving school-wide synergy – an uphill task

The findings reported in this chapter portray the intricate nature of the unequal but wide distribution of power in and around the schools, related to the beliefs and values shared by diverse groups of stakeholders inside and external to the SMTs and other staff. Heads were clearly the most powerful figures at school level, but very far from all powerful. Their authority gave them an advantage but their credibility, so necessary for support of staff and governors on which they depended, rested on far more than that. Support had to be gained and sustained through influence in a high-risk environment. For heads, seeking school-wide synergy meant that other SMT members, staff outside the team and governors had to support them in going down a path where the content of their comfort zone was increasingly dominated by central government reforms. The national policy thrust to create a high-risk environment where heads' survival depended on ensuring that the work of other staff meets externally imposed requirements militated against their opting for transformational leadership which extended much beyond the SMT. Inviting contributions from all staff to a shared vision makes much managerial sense only in an environment where there is sufficient school-level autonomy for realistic choice between alternative visions expressing different beliefs and values.

In this hostile context, SMTs offered a strategy for empowering the heads to impact on every aspect of the school in a more restrictive approach to transformational leadership. Meetings to achieve linkage subtasks enabled them to reach out through colleague SMT members towards other staff and, where deputies were involved, to governors. The heads had to find a balance that other staff would accept between top-down and bottom-up orientations to decision making. A top-down thrust lowered the risk that empowering other staff might result in their pursuing sectional interests which would not meet with external approval. But it also lowered the potential for school-wide synergy through staff ownership of decisions. A bottom-up thrust raised the risk of going off the externally approvable rails, but also increased the chance of achieving school-wide synergy. It seems that heads designed SMTs to extend their ability to promote their version of school-wide synergy by facilitating their omnipresence in the face of the complexities presented by the combination of institutional size, with the inevitability of some demarcation favouring perceptions of in-groups and out-groups; the plethora of management tasks; the potential minefield of sectional interests among a diversity of stakeholders; and the overarching priority to keep on the right side of central government on the one hand and parents and the local community on the other. How well did these contrasting team approaches to management work? Some tentative answers are sought in the final chapter.

Chapter 8

SMT synergy or bust?

A picture has been built up of the prevalence, characteristics and diversity of operation of senior management teams in large primary sector schools. The survey of headteachers provided a way into the world of primary school SMTs and suggested that they have become a central component of management structures in most of these institutions. They represent, in part, a response to expansion of management tasks in a high-risk environment of increasing external accountability brought by central government reforms. The four case studies of SMTs whose members professed a commitment to a team approach to management enabled details of teamwork to be explored from the differing perspectives of key players, backed by limited observation of SMTs at work. A combined cultural and political perspective on interaction has been employed as a tool for understanding the complexities of what goes on inside the SMTs and between their members and other staff. The largely qualitative research design was intended to enable the phenomenon of primary school SMTs to be examined in some depth, not to provide a basis for generalisation about the typical SMT.

Here themes from the introductory chapter are revisited and ideas brought together which emerged from the research findings. First, against the backdrop of difficulties inherent in any attempt to establish effectiveness of SMTs, the brief discussion in Chapter 3 of survey respondents' views of effectiveness is augmented through an account of judgements on the effectiveness of the case study SMTs, linking the criteria employed to the model of the SMT role. Second, ideas are developed about characteristics of SMTs, beginning with an assessment of how far the case study SMTs complied with the definitions of teams in the first chapter. An additional element is put forward which the research implies should be incorporated in definitions of teams. Third, a series of linked hypotheses is offered about effective SMT practice, informed by the research findings, as a stimulus for reflection and improving teamwork in the management of large primary schools. Fourth, a speculative contingency model of interaction within SMTs is offered which suggests how heads may most effectively work towards the holy grail of high synergy within teams, arguably offering the best chance of bringing about school-wide synergy while reducing some of the risks a team approach can entail. Fifth, implications for research and theory building are briefly aired, evaluating the combined cultural and political perspective as a heuristic device for getting beneath the surface of interaction in school management or other organisational settings. Finally, implications of the research are considered for four areas of policy: the managerialist thrust to reform management in the public sector; the relative disadvantage of primary school SMTs compared with their secondary counterparts because of their lower level of funding; the inequitable representation of women in senior management positions likely to include SMT membership; and provision of training which might promote effective teamwork.

Towards SMTs that work

It is important, initially, to clarify how far the scope of the research allows characteristics of effective SMTs to be identified. It is not possible to determine which team structures and processes will be effective under specific circumstances. Criteria for judging perceived effectiveness in management can be easily obtained (Bolam *et al.* 1993), but a gulf remains between effective management and effective education. The former does not necessarily produce the latter. Given the distribution of power within schools, it is as plausible to conceive of an effective SMT doing the right things in the face of poor quality teaching of uncommitted staff as it is to conceive of effective teaching by inspired staff which triumphs over poor leadership from a disorganised SMT. Further, though there has been massive international investment in school effectiveness research (Teddlie and Reynolds 1998) this edifice is constructed on the shaky foundation of slippery and ideologically driven notions of effectiveness (Slee and Weiner 1998). How many educationalists would value equally any style of management – top-down, bottom-up or hands off – as long as pupils learned effectively? How many central government ministers would regard a school as effective where staff worked synergistically to downplay or ignore their reforms?

Even if agreement could be obtained on what counts as effective management, teaching and learning, it is no simple task to prove that, say, headteachers' actions as SMT creators, principal developers and monitors at one end of the causal chain bring about valued pupil learning and social outcomes at the other. There are extra links – not least the constraining or enabling impact of mandatory national reforms on the parameters for school management – and intermediate links, like the impact of SMT management activity on teaching and the impact of teaching on pupil learning. Even a major correlational study, which might have identified which team practices were associated with which added-value measures of pupil learning, could not demonstrate conclusively that any coincidence between factors was causal and, if so, how this association worked. The causal chain according to which faith in SMTs has been constructed is too long for simple cause–effect linkages to be incontrovertibly established. It is possible, more modestly, to report perceptions of SMT effectiveness among staff and chairs of governors interviewed. Their views were as impressionistic as the responses of heads in the survey, staff with little or no management responsibility being least aware of the SMT contribution – and least interested at Kingsrise and Waverley, as long as they were not inhibited from doing their classwork. This source of evidence did yield a summary picture for each SMT consistent with findings presented in previous chapters:

- Winton – the team was regarded from inside and outside the SMT as fully or quite effective, the main criticism from other staff being that team members had not consulted them sufficiently following the merger;
- Pinehill – the team was seen by informants across the school as only moderately effective so far, though still evolving, because of disunity between the head and deputy partnership and the department leaders and, for the latter, lack of clarity about their individual management responsibilities;
- Kingsrise – the team was viewed by SMT members as fully effective but by others as only quite effective because the head was so forceful and SMT members did not disseminate enough information to staff outside the team;
- Waverley – the team was perceived as effective by informants throughout the institution, SMT members other than the head appreciating being able to have their say, though raising a question over the head's forcefulness, others having variable difficulty in pinpointing why the team worked so well apart from being appreciative of the supportive relationships established between them.

Criteria informing these judgements were implicit in the reasons given. Their variety was analysed by categorising reasons for judgements. There were no incompatibilities between those originating with interviewees from different schools, so a combined list was compiled (see Table 8.1). These criteria have been divided into positive, associated with perceived SMT effectiveness, and negative, linked with inhibition of effectiveness. They encompass:

- inputs to the teams – characteristics of individual members and the structure and combined features of the group;
- SMT process and tasks – embracing internal operation including team tasks and relationships with other staff and governors through linkage subtasks;
- SMT outputs – split into the direct and indirect outcomes of the teamwork process and tasks.

There was overlap between criteria employed by SMT members and others: those in normal type were mentioned solely by team members; those in

Table 8.1 Criteria for judging perceived effectiveness of case study SMTs

Aspect of SMT	Positive criteria	Negative criteria
Input: individual team members	competent in SMT role *individuals have good interpersonal skills* competent in classroom	lack of training in management *individuals unable to make good relationships*
Input: group	clearly defined responsibilities within SMT complementary skills	***unclear responsibilities within SMT*** SMT excluded from curriculum management
SMT role: teamwork process and team tasks	all members contribute to debate shared sense of humour positive relationships good communication head protected by other SMT members *all SMT members collaborate*	***head dominates internal hierarchy*** personal disputes within SMT fail to communicate openly some SMT members do not accept head's ultimate responsibility for decisions bogged down with detailed administration
SMT role: linkage subtasks	***good communication with others*** ***SMT members united in public*** ***SMT members approachable and accessible*** *SMT support and encourage involvement of other staff* *SMT members protect other staff* *SMT members foster consistent practice* representation of all other staff on SMT	***poor communication with other staff*** *SMT members disunited in public* *individual SMT members unapproachable or inaccessible* *fail to consult other staff sufficiently and harness their expertise* *head out of touch with other staff* *head and deputy exclude other staff from decision making* *head does not delegate enough to other staff* *individuals unpraising of other staff* fail to gain support of other staff no time to socialise with other staff
SMT outputs: direct	identify important issues abundance of joint decisions *develop good documentation*	fail to monitor implementation of SMT decisions
SMT outputs: indirect	*ensure educational provision is coherent* *ensure school runs smoothly*	

normal italic type were the exclusive concern of other staff and chairs of governors, and those in bold italic type were mentioned by both SMT members and others.

They complement criteria reported by heads in the survey (Table 3.12) and reflect findings from the case studies discussed earlier. Some positive criteria are matched by their negative correlate, as where the opportunity for all SMT members to contribute to debate is applauded by team members but strongly hierarchical team leadership by the head which excludes other members from full participation is rejected by team members and other staff alike. Others, such as sharing a sense of humour within the SMT, have no negative correlate because none was mentioned. The list is far from exhaustive, since it seems highly plausible that the opposite of any positive criterion would be given a negative rating (such as SMT members not sharing a sense of humour) and *vice versa*. Not surprisingly, informants dwelt on aspects of team operation with which they were most familiar. Conversely, the understandably limited breadth of their perspectives is suggested by the paucity of references to SMT outputs, whether direct, like making joint decisions, or indirect, as in bringing about a smoothly running institution. Criteria were almost entirely about input, process and tasks, no criteria mentioned relating to any effort to monitor team performance in terms of outputs. Team members emphasised areas intrinsic to fulfilling the SMT role: input, teamwork process and team tasks. Outsiders' criteria reflected their experience of SMT linkage subtasks, concentrating on external relationships and characteristics of individual team members' performance in relation to other staff. Greatest overlap occurred where insiders and outsiders interacted through these linkage subtasks (as indicated by the criteria in bold italic type in Table 8.1).

The crucial importance of establishing a positive relationship between the SMT and other staff discussed in the last chapter is underscored from the contrasting perspectives of these groups, mirroring the most common criterion expressed by survey respondents. Team members and others sought to realise somewhat different interests through the work of the SMTs, which were compatible only where a mutually desired balance was achieved between the top-down and bottom-up orientations underpinning team practice in decision making. Staff outside the SMTs looked to them for protection, and expected team members to be ready to respond to their needs, to consult them where their work would be affected, and to work harmoniously with each other in public. They disapproved where they were aware of heads operating hierarchically within the team and in relation to outsiders. Team members looked to carry out the SMT role through extensive participation, those other than heads – like other staff – being critical where heads were seen to deny them the opportunity to contribute fully, and both heads and team colleagues were acutely aware of their dependence on winning support of other staff. The relatively hierarchical approach to carrying out the SMT role adopted by three heads was less favoured by their team colleagues than the relatively egalitarian approach at Winton. These judgements suggest that the strong value within the staff professional culture placed on participating in management in recent decades remains strong despite the directive view of management centring on heads embodied in official documents, including those relating to inspection.

The inspection framework included scrutiny of the teams within a focus on 'leadership and management'. How did the case study SMTs fare in the eyes of inspectors? It should be remembered that this source of evidence about SMT effectiveness is as subject to limitations as were the interviews and observation. First, Winton and Kingsrise were inspected after fieldwork ended and practice in their SMTs was likely to have evolved; second, the operation of SMTs constituted a minor focus for inspectors; third, they could gather only a small amount of observational or interview data during their lightning tour on site; and finally, staff would have been aware when communicating with inspectors that the purpose of the exercise was to evaluate them, rather than to understand the trials and tribulations of their practice through research. Explicit reference to SMTs was brief but, as would be expected, the emphasis of their remarks echoed guidance for inspectors highlighted in Chapter 1 that senior staff and heads (together with governors) were there to set the direction for other staff to follow (see Table 8.2). Approval was given where SMT members were seen to work synergistically and strategically, with a clear division of individual responsibilities, and with directive links which extended to monitoring other staff but also allowed for some consultation. Conversely, criticism was aimed at heads judged not to have delegated enough tasks to their SMT colleagues, suggesting that there was a limit to the degree of hierarchical operation that inspectors deemed effective. There was minimal focus on SMT outputs.

To summarise: from the perspectives of staff inside and outside the teams and chairs of governors, coupled with the views of inspectors, the four teams were judged to be at least reasonably effective at Pinehill, effective though constrained by the heads' strong hierarchically oriented leadership at Kingsrise and Waverley, and generally effective at Winton. These evaluations are consistent with the limited observations of the teams for this study: most team members at Pinehill were attempting to put the earlier conflict behind them and to find mutually acceptable middle ground, and here, as elsewhere, the teamwork process framed by the head went fairly smoothly. SMT practice was also broadly in line with messages from handbooks and research on teams outside the education sphere set out in the first chapter, suggesting that their performance was affected by similar factors, at a high level of abstraction, as other kinds of team:

- heads' leadership of the team proved critical in creating and delimiting scope for colleague members to contribute – and especially how far they were empowered to lead within the team (Chapter 6);
- where heads managed to inculcate a shared culture of teamwork, whether relatively egalitarian or hierarchical, it provided the basis for different forms of synergy in teamwork (Chapter 5);
- individual contributions could be complementary rather than identical (Chapters 4 and 6);

Table 8.2 Inspectors' criteria for judging perceived effectiveness of case study SMTs

Aspect of SMT	Positive criteria	Negative criteria
Input: individual team members	good leadership of head (Winton)	need for training of SMT members in management (Waverley)
Input: group	clearly defined responsibilities within SMT (Kingsrise)	unclear responsibilities of department leaders within SMT (Pinehill)
SMT role: teamwork process and team tasks	head well supported by other SMT members (Winton) deputy plays pivotal part in management (Pinehill)	head delegates insufficiently (Pinehill, Waverley) SMT focus insufficiently strategic, need for vision statement (Waverley)
SMT role: linkage subtasks	SMT members started to monitor other staff (Winton) effective SMT consultation, communication and decision making (Kingsrise)	poor communication with other staff (Pinehill)
SMT outputs: direct	—	—
SMT outputs: indirect	SMT creates positive school-wide ethos (Waverley)	—

- where team members worked well together, the experience provided much valued opportunities for individual professional development which acted as a source of continued motivation (Chapter 5)
- difficult team decisions could be reached by making compromises on all sides where necessary to arrive at a working consensus (Chapter 6).

Identifying characteristics of effective SMTs

The differential judgements of perceived effectiveness of these SMTs, and the contrast between the relatively egalitarian practice at Winton and the more hierarchical approach in the other three teams raise a question over how far each SMT adds up to a 'team'. In Chapter 5 it was described how heads had created the SMTs at Winton and Pinehill, whereas the heads at Kingsrise and Waverley had adopted the team label at some point along a more evolutionary path. There was much 'loose talk' of teams in all four schools, any grouping of staff likely to be accorded the term – from SMTs, through departmental teams, to year group teams. How far SMTs in particular added up to teams was less clear-cut than free use of the term may have implied.

The four SMTs did meet criteria embedded in the two stipulative definitions of teams offered in Chapter 1 to different degrees. They were small, self-identified groups, whose members articulated a common purpose in contributing to shared leadership. This purpose had a narrower focus on supporting the head with his or her agenda in the three more hierarchical SMTs. Shared tasks were not broken down into specific performance goals. Team members varied in their efforts to monitor their effectiveness as a team, those at Winton being most self-critical but still basing judgements on performance of the SMT role, such as whether other staff expressed disquiet, rather than on more substantive team outputs such as the impact of SMT members' efforts on consistency and progression in teaching and learning throughout the school. Diversity in the scope of team meetings and the strong internal hierarchy reflected in meetings among subgroups in three teams suggests that the head's commitment to sharing leadership through teamwork was greater at Winton than elsewhere. Complementarity in terms of sharing expert knowledge linked with individual management responsibilities and in terms of individual team roles featured in all teams, but awareness of complementary skills was also greatest at Winton. Indirect evidence of team members sharing a sense of accountability for the SMT's work was offered by the varying degree to which members presented a united front to other staff and governors, even where there may have been internal disagreement. Complaints of department leaders at Pinehill to other staff about the headteacher suggest that they did not identify with his version of a team and did not feel accountable for its work. So, on these definitions, the four SMTs do add up to teams, though some demonstrate more characteristics than others.

The survey and case study evidence underlines distinguishing characteristics of SMTs on which the definitions of teams were silent. They concern the formal team leaders' approach to linked aspects of sharing the work of the team for which others' coordinated contributions were needed: *what* they were prepared to share; *with whom* they were prepared to share it; and *how equally* they were prepared to share it with some or all other team members. The headteacher at Winton shared most of the leadership burden, she shared it with all her SMT colleagues, and she did so relatively equally. The other headteachers shared less of this burden, shared less of it with more junior than with more senior colleague members, and shared it unequally with all of them. A fuller definition of teams could usefully include the criterion: *activity to realise a common purpose is shared among all members in such a way as to maximise their individual contribution to its achievement.* On this criterion, the SMT at Winton quite clearly operated more fully as a team than the others.

Rather than offer extravagant claims about the characteristics of team effectiveness, a 'top fifty' selection of linked hypotheses or hunches about effective SMTs in primary schools is offered in Table 8.3. They are based on findings presented throughout the book and ordered according to the model of the SMT role. Some hypotheses originate with positive judgements of informants or inspectors about features of the teams or their activities (like complementary skills of team members); others with what was deduced from negative judgements (such as becoming immersed in 'administrivia' at the expense of

Table 8.3 Linked hypotheses about effective SMTs in primary sector schools

Input: team members

Individual

1 Members are committed to teamwork and ready to compromise their individual interests if necessary for the sake of the team.
2 Members are competent in carrying out their individual management responsibility.
3 Members' individual management responsibility includes at least one major cross-school or departmental area.
4 Members are competent teachers who are able to offer a good example to others.
5 Members balance a focus on management tasks with sensitivity to the needs of team colleagues and others with and through whom these tasks are achieved.
6 Heads set explicit parameters for teamwork and take responsibility for monitoring whether they and other members operate within the boundaries of these parameters.
7 Heads work continually to develop and sustain a shared culture of teamwork.
8 New members receive a formal induction into the SMT.

Group

9 The knowledge, skills, attitudes and personalities of members are complementary.
10 The SMT is small enough to encourage in-depth debate and large enough to include all individuals necessary for developing a shared overview and making major decisions on behalf of staff.
11 All major cross-school and departmental individual management responsibilities are represented among SMT members.
12 Members are clear about their individual responsibilities, including their contribution to the SMT.
13 All members attend frequent and regular SMT meetings, and hierarchical 'inner cabinet' subgroup meetings are avoided.
14 All existing members are consulted during the selection of new SMT members, their contribution being subject to explicit ground rules.
15 Criteria for selecting members include promotion of equal opportunities for women and men and the main ethnic groups represented among pupils and staff.
16 Structured development activities and opportunities for unstructured development are undertaken to foster the development of individual members and the SMT as a whole.
17 Members offer mutual support to protect each other's ability to contribute to the SMT's work.

SMT role: process and tasks

Teamwork process and team tasks

18 Heads create conditions which encourage all members to make a full contribution to the SMT while establishing and negotiating the boundaries of acceptable behaviour.
19 Other members support the head through followership behaviour which includes checking that their actions lie within the comfort zone of the head.
20 Members are committed to the frank exchange of views while being sensitive to individuals' feelings.
21 Individual educational and managerial beliefs and values are freely expressed and consensus is reached on broad SMT goals within the established school aims.

Table 8.3 Continued

22 The form of complementarity between the individual team roles of 'leadership of the team' and 'team membership' maximises the opportunity for all members to lead within the team and make an equal contribution to debate and decision making.
23 Heads maximise the range of agenda items falling within the SMT remit and other members are encouraged to contribute to setting the SMT agenda.
24 Members attempt to keep the SMT agenda and time spent on joint work within manageable bounds.
25 Arrangements for chairing meetings do not inhibit any member from making an equal contribution to debate.
26 The content of team tasks embraces all areas of school-wide policy, strategic planning, major decision making and routine organisation.
27 Members make an equal contribution to major decisions and to sustaining a shared overview.
28 Major decisions are made by reaching a working consensus reached through open expression of individual views.
29 Contingency procedures are established in case a working consensus cannot be reached.
30 Members balance keeping to task with providing sufficient relief to sustain concentration.
31 Members gain intrinsic benefit from being in the SMT which includes enjoying a shared sense of humour.
32 There is a high degree of mutual trust, respect and cordiality among members, and disagreements are SMT issue based rather than personal.
33 Members avoid entering into enduring subgroups or coalitions which exclude SMT colleagues.
34 All members – including heads – seek constructive feedback from colleagues on their contribution to team performance.

Linkage subtasks

35 A two-way monitoring and communication structure is established enabling other staff to contribute, face to face and through representation, to school aims, policies, strategic planning, major decisions and routine organisation.
36 The design of the communication structure ensures that all staff are represented in meetings about matters affecting their work.
37 Ground rules for involvement of other staff in the initiation, consultation, proposal, ratification and final stages of major decision making are negotiated and respected.
38 Other staff are able to participate in consultation, ratification and making of final decisions which directly affect their work.
39 Other staff are encouraged to consider their sectional interests within a school-wide perspective as far as possible.
40 Members attend to the implementation of major decisions, including monitoring the work of other staff.
41 Members attend to sustaining a permeable demarcation between the SMT and others by being approachable, accessible, acknowledging effort and achievement, and gathering views.
42 A balance is struck between minimising the private SMT arena and avoiding overload for other staff through involving them in management.
43 Team activity in the private SMT arena is consistent with the public account of it given by SMT members.

Table 8.3 Continued

---

44   SMT members present a united front to other staff, which extends to their commitment to shared decisions while acknowledging the range of views taken into account.

SMT Direct Outputs

---

45   The SMT has strong credibility with other staff and governors according to the evidence of members' joint work that is available to them.

46   National reforms and other externally initiated changes are assessed against established school aims and a strategic and coordinated response is made.

47   Members address all areas of school-wide policy, strategic planning, major decision making and routine organisation.

48   The necessary range of policies, strategic plans, major decisions and arrangements for routine organisation are made and their implementation assured.

49   Other staff are aware of all aspects of management affecting their work and of where they can obtain relevant information.

50   Governors are well informed about and approve of SMT activity and outputs.

---

working more strategically); yet others with the researchers' judgements, informed by the research and handbook literature on teams, on the consequences of what did or did not happen on the ground (as in the claim that existing SMT members should contribute to selection of new team colleagues). The list is intended as an *aide-mémoire* for practitioners in primary schools and management trainers involved in designing, reviewing and developing SMTs, not as a blueprint guaranteeing success in every context! If it is to serve its purpose as a trigger for practical reflection, several features should be borne in mind:

- the assumption is made that a school is large enough to allow for the SMT to constitute a subset of the staff;
- the hypotheses constitute a set of linked criteria which should be considered together since they comprise an integrated approach to inputs, the process and tasks incorporated in the shared SMT role, and direct outputs;
- some, such as unified commitment of SMT members to teamwork (No. 1) may be necessary for effectiveness; others, like planned induction and team training (Nos. 8 and 16), are probably optional;
- some, say, heads setting explicit parameters for teamwork (No. 6) imply taking planned action; others, including avoiding subgroups or coalitions (Nos. 13 and 33), imply deliberately withholding from action;
- certain hypotheses, perhaps the idea that all members participate in all meetings within the SMT (No. 13), will be contentious, providing something to aim for or something to reject according to beliefs and values about team effectiveness;
- several, like minimising the private SMT arena while avoiding overloading

other staff (No. 42), imply trying to find the best balance between contradictory values;

- many, such as members having cross-school or departmental responsibility (No. 3) are dependent on contextual factors like school size and budget.

When put together, the hypotheses provide a speculative vision of a 'dream team' which, nevertheless, has modest empirical grounding. In reacting to this vision, practitioners may accept, modify or reject aspects of it in the light of the national and local context, the institutional history of the school, and their managerial beliefs and values. Engaging in this exercise should help them articulate a personalised team vision which could form the framework for developing an SMT that merits the 'team' label and stands a good chance of making a positive impact on management and, indirectly, on teaching and learning.

Synergy without tears

Here an ambitious and complex hypothesis is developed in the form of a contingency model explaining patterns of interaction within the case study SMTs and their implications for different levels of synergy within the teams. The research suggests that team approaches to managing medium-sized and large primary sector schools through an SMT which acts on behalf of the staff have considerable potential as a means of achieving close managerial coordination and coherence that national reforms virtually dictate; maximising the range of factors taken into account in making major decisions; and providing a fulfilling and developmental professional experience for SMT members. Amongst the case study schools this potential appeared to be most fully realised at Winton through the relatively egalitarian way SMT members operated, with greater commitment of time to a team approach than staff in the other three teams. They were able to achieve a higher degree of synergy because all members were given scope to give their all, with the proviso that they kept within the head's comfort zone, and they were willing to operate within these parameters. Yet a moderate degree of synergy was also achieved in the more hierarchical teams, reliant on willingness of other members to support the heads in taking a strong, hierarchically oriented lead. These heads were not 'control freaks': they fostered the kind of support from colleague members that they valued while also delimiting the boundaries of this contribution tightly enough to retain a high level of control over management of the school in a high-risk environment.

A key factor distinguishing the four heads was, therefore, how ready they were to risk losing control by sharing and delegating tasks. The extent of sharing has implications for the potential contribution of other team members, the degree of synergy attainable, and also the level of risk of things going wrong from the perspective of the headteachers as team leader. Figure 8.1 is a matrix

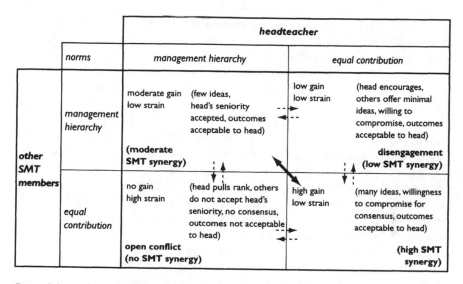

Figure 8.1 Interaction between headteacher and other SMT members

comparing norms relating to belief in a management hierarchy and in equal contribution to which the head subscribes (the left- and right-hand columns) with the equivalent norms to which other SMT members subscribe (the upper and lower rows). Each cell depicts the combination of norms held by the head and other SMT members. (For simplicity, it is assumed that other SMT members share allegiance to the same norm at any time.) The upper-left-hand cell represents the situation at Kingsrise and Waverley, where the heads adopted a strongly hierarchical team approach accepted by other SMT members. This was a 'low gain, low strain' approach where interaction was harmonious since there was congruence between norms followed by all members. The heads took a low risk of loss of control by restricting the contribution of other members, but the potential for SMT-wide synergy was only moderate. The range of shared tasks was limited and other members were not encouraged to take initiatives and to contribute their ideas beyond responding to the heads' proposals.

The lower-right-hand cell represents the situation at Winton, where the head encouraged other members to make an equal contribution and they accepted the invitation. Here the potential for SMT synergy was high because all members were involved in a very wide range of tasks and were encouraged to take their own initiatives. The risk of the head losing control was low as long as other members sought outcomes within the head's comfort zone and were willing to compromise if necessary to achieve this situation. It is important to note interaction is harmonious in both cells where there is congruence between the norms followed by all members, but that the level of synergy is likely to be higher where all involved can make an equal contribution, on the assumption that neither headteachers nor any other members of staff have a monopoly on the best ideas for managing a school in the complex reform-laden UK environment. A team may sustain harmonious interaction and reap as much synergy as possible at any time through all members working towards making an equal contribution. If the contingency arises where one or more other members advocate a course of action lying outside the head's comfort zone, and they can accept the head pulling rank (regressing temporarily to the upper left hand cell in Figure 8.1), withdrawing a decision from the domain of the team, and making it unilaterally as the team leader who is externally accountable for the work of the SMT, then harmony may be retained. The key to smooth operation and maximising synergy is for both head and other SMT members to be flexible enough to switch together, for such contingencies, from adherence to the norm of equal contribution to the norm of a management hierarchy, then being ready to switch back.

The remaining two cells indicate alternative ways where synergy may be compromised through disjunction between norms followed by the head and other SMT members. The lower-left-hand cell covers situations where the head operates hierarchically by pulling rank according to her or his position in the management hierarchy but other members do not accept this move because it transgresses their belief in their entitlement to make an equal contribution. Internal team conflict may ensue, as happened at Pinehill, creating a situation temporarily devoid of SMT synergy. The upper-right-hand cell captures circumstances where the head encourages other members to make an equal contribution, but they act according to their subordinate position in the management hierarchy. The result is disengagement of other members, as they hold back from contributing in the way nurtured by the head. This kind of situation happened in the relatively hierarchical SMTs where the heads encouraged colleague members to participate in monitoring other staff but they declined the invitation, implying it was the heads' task as top manager. Low synergy was possible in so far as other staff were willing to support the head in doing all the work.

The matrix explains major findings, though further research would be needed to test and refine it. Prescriptions for practice which might follow from this elaborate hypothesis seem clear. First, arguments for the principle of sharing school management widely and equally may be persuasive in an ideal world, but they fail to take into account two features of the real world, at least in Britain: the possibility that sharing might result in ineffective management which is unacceptable because of the potential negative impact on pupils' education; and the strict hierarchy of accountability where the headteacher may have to answer for empowering colleagues if things go wrong. Given this less than ideal situation, the study shows how sharing school management through a team approach is very worthwhile but it can be risky. Heads should therefore consider a contingency approach dependent on school circumstances, but aiming towards the most potent high-gain, low-strain approach based on belief in equal contribution while allowing for contingent reversion to the management hierarchy.

Second, where they inherit a team (as most newly appointed heads do) or wish to develop one with existing colleagues, an initial task should be to carry out a 'team culture audit', perhaps through a round of informal interviews with individuals, checking out the beliefs and values about team approaches to management to which present and any prospective SMT members subscribe. In the light of this information, heads may decide whether to begin by operating in line with with their beliefs and values. Where most or all colleagues concerned give precedence to the management hierarchy, it will probably be feasible to start down the 'low-gain, low-strain' road (represented by the upper-left-hand cell in Figure 8.1) which offers a moderate level of synergy, gradually inviting colleagues to make a more equal contribution (so inching towards the position represented by the lower-right-hand cell). The risk will have to be accepted that the latter may not immediately take up the invitation (such situations are represented by the upper-right-hand cell). Where other members more strongly support the norm of equal contribution, it may be possible to move directly into the potentially most effective 'high-gain, low-strain' mode, encouraging colleagues to accept the possibility of an occasional temporary regression to the more hierarchical approach.

Third, whenever the opportunity arises to appoint staff who will join the SMT, or where a brand new team is being created, criteria for selection should include the beliefs and values of candidates about team approaches to management, and especially how far they subscribe to the norm of equal contribution and, if so, whether they accept the contingent need of heads for regression to the norm of a management hierarchy because of their unique accountability for the SMT. Selection procedures should be designed to explore these beliefs and values.

Fourth, proceeding with caution can minimise, though never remove, the risk of debilitating conflict or frustrating disengagement. Unpredictability of interaction – not least because of the widespread coexistence of the contradictory norms of a management hierarchy and equal contribution among team members including heads – militates against any guarantee that such situations will never arise. Circumstances when heads perceive it to be necessary to pull rank with colleagues who are used to making an equal contribution will always have potential to jeopardise SMT synergy if other members do not switch norms accordingly (the lower-left-hand position in Figure 8.1). There is no sure-fire and risk-free recipe for high SMT synergy: the low-gain, low-strain hierarchical approach developed incrementally and followed harmoniously in two case study schools is likely to be more effective in a context of stringent external accountability than a headlong rush towards equal contribution, risking consequences that heads cannot afford in a high external accountability environment.

Finally, structured and unstructured development opportunities should be considered which may facilitate teamwork and support a gradual shift in the culture of teamwork where necessary to promote more equal contribution with the safeguard of contingent regression to the management hierarchy. Heads at the SMT design stage, whether moving towards a team approach or taking up a new post, could use the linked hypotheses about effective SMTs as a starting point for elaborating a vision of good teamwork practice, where possible in consultation with potential SMT members. The contingency model offers a starting point for considering how to get there. Twenty questions about SMT design and implementation that face heads embarking on a team approach are listed in Table 8.4.

Table 8.4 Twenty questions for SMT designers

1	Why am I opting for a team approach involving an SMT?
2	How extensive should be the shared SMT role in managing the school?
3	What educational and managerial values should underpin its work?
4	How far should recent institutional history and beliefs and values of prospective team members be taken into account in considering the membership and mode of operation of the SMT?
5	How far will the SMT's initial operation reflect the management hierarchy and how far will members be encouraged to make an equal contribution to debate and decision making?
6	What criteria should be used in selecting SMT members?
7	How far should prospective members be consulted about their own and colleagues' membership?
8	What range of individual management responsibilities should be covered by SMT members and should all staff be represented by them?
9	How far do prospective members have knowledge, skills, attitudes and personalities that are likely to be complementary?
10	How will two way communication links be established between the SMT, other teaching and support staff, and governors?
11	What pattern of meetings will be required for team meetings and for linkage with other staff?
12	How will the team agenda be set and what procedures will be needed to address it?
13	What procedures will be adopted initially for making major decisions and for resolving disagreements?
14	What part of the SMT operation should be conducted behind closed doors?
15	What ground rules for SMT operation in private and in public should be negotiated at the outset?
16	How may a shared culture of teamwork be promoted within the SMT?
17	How may constructive and friendly relationships between SMT members and other staff be fostered?
18	How may the credibility of the SMT with other staff and governors be assured?
19	What activities could help nurture the development of individuals and their ability to work together productively?
20	How will the team's operation and outcomes of its work be monitored and steps taken, where necessary, to modify practice?

Implications for research and theory

This, the first substantial study of primary school SMTs in the UK, has generated many hypotheses which would benefit from further examination. The contingency model, in particular, needs testing through examination of a much wider range of SMTs and, ideally, tracking factors affecting the development of newly formed teams over a period of years. Another profitable avenue of enquiry would be to operationalise direct SMT outcome measures, which was not attempted in the present research, so that team performance could be compared with more precision than the impressionistic criteria that informants and inspectors may employ. A third would be to explore further the notion of different forms of complementarity between preferred individual team roles through observational studies.

It is surprising how little research has been carried out on team approaches to management in other education sectors, where organisations tend to be larger and to feature more elaborate management structures, where heavier reliance must be placed on consultation and ratification of major decisions through representation of interested parties rather than institution-wide participation, and where more communication is by indirect means rather than face to face. More knowledge is needed about the articulation in these more complex institutions between teams formed at different institutional levels. It is probable that team approaches are as problematic in other sectors as found in the research into secondary and primary SMTs, even where conditions were reasonably favourable. Despite the decision to investigate schools where all SMT members professed commitment to a team approach, teamwork was not hassle-free in any situation. How may team approaches be developed where the prospects are less good, as in situations reported in the literature (see Chapter 1) where individuals end up in SMTs because of their formal status in the management hierarchy but the close relationship and greater accountability to colleagues that teamwork implies lies outside their comfort zone? How might a shared culture of teamwork be fostered under such inauspicious circumstances? In the first chapter, research on teamwork in the commercial sector was criticised which extrapolates from simulation exercises or the retrospective accounts of members from teams judged by some output measure to be successful. This work needs to be complemented by observational studies that get closer to teamwork as it happens in real time in the real workplace.

The picture of SMTs in action was framed by the combined cultural and political perspective. It was adopted to facilitate exploration of some of the complexities of interaction, including:

- the coexistence of contradictory beliefs and values held by individuals and groups;
- the expression of these contradictory beliefs and values without necessarily inducing conflict;

- the degree to which different sets of beliefs and values were shared;
- differential use of power in contexts which might range from the synergistic to the conflictual;
- the unequal but extensive distribution of power where each party to action has some resources that can be brought to bear, so all involved are interdependent and actions may be delimited rather than determined;
- the reciprocal link between cultural determinants of the use of power and the impact of differential uses of power on the shaping of team culture.

Certain limitations could be avoided of single cultural or political perspectives reviewed in Chapter 2, especially prejudging whether shared cultural allegiances bounded surface conflict or whether surface accord masked underlying conflict. The interpretive framework facilitated analysis of situations where there could be elements of both conflict and consensus. In Chapter 6 it was shown how, at Winton, the head and an SMT colleague might hold incompatible views on a team decision and the latter would initiate a resolution by switching cultural norms and handing the decision back to the head. Adopting a stipulative definition of power as transformative capacity rather than a zerosum notion proved critical to understanding how parties to interaction could use resources to further shared interests and so benefit from mutual empowerment. The different forms of complementarity between preferred individual team roles which marked most interaction observed were understood as following from the synergistic use of power among all members. Acquiescence to a hierarchically oriented head was as much a use of power to enable the head to operate in this way as was another head's setting of conditions which fostered equal contribution by other members of the team.

The dual perspective proved sophisticated enough to grasp such details of interaction but it did have limitations, as heralded in Chapter 2. First, the wider range of concepts involved than would generally be used in either constituent single perspective, and the intricate ways in which they articulated together, made it conceptually hard work to use. Second, some depth of analysis possible from within each single perspective was lost, since only a restricted range of concepts could be employed. Third, the multiple metaphor approach precluded combining single perspectives resting on incompatible assumptions. As Bolman and Deal (1991) recognised, a political perspective based on a conflictual view of interaction would not sit easily alongside a cultural perspective based on a view of interaction as promoting accord through a largely irrational, implicit and deeply symbolic process. Broadening conceptual horizons by combining perspectives meant eschewing their approach to entertaining first one set of assumptions under, say, a conflictual political perspective, then another set under a cultural perspective which is incompatible with the first.

Nevertheless, such an approach evidently has potential for wider application in exploring interaction (Hall 1996; Wallace 1996). An agenda for further conceptually oriented research could profitably include: empirical investigations using the cultural and political perspective, whether at the same or across different system levels, amongst diverse institutional settings in different sectors of education; extension and refinement of the range of concepts and their articulation which might be incorporated in this dual metaphor; and conceptual bridgework both to explore the possibility of creating other multiple metaphors by seeking compatible areas of linkage, and to assess their fitness for different analytical purposes.

Policy implications

The research findings not only gave insights into the detailed picture of SMT members' collective practice but also highlighted the significance of the big picture: the wider social and political context in which SMTs were set. The impact of central government reforms on primary schooling was pervasive, as witnessed by the rationales articulated by heads in the survey and case studies for creating SMTs or reconceiving practice in these terms, allocating individual management responsibilities of team members, and setting the content of the SMT agenda. Adoption of team approaches reflected expansion of the chief executive aspect of headteachers' role rooted in national reforms (see Chapter 1). There was plentiful evidence that they held onto the leading professional aspect of the role, though they were attempting to express their educational beliefs and values exclusively through other staff as their own teaching input was now minimal, and national reforms impinged on their view of good practice. There were also local- and site-level factors, like the mergers at Winton and Kingsrise, which affected the creation of such teams.

Four policy issues stand out. The first concerns the rise of managerialism. In Chapter 1 the claim was discussed that primary school heads have created SMTs as a managerialist tool to help them tighten their hierarchical control over other staff, as part of their complicity in implementing the central government reforms designed to marketise education. (It is, perhaps, a moot point how far a strongly hierarchical approach is actually on the increase. The research reviewed in the first chapter gives evidence of a long tradition of hierarchical primary headship but the attempt to bring the zones of policy and practice together is new.) The present findings support the thesis that elements of managerialism have been introduced into primary schools within a wider policy thrust to reform the public sector through 'new public management' practices common to many western governments (Foster and Plowden 1996). Some mandatory reforms of management, like the LMS budget, set parameters framing the creation of SMTs; others, like staff appraisal, constituted part of the management burden that heads in this study sought to share through a team approach. Central government strategy for driving home these and other reforms through mandates and, more recently, policing their implementation through inspection had reduced the power of heads and other staff to decide whether to introduce many practices following from reforms, leaving only the power of decision over how they should be introduced. The magnitude of this external intervention also left little space to consider alternative agendas originating at school level which were prevalent before the reforms (Wallace 1991c). A major proportion of the top-down agenda curtailing the collective autonomy of teachers was therefore not of heads' making. Despite central government rhetoric about self-management and local determination, the parameters for site-based decision making were now heavily delimited, constraining – though not entirely removing – potential for extensive transformational leadership. In this sense, externally imposed managerialism had narrowed the parameters of heads' room to manoeuvre to express their beliefs and values to promote school development in their own image. If Webb and Vulliamy (1996b) are correct that the propensity towards directive, strongly hierarchical primary school headship is on the increase, it seems likely that this shift is a consequence of heads now being subject to much stronger hierarchical and directive forces originating with the past central government (and augmented by the even greater centralising tendency of its successor).

Yet the evidence also suggests that such managerialist forces did not tell the whole story behind heads' adoption of team approaches and the form they took. Rather, these forces created conditions which favoured the search by heads for support with the increased management burden, but which also made it a high-stakes strategy because heads stood to be held uniquely accountable for the work of their team colleagues and other staff. Power within the system-wide dialectic of control was distributed to the extent that there was some room to manoeuvre for heads to express their managerial beliefs and values where they did not align with managerialism. The survey findings suggest that heads were empowered to opt for highly variable involvement of SMT colleagues and other staff in making major decisions, from the relatively top-down hierarchical approach labelled by Webb and Vulliamy as expressing managerialist leadership to the more bottom-up approach where staff outside the team could initiate the decision procedure and participate in making final decisions.

The case studies showed how the head at Winton found considerable room to manoeuvre within parameters imposed by the reforms to promote her managerial beliefs and values through a relatively egalitarian team approach while the other three heads chose a more hierarchical approach according to their beliefs and values, more in tune with managerialist leadership as conceived by Webb and Vulliamy. In other words, the distribution of power did allow some mediation of the externally imposed policy agenda where a powerful actor at the school level subscribed to a managerial culture that did not resonate closely with beliefs and values claimed to underpin managerialism. At the same time, the forces of managerialism could certainly not be ignored: the head at Winton led the staff in implementing externally imposed reforms and working to meet the expectations of inspectors, just as did the heads in the other case study schools. She exemplified the approach to management of the women heads studied by Hall (1996) which, as discussed in Chapter 1, Hall argued was not managerialist. The head was highly entrepreneurial, striving for the success of the merged school in the reform environment. She was ready to embrace reforms of which she approved and to co-opt others to suit her interests by harnessing opportunities presented by particular reforms to express beliefs and values that ran counter to their instigators' intentions. She worked with other SMT members rather than seeking to exert directive power over them, fostering a shared culture of teamwork based on a high degree of reciprocity.

In sum, the managerialist thrust of past and present central government policies has impacted on primary school management, including the widespread adoption of SMTs, but its implementation is not a *fait accompli*. There are pockets of mediation at school level, though it is uncertain how common they are, consistent with the idea that managerialism interacts with pre-existing professional practices but does not necessarily replace them:

> Generic managerialism has to be enacted within the context of producing particular public goods and services. Its own 'mission' (the pursuit of greater productivity or efficiency) cannot effectively substitute for specific service goals and the forms of expertise needed to achieve them.
>
> (Clarke and Newman 1997: 103)

The retention by heads of a leading professional role and its expression through their SMTs, even though circumscribed by reforms, suggests that managerialist imperatives may well continue to coexist uneasily with long-standing professional practices.

The second policy issue is about money – or lack of it. When observing the case study SMT meetings, their distinctive character as primary school teams was sometimes poignantly brought home. While holding an SMT meeting after school at Winton, the head took responsibility for looking after a pupil while she waited to be collected by a social worker. This girl had been abused and was now subject to child protection proceedings. The head produced a box of toys for the girl, who came in and out of the head's office during the team meeting with a toy cup of tea for each SMT member. Seamlessly, without deflection from the team debate, SMT members entered into role with the pupil, thanking her, drinking the imaginary tea, and returning the cup for her to pretend to wash up or refill. This incident was indicative, not only of the pastoral role played by all staff in primary schools, but also of the level of resourcing within which primary sector SMTs have to operate. The research showed clearly how the longstanding central and local government policies of funding primary schools at a lower rate than secondary schools inhibited the development of thoroughgoing team approaches to primary school management. Despite repeated efforts to persuade politicians that the level of this differential is unjustified and counterproductive (eg House of Commons 1986, 1994; Alexander *et al.* 1992; Alexander 1997), primary schools remain the poor neighbours of their secondary counterparts and so do their SMTs. Members of the secondary SMTs investigated in the study by Wallace and Hall (1994) enjoyed much more favourable resourcing which greatly facilitated their work.

The relative disadvantage for primary SMTs imposed by the lower level of resourcing was twofold. First, tight parameters set by the LMS budget and system of salary differentials meant that fewer staff with promoted posts had to shoulder a wider range of responsibilities. The analysis of SMT members' responsibilities and their location in the case study school management structures in Chapters 3 and 4 revealed how, on top of teaching a class, a member might have cross-school, departmental and curriculum coordination management responsibilities – and all in return for two or three increments above the basic salary scale. The largest primary schools cater for a similar number of pupils as the average secondary school, yet the distribution of management responsibilities will be spread more widely amongst a greater number of staff in the latter institution.

Second, compounding the multiplicity of individual management responsibilities was the scarcity of non-contact time for individual members and the whole team to carry out the shared SMT role (Chapters 3 and 6). If senior staff were not to have a class or to be relieved from some of their teaching each week, their time during the school day spent on management work had to be covered by other teachers. The low ratio of staff to pupils in primary schools that their LMS budget would allow precluded SMTs in these schools from doing much joint work during the school day. Chapter 3 showed how most meetings of SMTs in the survey took place before or after lesson time, or even during the lunch break. All meetings between SMT members and other staff in the case study schools happened at such times. Only the most senior staff in the larger case study schools did not have a class, and, even in the largest (Winton), the tight budget forced one SMT member to assume class teaching responsibility at the expense of her contribution to management. All SMT members in the secondary SMTs studied by Wallace and Hall had a substantial allocation of non-contact time, a substantial minority of their meetings were held during the school day – and they were paid more than their opposite numbers in the primary schools!

The implication for policy makers is that, for team approaches to management to succeed, their members need quality time to meet together and carry out their multiple individual management responsibilities on a par with their secondary colleagues. One reason that the disparity in primary and secondary school funding in the UK has not been tackled is that it is expensive: it would be political suicide to rob secondary school budgets to pay for levelling up the resourcing of primary schools. The alternative is to increase overall investment of public money in education by increasing primary school budgets but such a strategy would fly in the face of the new public management policy thrust where more means less: public sector institutions are required to be more effective and efficient while there has been a net decline in public spending (Foster and Plowden 1996). Recently central government ministers have announced a substantial increase in expenditure on education, but this money is targeted on other priorities including school improvement. The potential of SMTs for achieving a high level of internal synergy as a route to promoting the school-wide synergy necessary for effectiveness – by any definition – will remain untapped unless they receive a more favourable funding level.

The third policy issue concerns the relative disadvantage of women in acquiring the status and experience required for SMT membership. The survey results mirrored the national picture where, despite primary school teaching being a profession predominantly staffed by women, they are under-represented in management positions, and therefore in SMTs. There is no evidence that women and men are not equally capable of contributing effectively to a team approach to management, and so there is a strong argument on technical grounds alone against excluding members of either gender. The dominant ethic governing selection of SMT members in the case study schools was the 'best person for the job', which begs the question of criteria for judging who will best fit the SMT bill. The commonly employed criterion that prospective members should have prior experience in management positions pushes the problem of under-representation of women back down the career path. Since far more women than men take a career break, proportionately fewer women can rack up the same number of years of experience in such management positions as the men with whom they compete for senior posts that are likely to carry SMT membership. A radical rethink is needed of how to interpret the professional value of a career break so that more women returners can gain management positions immediately rather than having to fight their way back into the profession through supply teaching. In addition – another worthwhile expense for central government – re-entry training support for women returners which includes a substantial focus on management would help them get up to speed with their contemporaries who had stayed in the profession.

The final policy issue is about the need for greater structured development support for SMTs. Ironically, given the central government focus on school improvement and effectiveness and the imperative for school staff to co-ordinate their work closely just to survive in a context of perennial reform, SMTs hardly feature in central government policy. Heads are the prime targets for accreditation and training under the auspices of the Teacher Training Agency. As mentioned in Chapter 1, the individualistic and directive official conception of headship is embodied in the national standards for headteachers (TTA 1997) which require them to be able to create and operate within a team in managing the school. Heads receive all the attention, and it appears to be assumed that training for them alone is sufficient to bring about 'a high performing team'. The case studies suggest that this confidence in heads being able to build effective teams without team training support being available for all members may be misplaced (as in the experience at Pinehill). Chapter 5 showed how little structured development for teamwork had been experienced by any member in the three schools with a more hierarchically organised SMT, let alone development for the team as a whole. Yet abundant evidence from research and training experience (Joyce and Showers 1988; Wallace 1991a) implies that a necessary condition for learning to manage effectively, whether developing a team or acting as a team member, is by doing the real job. Team members ultimately learn how to collaborate effectively by working together in school. Awareness of possibilities and pitfalls can be raised through preparatory training (as in the National Professional Qualification for Headship in the UK), but much of the learning can be done only *in situ*. Structured development activities may not be necessary for SMTs to operate, but they can greatly facilitate team development. This study and others' research show just how difficult effective teamwork can be to achieve; the signs are that maybe a quarter or more of SMTs are not effective teams. There is clearly a case for a central government initiative to provide stronger team development support. The matrix (Figure 8.1) discussed above implies that one valuable focus would be to raise SMT members' awareness of their contradictory managerial beliefs and values. Assistance could be offered with learning to live with this contradiction and switching between alternative beliefs and values as contingencies arise. Instead of advocating simplistic solutions (usually, in the past, pushing towards extensive sharing of management), heads could be advised to adopt a contingency approach, depending on an ongoing situational analysis.

Research on professional development and training suggests that structured development activities should give priority to sustained programmes, rather than one-off workshop-type events; to support for intact teams, rather than training for one or more individuals within them; and to in-house consultancy where teams may be observed at work and offered feedback on their actual performance, rather than playing at teamwork through off-site simulations. High-quality support of this kind does not come cheap but could make a real difference to the ability of SMTs to achieve their potential for synergy.

Before the 1997 UK general election, the present British Prime Minister memorably proffered the ringing soundbite that the New Labour Party priorities in government would be 'education, education, education'. The present study implies that the keys to achieving more effective primary education are – less lyrically – 'synergy, synergy, synergy' among school staff. Their minimal compliance can probably be achieved by mandates policed by external accountability measures. High-level synergy necessary to make the most dramatic difference to effectiveness means something different: voluntarily entering into the spirit of reform with a degree of power to contribute as an equal to the direction of improvement efforts. This is where teamwork comes in.

References

Alexander, R. J. (1984) *Primary Teaching*, London: Cassell.
—— (1997) *Policy and Practice in Primary Education: Local Initiative, National Agenda* (2nd edn), London: Routledge.
Alexander, R. J., Rose, J. and Woodhead, C. (1992) *Curriculum Organisation and Classroom Practice: a Discussion Paper*, London: Department of Education and Science.
Bacharach, S. and Lawler, E. (1980) *Power and Politics in Organisations*, San Francisco: Jossey-Bass.
Ball, S. (1987) *The Micropolitics of the School*, London: Methuen.
Belbin, M. (1981) *Management Teams: Why They Succeed or Fail*, London: Heinemann.
—— (1993) *Team Roles at Work*, Oxford: Butterworth-Heinemann.
Bell, L., Halpin, D. and Neill, S. (1996) 'Managing self governing primary schools in the locally maintained, grant maintained and private sectors', *Educational Management and Administration* 23, 3: 253–61.
Bell, L. and Rhodes, C. (1996) *The Skills of Primary School Management*, London: Routledge.
Blanchard, K., Carew, D. and Parisi-Carew, E. (1992) *The One Minute Manager Builds High Performing Teams*, London: HarperCollins.
Blase, J. and Anderson, G. (1995) *The Micropolitics of Educational Leadership: from Control to Empowerment*, London: Cassell.
Board of Education (1937) *Handbook of Suggestions for Teachers*, London: His Majesty's Stationery Office.
Bolam, R., McMahon, A., Pocklington, K. and Weindling, D. (1993) *Effective Management in Schools*, London: Department for Education.
Bolman, L. and Deal, T. (1991) *Reframing Organisations: Artistry, Choice and Leadership*, San Francisco: Jossey-Bass.
Bottery, M. (1992) *The Ethics of Educational Management*, London: Cassell.
Bowe, R. and Ball, S. with Gold, A. (1992) *Reforming Education and Changing Schools*, London: Routledge.
Bower, M. (1966) *The Will to Manage: Corporate Success through Programmed Management*, New York: McGraw-Hill.
Burns, J. (1978) *Leadership*, New York: Harper & Row.
Bush, T. (1995) *Theories of Educational Management* (2nd edn), London: Paul Chapman.
Campbell, R. J. (1985) *Developing the Primary School Curriculum*, London: Cassell.

Central Advisory Council for Education (England) (1967) *Children and their Primary Schools*. Plowden Report, London: Her Majesty's Stationery Office.

Clarke, J. and Newman, J. (1997) *The Managerial State*, London: Sage.

Cohen, M. and March, J. G. (1974) *Leadership and Ambiguity*, New York: McGraw-Hill.

Coleman, G. (1991) 'Investigating Organisations: a Feminist Approach', Occasional Paper 37, University of Bristol: School for Advanced Urban Studies.

Coulson, A. A. (1980) 'The role of the primary head', in T. Bush, R. Glatter, J. Goodey and C. Riches (eds) *Approaches to School Management*, London: Harper & Row.

—— (1990) 'Primary school headship: a review of research', in R. Saran and V. Trafford (eds) *Research in Education Management and Policy: Retrospect and Prospect*, London: Falmer Press.

Coulson, A. A. and Cox, M. V. (1975) 'What do deputies do?', *Education 3–13* 3, 2: 100–3.

Cox, C. B. and Dyson, A. E. (eds) (1969) *Fight for Education: a Black Paper*. London: Critical Quarterly Society.

Cuthbert, R. (1984) 'The management process', Block 3, Part 2, E324 *Management in Post-Compulsory Education*, Milton Keynes: Open University Press.

Dahl, R. (1957) 'The concept of power', *Behavioural Science*, 2: 201–15.

Davies, B. and Ellison, L. (eds) (1994) *Managing the Effective Primary School*, Harlow: Longman.

Day, C., Johnston, D. and Whitaker, P. (1985) *Managing Primary Schools: a Professional Development Approach*, London: Harper & Row.

Department for Education (1994) *School Teachers' Pay and Conditions Document 1994*, London: Her Majesty's Stationery Office.

Department for Education and Employment (1996) *Statistics of Education, England and Wales: 1996 Edition*, London: Department for Education and Employment.

—— (1997) *Statistics of Education, Schools in England: 1996*, London: Department for Education and Employment.

Department of Education and Science (1978) *Primary Education in England*, London: Her Majesty's Stationery Office.

—— (1982) *Education 5 to 9: an Illustrative Survey of 80 First Schools in England*, London: Her Majesty's Stationery Office.

—— (1985) *Education 8–12 in Combined and Middle Schools*, London: Her Majesty's Stationery Office.

—— (1987) *School Teachers' Pay and Conditions Document 1987*, London: Her Majesty's Stationery Office.

Evers, C. W. (1990) 'Schooling, organisational learning and efficiency in the growth of knowledge', in J. Chapman (ed.) *School Based Decision Making and Management*, London: Falmer Press.

Evetts, J. (1990) *Women in Primary Teaching: Career Contexts and Strategies*, London: Unwin Hyman.

Foster, C. and Plowden, F. (1996) *The State under Stress*, Buckingham: Open University Press.

Fullan, M. with Stiegelbauer, S. (1991) *The New Meaning of Educational Change*, London: Cassell.

Garrett, V. (1997) 'Principals and headteachers as leading professionals', in P. Ribbins (ed.) *Leaders and Leadership in the School, College and University*, London: Cassell.

Giddens, A. (1976) *New Rules of Sociological Method*, London: Hutchinson.

—— (1984) *The Constitution of Society*, Cambridge: Polity.

Grace, G. (1995) *School Leadership: Beyond Education Management*, London: Falmer.

Hall, V. (1993) 'Women in educational management: a review of research in Britain', in J. Ouston (ed.) *Women in Educational Management*, Harlow: Longman.

—— (1996) *Dancing on the Ceiling: a Study of Women Managers in Education*, London: Paul Chapman.

Hall, V. and Wallace, M. (1993) 'Collaboration as a subversive activity: a professional response to externally imposed competition between schools?' *School Organisation* 13, 2: 101–17.

Hargreaves, A. (1994) *Changing Teachers, Changing Times: Teachers' Work and Culture in the Post-Modern Age*, London: Cassell.

Harrison, M. and Gill, S. (1992) *Primary School Management*, Oxford: Heinemann.

Harvey, T. and Drolet, B. (1994) *Building Teams, Building People*, Lancaster, PA: Technomic.

Hayes, D. (1996) 'Taking nothing for granted: the introduction of collaborative decision making in a primary school', *Educational Management and Administration* 24, 3: 291–300.

Hearn, J., Sheppard, D., Tancred-Sheriff, P. and Burrell, G. (1989) *The Sexuality of Organisation*, London: Sage.

Hill, T. (1989) *Managing the Primary School*, London: Fulton.

Hilsum, S. and Start, K. (1974) *Promotion and Careers in Teaching*, Slough: NFER.

House, E. (1981) 'Three perspectives on innovation', in R. Lehming and M. Kane (eds) *Improving Schools: Using What We Know*, Beverly Hills, CA: Sage.

House of Commons (1986) *Achievement in Primary Schools: Third Report from the Education, Science and Arts Select Committee*, London: Her Majesty's Stationery Office.

—— (1994) *The Disparity in Funding between Primary and Secondary Schools: Education Committee Second Report*, London: Her Majesty's Stationery Office.

Hoyle, E. (1986) *The Politics of School Management*, London: Hodder and Stoughton.

Hughes, M (1985) 'Leadership in professionally staffed organisations', in M. Hughes, P. Ribbins and H. Thomas (eds) *Managing Education: the System and the Institution*, Eastbourne: Holt, Rinehart and Winston.

Inner London Education Authority (1985) *Improving Primary Schools, Report of the Committee of Inquiry Chaired by N. Thomas*, London: Inner London Education Authority.

Jirasinghe, D. and Lyons, G. (1996) *The Competent Head*, London: Taylor and Francis.

Jones, A. (1987) *Leadership for Tomorrow's Schools*, Oxford: Blackwell.

Joyce, B. and Showers, B. (1988) *Student Achievement through Staff Development*, London: Longman.

Joyce, B., Murphy, C., Showers, B. and Murphy, J. (1989) 'School renewal as cultural change', *Educational Leadership*, November: 70–7.

Katzenbach, J. and Smith, D. (1993) *The Wisdom of Teams: Creating the High Performance Organisation*, Boston, MA: Harvard Business School Press.

Kharbanda, O. and Stallworthy, E. (1990) *Project Teams: the Human Factor*, Oxford: Blackwell.

Kickert, W. (1991) 'Steering at a distance: a new paradigm of public governance in Dutch higher education', paper for the European Consortium for Political Research, March 1991, University of Essex.

Langdon, K. (1905) *School Management*, London: Kegan Paul, Trench, Trubner.

Larson, C. and LaFasto, F. (1989) *Teamwork: What Must Go Right, What Can Go Wrong*, London: Sage.

Lindle, J. C. (1994) *Surviving School Micropolitics: Strategies for Administrators*, Lancaster, PA: Technomic.

Lortie, D. (1969) 'The balance of control and autonomy in elementary school teaching', in A. Etzioni (ed.) *The Semi-Professions and their Organisation*, New York: Free Press.

Louis, K. S. and Miles, M. (1990) *Improving the Urban High School: What Works and Why*, New York: Teachers College Press.

McEwen, E. (1997) *Leading your Team to Excellence: How to Make Quality Decisions*, Thousand Oaks, CA: Corwin Press.

MacGilchrist, B., Mortimore, P. , Savage, J. and Beresford, C. (1995) *Planning Matters: the Impact of Development Planning in Primary Schools*, London: Paul Chapman.

Maclure, S. (1970) 'The control of education', in The History of Education Society (ed.) *The Government and Control of Education*, London: Methuen.

Maeroff, G. (1993) *Team Building for School Change: Equipping Teachers for New Roles*, New York: Teachers College Press.

Menter, I., Muschamp, Y., Nicholls, P. and Ozga, J. with Pollard, A. (1997) *Work and Identity in the Primary School: a Post-Fordist Analysis*, Buckingham: Open University Press.

Merriam, S. (1988) *Case Study Research in Education*, London: Jossey-Bass.

Miles, M. and Huberman, M. (1994) *Qualitative Data Analysis* (2nd edn), London: Sage.

Morgan, G. (1986) *Images of Organisation*, Newbury Park, CA: Sage.

Mortimore, P., Sammons, P., Stoll, L., Lewis, D. and Ecob, R. (1988) *School Matters: the Junior Years*, Wells: Open Books.

Newman, E. and Pollard, A. (1994) 'Observing primary school change: through conflict to whole-school collaboration?', in D. Hargreaves and D. Hopkins (eds) *Development Planning for School Improvement*, London: Cassell.

Nias, J. (1987) 'One finger, one thumb: a case study of the deputy head's part in the leadership of a nursery/infant school', in G. Southworth (ed.) *Readings in Primary School Management*, Lewes: Falmer.

Nias, J., Southworth, G. and Yeomans, R. (1989) *Staff Relationships in the Primary School*, London: Cassell.

Nias, J., Southworth, G. and Campbell, P. (1992) *Whole School Curriculum Development in Primary Schools*, London: Falmer Press.

Office for Standards in Education (1994) *Handbook for the Inspection of Schools*, London: Her Majesty's Stationery Office.

—— (1997) *The Annual Report of Her Majesty's Chief Inspector of Schools: Standards and Quality in Education 1995/96*, London: The Stationery Office.

Perrow, C. (1986) *Complex Organisations: a Critical Essay* (3rd edn), New York: Random House.

Peters, T. and Waterman, R. (1982) *In Search of Excellence*, London: Harper and Row.

Pollard, A., Broadfoot, P., Croll, P., Osborn, M. and Abbott, D. (1994) *Changing English Primary Schools? The Impact of the Education Reform Act at Key Stage One*, London: Cassell.

Powney, J. and Weiner, G. (1991) *Outside of the Norm: Equity and Management in Educational Institutions*, London: South Bank Polytechnic Department of Education.

Reitzug, U. and Reeves, J. (1992) ' "Miss Lincoln doesn't teach here": a descriptive narrative and conceptual analysis of a principal's symbolic leadership behaviour', *Educational Administration Quarterly*, 28, 2: 185–219.

Robinson, M. (1983) 'The role of the year leader: an analysis of the perceptions of year leaders and deputy heads in 8–12 middle schools', *School Organisation* 3, 4: 333–44.

Shakeshaft, C. (1989) *Women in Educational Administration* (2nd edn), Newbury Park, CA: Sage.

Slee, R. and Weiner, G. with Thompson, S. (eds) (1998) *School Effectiveness for Whom?* London: Falmer Press.

Smith, D. (1991) 'Hystmount Junior School', in P. Mortimore and J. Mortimore (eds) *The Primary Head: Roles, Responsibilities and Reflections*, London: Paul Chapman.

Southworth, G. (1995) *Looking into Primary Headship: a Research Based Interpretation*, London: Falmer Press.

—— (1998) *Leading Improving Primary Schools: the Work of Headteachers and Deputy Heads*, London: Falmer Press.

Spencer, J. and Pruss, A. (1992) *Managing your Team: How to Organise People for Maximum Results*, London: Piatkus.

Stronach, I. and Morris, B. (1994) 'Polemical notes on educational evaluation in the age of "policy hysteria"', *Evaluation and Research in Education* 8, 1/2: 5–19.

Tannenbaum, R. and Schmidt, W. H. (1958) 'How to choose a leadership pattern', *Harvard Business Review* 51: 3.

Teacher Training Agency (1997) *National Standards for Headteachers*, London: Teacher Training Agency.

Teddlie, C. and Reynolds, D. (eds) (1998) *International Handbook of School Effectiveness Research*, London: Falmer Press.

Times Educational Supplement (1993) 'Mad about big friendly giants', December 3: 22.

Wallace, M. (1986a) 'Towards an Action Research Approach to Educational Management', unpublished Ph.D. thesis, Centre for Applied Research in Education, University of East Anglia.

—— (1986b) 'The rise of scale posts as a management hierarchy in schools', *Educational Management and Administration* 14: 203–12.

—— (1989) 'Towards a collegiate approach to curriculum management in primary and middle schools', in M. Preedy (ed.) *Approaches to Curriculum Management*, Milton Keynes: Open University Press.

—— (1991a) *School-Centred Management Training*, London: Paul Chapman.

—— (1991b) 'Contradictory interests in policy implementation: the case of LEA development plans for schools', *Journal of Education Policy* 6, 4: 385–99.

—— (1991c) 'Coping with multiple innovations: an exploratory study', *School Organisation* 11, 2: 187–209.

—— (1992) 'The management of multiple innovations', Module 1, Unit 3, Part 2, Open University Course E326 *Managing Schools*, Milton Keynes: Open University.

—— (1996) 'A crisis of identity: school merger and cultural transition', *British Educational Research Journal* 22, 4: 459–73.

Wallace, M. and Hall, V. (1989) 'Management development and training for schools in England and Wales: an overview', *Educational Management and Administration* 17, 4: 163–75.

—— (1994) *Inside the SMT: Team Approaches to Secondary School Management*, London: Paul Chapman.

Wallace, M. and McMahon, A. (1994) *Planning for Change in Turbulent Times: the Case of Multiracial Primary Schools*, London: Cassell.

Webb, R. and Vulliamy, G. (1996a) *Roles and Responsibilities in the Primary School: Changing Demands, Changing Practices*, Buckingham: Open University Press.

—— (1996b) 'A deluge of directives: conflict between collegiality and managerialism in the post-ERA primary school', *British Educational Research Journal* 22, 4: 441–58.

Weindling, D. and Earley, P. (1987) *Secondary Headship: the First Years*, Windsor: NFER-Nelson.

Welsh Office (1996) *Statistics of Education and Training in Wales: Schools No. 4 1996*, Cardiff: Welsh Office.

West, N. (1992) *Primary Headship: Management and the Pursuit of Excellence*, London: Longman.

Index

Printed in the United States
by Baker & Taylor Publisher Services